DAILY LIVES OF

Civilians in Wartime Twentieth-Century Europe

**Recent Titles in the
Greenwood Press "Daily Life Through History" Series**

Civilians in Wartime Europe, 1618–1900
Linda S. Frey and Marsha L. Frey, editors

The Vietnam War
James E. Westheider

World War II
G. Kurt Piehler

Immigrant America, 1870–1920
June Granatir Alexander

Along the Mississippi
George S. Pabis

Immigrant America, 1820–1870
James M. Bergquist

Pre-Columbian Native America
Clarissa W. Confer

Post–Cold War
Stephen A. Bourque

The New Testament
James W. Ermatinger

The Hellenistic Age: From Alexander to Cleopatra
James Allan Evans

Imperial Russia
Greta Bucher

The Greenwood Encyclopedia of Daily Life in America, Four Volumes
Randall M. Miller, general editor

DAILY LIVES OF

Civilians in Wartime Twentieth-Century Europe

Edited by Nicholas Atkin

The Greenwood Press "Daily Life Through History" Series

Daily Life of Civilians during Wartime
David S. Heidler and Jeanne T. Heidler, Series Editors

GREENWOOD PRESS
Westport, Connecticut • London

Library of Congress Cataloging-in-Publication Data

Daily lives of civilians in wartime twentieth-century Europe / edited by Nicholas Atkin.
    p. cm. — (Daily life of civilians during wartime, ISSN 1080–4749)
  Includes bibliographical references and index.
  ISBN-13: 978–0–313–33657–7 (alk. paper)
  1. War and society—Europe—History—20th century.   2. Civilians in war—Europe—History—20th century.   I. Atkin, Nicholas.
  HM554.D35   2008
  303.6'60940904—dc22   2008012986

British Library Cataloguing in Publication Data is available.

Library of Congress Catalog Card Number: 2008012986
ISBN-13: 978–0–313–33657–7
ISSN: 1080–4749

First published in 2008

Greenwood Press, 88 Post Road West, Westport, CT 06881
An imprint of Greenwood Publishing Group, Inc.
www.greenwood.com

Printed in the United States of America

The paper used in this book complies with the Permanent Paper Standard issued by the National Information Standards Organization (Z39.48–1984).

10   9   8   7   6   5   4   3   2   1

The publisher has done its best to make sure the instructions and/or recipes in this book are correct. However, users should apply judgment and experience when preparing recipes, especially parents and teachers working with young people. The publisher accepts no responsibility for the outcome of any recipe included in this volume.

To Ben

Contents

Series Foreword

Few scenes are as poignant as that of civilian refugees torn from their homes and put to plodding flight along dusty roads, carrying their possessions in crude bundles and makeshift carts. We have all seen the images. Before photography, paintings and crude drawings told the story, but despite the media, the same sense of the awful emerges from these striking portrayals: the pace of the flight is agonizingly slow; the numbers are sobering and usually arrayed in single file along the edges of byways that stretch to the horizon. The men appear hunched and beaten, the women haggard, the children strangely old, and usually the wide-eyed look of fear has been replaced by one of bone-grinding weariness. They likely stagger through country redolent of the odor of smoke and death as heavy guns mutter in the distance. It always seems to be raining on these people, or snowing, and it is either brutally cold or oppressively hot. In the past, clattering hooves would send them skittering away from the path of cavalry; more recently, whirring engines of motorized convoys push them from the road. Aside from becoming casualties, civilians who become refugees experience the most devastating impact of war, for they truly become orphans of the storm, lacking the barest necessities of food and clothing except for what they can carry and eventually what they can steal.

The volumes in this series seek to illuminate that extreme example of the civilian experience in wartime and more, for those on distant home fronts also can make remarkable sacrifices, whether through their labors to support the war effort or by enduring the absence of loved ones far from home and in great peril. And war can impinge on indigenous populations in eccentric ways. Stories of a medieval world in which a farmer fearful about his crops could prevail on armies to fight elsewhere are possibly exaggerated, the product of nostalgia for a chivalric code that most likely did not hold much sway during a coarse and vicious time. In any period and at any place, the fundamental reality of war is that organized violence is no less brutal for its being structured by strategy and tactics. The advent of total war might have been signaled by the famous *levée en masse* of the French Revolution, but that development was more a culmination of a trend than an innovation away from more pacific times. In short, all wars have assailed and will assail civilians in one way or another to a greater or lesser degree. The Thirty Years' War displaced populations just as the American Revolution saw settlements preyed upon, houses razed, and farms pillaged. Modern codes of conduct adopted by both international consent and embraced by the armies of the civilized world have heightened awareness about the sanctity of civilians and have improved vigilance about violations of that sanctity, but in the end such codes will never guarantee immunity from the rage of battle or the rigors of war.

In this series, accomplished scholars have recruited prescient colleagues to write essays that reveal both the universal civilian experience in wartime and aspects of it made unique by time and place. Readers will discover in these pages the other side of warfare, one that is never placid, even if far removed from the scenes of fighting. As these talented authors show, the shifting expectations of governments markedly transformed the civilian wartime experience from virtual non-involvement in early modern times to the twentieth century's expectation of sacrifice, exertion, and contribution. Finally, as the Western powers have come full circle by asking virtually no sacrifice from civilians at all, they have stumbled upon the peculiar result that diminishing deprivation during a war can increase civilian dissent against it.

Moreover, the geographical and chronological span of these books is broad and encompassing to reveal the unique perspectives of how war affects people whether they are separated by hemispheres or centuries, people who are distinct by way of different cultures yet similar because of their common humanity. As readers will see, days on a home front far from battle usually become a surreal routine of the ordinary existing in tandem with the extraordinary, a situation in which hours of waiting and expectation become blurred against the backdrop of normal tasks and everyday events. That situation is a constant, whether for a village in Asia or Africa, or Europe or the Americas.

Consequently, these books confirm that the human condition always produces the similar as well the singular, a paradox that war tends to amplify. Every war is much like another, but no war is really the same as any other. All places are much alike, but no place is wholly separable from its matchless identity. The civilian experience in war mirrors these verities. We are certain that readers will find in these books a vivid illumination of those truths.

David S. Heidler and Jeanne T. Heidler
General Editors

Preface

This collection of essays examines the manner in which the wars of the twentieth century have impacted on Europe's civilians. It might be thought that this is well-worn territory. Though the social context of World War Two is beginning to receive the coverage it deserves, the civilian experience of the other conflicts under review here—World War One, the Russian and Spanish Civil Wars, the post-Yugoslav Wars, and the Cold War—has received far less attention. There are several reasons why this might be so: a long-standing reluctance on the part of historians to tackle daily life; the conservative traditions of military history writing; lingering political sensibilities; and an unevenness of primary sources. It is a credit to the following essays that they overcome such drawbacks to rescue people's day-to-day lives from obscurity and to place these experiences at the forefront, always recognizing that there can never be a specific civilian type and that Europe's twentieth-century military campaigns have been lived through in different ways.

The opening chapter assesses the ways in which historians have tackled daily life during wartime and, at the same time, explains how battle has changed over the modern period. Without necessarily subscribing to the belief that the period since the French Revolutionary and Napoleonic upheavals (1792–1815) has witnessed an unstoppable march towards "total war," it is difficult to deny that the more recent the conflict the more likely it has been to have disrupted the rhythms of daily life.

This was especially true of World War One. Though it was envisaged that this would be of short duration, over by Christmas 1914, it proved an arduous drawn-out affair that increasingly encroached upon day-to-day life. In a wide-ranging essay, taking in Britain, France, Belgium, and Germany, chapter 2 by François Cochet illustrates how civilians increasingly came to appreciate that they were at war. This was evidenced in material shortages; the mobilization of the home fronts; the spread of government propaganda; increasing state interference into ordinary activities; and the threat of death on an unprecedented scale. Not everywhere was equally affected—much depended on where in Europe one lived and how close people were to the actual fighting—yet it was increasingly hard to escape the privations and dangers of war.

Given Russia's huge geographical size, it might have been thought that civilians had a good chance of escaping the upheavals brought about by the Russian Civil War. Yet, as Sam Johnson shows in chapter 3, this was a fratricidal and ideological struggle that affected a majority of the population. First to suffer were those who lived in the cities, where men, women, and children were engaged in a daily tussle for survival. Thanks to the fluidity of the battle lines, before long the countryside was also affected. The Civil War culminated in famine and the creation of millions of refugees.

The Spanish Civil War (1936–39) was another conflict in which communities were pitted against one another and where, again, dogma impinged on civilian life as the Nationalist and Republican forces endeavored to capture the nation, both in an institutional and ideological sense. In this feverish atmosphere, everyone's loyalties were suspect and frequently called into question, threatening the Republicans' aim of building a new society. As Michael Richards demonstrates, this ambition had to be reconciled with the demands of fighting the military campaign, as losses and devastation began to mount.

Chapter 5 examines the dimensions of World War Two, a conflict that dwarfed all others, including that of 1914–18, and that perhaps genuinely deserves the label "total," always excepting that no conflict can ever be entirely total. Though the magnitude of the fight makes any generalization hazardous, the chapter identifies a series of key factors that influenced the civilian experience, notably displacement, government, adjustment, and comportment.

World War Two, of course, bequeathed a Europe divided between east and west and a new world order dominated by the superpowers, the United States and the Soviet Union. Largely because of the advent of nuclear weapons, the subsequent Cold War never became a "hot war," yet it nonetheless had a tremendous impact on the peoples of Europe. Revisiting several of the historiographical issues and approaches explored throughout this volume, chapter 6 by Frank Tallett examines how the Cold War was experienced on the ground and elaborates some innovatory lines of enquiry for future research.

Writers are just beginning to make sense of the irrational and unspeakable acts that took place with the collapse of the former Yugoslavia.

Drawing on newspaper accounts, personal letters, documentary film footage, and extensive oral testimonies, chapter 7 in this study, by Maja Povrzanović Frykman, focuses not on refugees but on those civilians in Croatia and Bosnia-Herzegovina who, in 1992–95, stayed in their homes, a group of people whom she has termed the "forgotten majority," and who witnessed death, rape, destruction, and trauma.

The themes of this book are not, for the most part, uplifting ones. Though each of the conflicts under consideration here had its own characteristics and though civilians underwent their own personal experiences, they shared in a wider misery. Cold, hunger, fear, material deprivation, the threat of sexual assault, arbitrary violence, death—these are the common elements that feature in each of the chapters.

The book closes with a glossary of terms, to help the reader better understand some of the concepts, events, and places discussed in the chapters, and a narrative bibliography to guide the user to more resources that will help build a better understanding of the lives of European civilians in wartime in the twentieth century.

Acknowledgments

My thanks go first to David and Jeanne Heidler for commissioning me to edit this book. At Greenwood, Michael Hermann and then Anne Thompson saw the manuscript through into production. Thanks also extend to all the contributors. Frank Tallett read the introduction, while my colleague Linda Risso kindly made suggestions to chapter 5. Brian Sudlow translated chapter 2 from the original French. A much shorter version of Maja Povrzanović Frykman's chapter appeared in *Ethonologie Française* and thanks are extended to the journal for permission to reproduce material already in print. As always, my biggest debt is to my family: Claire, Charlotte, and Ben.

Abbreviations

AEG	Allgemeine Elektrizitäts-Gesellschaft
AMA	Agrupación de Mujeres Antifascistas
ARA	American Relief Association
BBC	British Broadcasting Corporation
CIA	Central Intelligence Agency
CNT	Confederación Nacional del Trabajo
DM	German Marks
DORA	Defence of the Realm Act
DPs	Displaced Persons
EC	European Community
EEC	European Economic Community
FAI	Federación Anarquista Ibérica
FET de las JONS	Falange Española Tradicionalista de las Juntas de Ofensiva Nacionalsindicalista
FETE	Federación Española de Trabajadores de la Enseñanza
FUE	Federación Universitaria Española
GDP	Gross Domestic Product
GI	Government Issue, synonym for American soldiers (wearing government-issued uniforms)

GNP	Gross National Product
HDZ	Croatian Democratic Union
ICTY	International Criminal Tribunal for Yugo-slavia
IRO	International Refugee Organization
JNA	Yugoslav People's Army
LVF	Légion des Volontaires Français contre le Bolchevisme
MP	Member of Parliament
NATO	North Atlantic Treaty Organization
NEP	New Economic Policy
OT	Organisation Todt
PCE	Partido Comunista de España
POUM	Partido Obrero de Unificación Marxista
POW	Prisoner of War
PSOE	Partido Socialista Obrero Español
PSUC	Partit Socialista Unifacat de Catalunya
RAF	Royal Air Force
SDA	Democratic Action Party
SDS	Serbian Democratic Party
SEATO	Southeast Asia Treaty Organization
SF	Sección Femenina
SS	Schutzstaffel
UGT	Unión General de Trabajadores
UN	United Nations
UNHCR	United Nations High Commissioner for Refugees
UNPROFOR	United Nations Protection Forces
UNRRA	United Nations Relief and Rehabilitation Administration
USSR	Union of Soviet Socialist Republics
VD	Venereal Disease

Chronology

WORLD WAR ONE

1914

June 28	Franz Ferdinand assassinated in Sarajevo
July 23	Austrian ultimatum to Serbia
July 28	Declaration of war by Austria-Hungary on Serbia
July 29	Austria invades Serbia
July 30	Russia orders mobilization
July 31	Austria-Hungary mobilizes
August 1	German empire declares war on Russia/French and German mobilization
August 3	German empire declares war on France/Italian declaration of neutrality
August 4	Britain declares war on German empire/Germany invades Belgium
August 6	Austria-Hungary declares war on Russia
August 7	British Expeditionary Force begins to land in France

August 12	French and British declaration of war on Austria-Hungary
August 14–25	Battle of the Frontiers (Lorraine)
August 20	Battle of Gumbinnen
August 21–24	Battle of Charleroi
August 23	Battle of Mons
August 24	German armies enter France
August 29	Battle of Guise
August 26–30	Battle of Tannenberg
September 5–12	Germans pushed back in the battle of the Marne
September 6–15	Battle of the Masurian Lakes
September 17–October 18	Race to the sea
September 27–October 10	First Battle of Artois
October 9–20	Battles of Warsaw and Ivangorod
October 12–November 11	First battle of Ypres
November 2	Russia declares war on Turkey
November 6	France and Britain declare war on Turkey
December 2	Austria-Hungary captures Belgrade
December 20	First Battle of Champagne begins

1915

January 3	Germans first use gas shells
February 7–22	Second Battle of the Masuria Lakes
April 22–May 27	Second battle of Ypres
April 26	Allies and Italy sign the Treaty of London
May 2	Austro-Hungarian offensive in Galicia
May 7	Sinking of the *Lusitania*
May 9–June 18	Second battle of Artois
May 23	Italy declares war on Austria-Hungary
June 23	Start of the Battle of Isonzo
August 25	Italian declaration of war on Turkey
August 26	Italian declaration of war on Germany
September 25–October 14	Third Battle of Artois

September 25–October 14	French offensive in the Champagne
October 7	Start of Austro-Hungarian invasion of Serbia
October 14	Bulgaria joins the Central Powers

1916

January 6	Conscription introduced in Britain
February 21–December 18	Battle of Verdun
April 24–29	Easter Rising in Dublin
June 4–September 20	Brusilov Offensive
May 31–June 1	Battle of Jutland
July 1–November 13	Battle of the Somme
August 27	Rumania enters the war on the Allied side
September 1	Central Powers march into Rumania

1917

February 1	Germany starts campaign of unrestricted submarine warfare
March 2	Nicholas II abdicates
April 6	United States enters the war
April 16–29	Chemin des Dames offensive
May	Mutinies in the French army
June 18	Start of the Kerensky offensive
July 31–November 10	Third Battle of Ypres (Passchendaele)
October 24–November 10	Battle of Caporetto
November 20–December 8	Battle of Cambrai
December 3	Bolsheviks sign Armistice

1918

January 8	President Wilson publishes the Fourteen Points
March 3	Signing of Brest-Litovsk
March 21–July 18	German offensive in the west
July 18	Beginning of Allied counter-offensive
May	Start of Allied intervention in northern Russia

September 30	Allies sign Armistice with Bulgaria
October 24	Start of the Battle of Vittorio Veneto
October 27	Austria-Hungary sues for an armistice with Italy
November 9	Abdication of the Kaiser
November 11	Armistice between the Allies and Germany

RUSSIAN CIVIL WAR

1917

January	Widespread strikes across Russia
February 14	Duma reconvened
February 19	Bread rationing to be introduced from March 1
February 23	Beginning of revolution
February 26	Nicholas II orders the dissolution of the Duma, an order which was ignored. Instead Duma establishes Provisional Government.
March 2	Abdication of Nicholas II
Early April	All Russian Consultation of Soviets gathers in Petrograd
April 3	Return of Lenin to Russia
April 4	Lenin issues "April Theses"
April 21	Bolshevik demonstrations in Petrograd and Moscow
April 28	Bolsheviks set up the Red Guard
May 4	Return of Trotsky to Russia
June 3	First All-Russian Congress of Soviets
June 29	Lenin leaves Russia for Finland, returning on July 4
July 3–6	Pro-Bolshevik protests in Petrograd, suppressed by Provisional Government
July 11	Kerensky becomes prime minister
July 18	Kornilov appointed Commander-in-Chief
July 19	Provisional Government orders arrest of Bolshevik leaders
August 9	Provisional Government plans elections for November

August 26–30	Kornilov Affair
September 25	Bolsheviks emerge the majority in the Workers' Section of the Petrograd Soviet
October 10	Bolshevik Central Committee meets in Petrograd and votes in favor of taking power by force
October 24–25	Bolsheviks stage revolution/convening of the Second All-Russian Congress of Soviets/arrest of members of the Provisional Government
October 26	Congress issues Decree on Peace, promising to pull Russia out of World War One and Land Decree confiscating property of large landowners
November 2	Proclamation of the right of self-determination of the peoples of Russia
November 10	Abolition of ranks and titles
Mid-November	Elections to the Constituent Assembly/Bolsheviks in the minority
December 7	Cheka established
December 27	Counter-revolutionary Volunteer Army founded by Generals Alekseev and Kornilov

1918

January 5	Constituent Assembly opens
January 6	Closure of Constituent Assembly
January 8	Third Congress of Soviets opened, dominated by Bolsheviks
January 15	Establishment of the Red Army
January 19	Polish Legion declares war on the Bolsheviks
January 22	Rada announces Ukrainian independence
February 9	Private ownership abolished and land socialized
February 18	Red Army seizes Kiev
February 21–22	Lenin authorizes the summary execution of the revolution's opponents
February 23	Conscription begins for Red Army
March	People's Courts created
March 3	Signing of Brest-Litovsk
March 6–8	Seventh Congress of the Bolshevik Party
March 9	Allied forces land at Murmansk

March 11	Capital transferred from Petrograd to Moscow
March 25	Germans establish Belarusian National Republic
April 22	Transcaucasian Federation declares its independence
May 26	Czech Legion revolts against Bolsheviks/Transcaucasian Federation splits into the Republics of Georgia, Armenia, and Azerbaijan
June 28	Introduction of War Communism
July 10	Soviet Constitution introduced
September 3	Official declaration of the Red Terror
October 21	Conscription of labor
November 29	Northern Estonian War of Independence
December	Start of Latvian War of Independence

1919

January 1	Establishment of Byelorussian Soviet Socialist Republic
February 14	Polish-Soviet war begins
March 4	Comintern founded in Moscow

1920

March 26	Volunteer Army retreats to Crimea to join with armies of Wrangel
November 14	Wrangel flees Russia

1921

February 16	Red Army enters Georgia
February 28	Kronstadt uprising
March 18	End of Polish-Soviet War
March 21	War Communism replaced by the New Economic Policy
July 13	Famine officially acknowledged by Soviet Union

1922

December 29	Creation of the USSR

SPANISH CIVIL WAR

1875

                    Constitutional monarchy founded

1923

September 13–14   Putsch of Miguel Primo de Rivera

1930

January 28   Dismissal of Primo de Rivera by the king

August 17   Republican leaders meet and agree to create a Provisional Government and overturn the monarchy

December 12   Failed military coup

1931

February 14   Resignation of Berenguer government

February 18   Aznar interim government

April 12   Municipal elections bring victories for the Republicans in large cities

April 14   Proclamation of the Second Republic/departure of the king

May-June   Decrees on secular education and rural rents

May 11   Burning of Madrid convents

June 28   Elections for the Cortes

July 14   Opening of the Cortes

July 20–27   July general strike

December 9   Proclamation of new constitution

1932

January   Spain hit by widespread strikes/dissolution of the Jesuit order

August 10   Further failed military coup by General Sanjurjo

1933

January   Anarchist rising in Catalonia

April	Municipal elections go against Azaña
May	Law on congregations
October 29	Founding of the Falange
November 19	Victory of the Right in Elections
December 8–11	Anarchist risings in Catalonia and Aragon

1934

| February 13 | Falange joins JONS |
| October | Asturian rebellion repressed under orders of Franco |

1935

| April | Beginnings of severe cabinet instability |

1936

February 16	Election of the Popular Front
April 7	Zamora deposed as president and replaced by Azaña
May 10	Azaña becomes president
July 17	Military coup in Morocco
July 18	Start of the Civil War in mainland Spain
July 27	Pledge of Mussolini and Hitler to assist Franco
July 28–30	German aircraft arrive in Morocco and Seville
August 2	Britain and France adopt a policy of nonintervention
September 4	Forming of Largo Caballero's government
September 12	Insurgents take San Sebastián
September 30	Bishop of Salamanca describes the Nationalist campaign as a "crusade"
October 1	Franco named generalissimo
October 12	USSR lends support to the Loyalists
November 8	Nationalist advance on Madrid
December	Formation of Condor Legion

1937

| February 6–15 | Battle of Jarama |
| | Nationalist forces capture Málaga |

March 8–18	Battle of Guadalajara
April 19	Right-wing forces fused together by Franco
April 26	Bombing of Guernica
May 3	Fall of Caballero government
May 17	Negrín government
June 18	Fall of Bilbao
July 6	Battle of Brunete
August 24	Republican forces launch Zaragoza offensive
October 31	Negrín government moves to Barcelona

1938

March 10	Franco initiates Aragon offensive
April 15	Franco's armies capture Vinaroz
May 1	Publication of Negrin's Thirteen Points
July 25	Republican Ebro offensive
October 4	International Brigades withdraw
December 23	Intensive Nationalist aerial attacks on Barcelona and Valencia

1939

January 26	Nationalists capture Barcelona
January 27	Franco's government recognized by Britain and France
March 4	Naval revolt at Catagena
March 27	Nationalist troops enter Madrid
April 1	Franco declares the end of hostilities
September 4	Franco declares Spanish neutrality

WORLD WAR TWO

1938

March 12	Anschluss between Germany and Austria
September 29	Munich Agreement
October 1	Germany enters Czech Sudetenland
November 9	Kristallnacht

1939

March 15	Dismemberment of Czechoslovakia
April 7	Germany, Italy, Spain, and Japan sign anti-Comintern pact
August 23	Signing of Nazi-Soviet Pact
September 1	Germany invades Poland
September 3	Britain and France declare war on Germany
September 17	USSR invades Poland
September 27	Fall of Warsaw
September 28	USSR and Nazi Germany divide Poland
November 30	War declared between Finland and the USSR

1940

January 1	USSR attacks Finland
March 12	End of Soviet-Finnish War
April 9	German invasion of Norway and Denmark
May 1	Norwegian surrender
May 10	German offensive in Belgium, Holland, and Luxemburg/Churchill replaces Chamberlain as prime minister
May 12	German troops cross into France
May 15	Surrender of Dutch army; RAF begins its bombing campaign against Germany
May 16	French lines broken at Sedan
May 26	Beginning of the Dunkirk evacuations (end June 3)
May 27–28	Capitulation of Belgium
June 4–8	Allies leave Norway
June 10	Italy enters the war against France and Britain
June 14	Germans arrive in Paris
June 15	USSR occupies Lithuania, Latvia, and Estonia
June 16	Pétain becomes prime minister
June 21	Italy attacks France
June 22	Signing of Franco-German armistice

June 28	Russian occupation of Bessarabia and northern Bukovina
July 10	Start of the Battle of Britain
July 11	Pétain becomes head of the Vichy regime
July 14	Baltic states appropriated by the USSR
August 25	RAF attacks Berlin
September 7	Start of the Blitz
September 25	Quisling government created in Norway
September 27	Germany, Italy and Japan sign Tripartite Pact
October 7	Germans enter Rumania
October 12	Hitler suspends plans to invade Britain (Operation Sealion)
October 22	Slovakia allies with Germany; Jews deported from Alsace-Lorraine
October 28	Italy invades Greece
November 1	Jews prohibited from leaving Warsaw Ghetto
November 14	Luftwaffe's bombing of Coventry
November 20–25	Hungary, Rumania, and Slovakia join Tripartite Pact

1941

January 10	Lend-Lease introduced in U.S. Congress
March 1	Bulgaria joins Axis
March 11	U.S. president approves Lend-Lease
April 6	German invasion of Yugoslavia
April 6–8	Axis forces invade Greece and Yugoslavia
May 10-11	Last major air raid on London for three years
May 14	First round-up of Jews in Paris
May 20	Germans invade Crete
June 22	Germany invades the Soviet Union
June 26	Finland declares war on the Soviet Union
July 12	British-Soviet mutual aid pact
July 21	Luftwaffe attack Moscow
August 12	Atlantic Charter

September 8	Start of the siege of Leningrad
September 19	Kiev and Poltava fall to the Germans
November 3	Germans capture Kursk
November 6	United States extends Lend-Lease to the USSR
December 6	Britain declares war on Bulgaria, Finland, and Rumania
December 7	Pearl Harbor attacked by Japan
December 8	United States and Britain declare war on Japan
December 11	Germany and Italy declare war on the United States

1942

January 1	26 nations sign UN Declaration
January 13	Recapture of Kiev by Red Army
January 20	Conference at Wannsee on the Final Solution
March 27	First French Jews sent to Auschwitz
April 24	German air raids on British cathedral cities (Baedeker raids)
May 30	Start of heavy RAF bombing raids on Germany
July 16	Mass roundup of Jews in France
July 22	First deportations from Warsaw ghetto
October 22	RAF bombs Italian cities
November 8	Allies invade North Africa
November 11	Germany occupies all of France
December 12	Slovakia declares war on the United States
December 13	Hungary declares war on the United States

1943

January 14–24	Casablanca Conference
January 27	First USAAF raids on Germany
January 30	Founding of the Milice
February 2	German armies surrender at Stalingrad
February 8	Soviets triumph at Kursk
April 19	First Warsaw uprising

May 23–29	Heavy RAF raids on German cities
June 8	Comintern disassembled
July 5	Germans attack Kursk
July 11	Allies invade Sicily
July 19	Bombing of Rome
July 24	RAF bombs Hamburg
July 25	Fall of Mussolini
August 8	Capitulation of Italy
September 3	Allies land in mainland Italy
September 5	Liberation of Corsica
September 7	Germans start to leave Ukraine
September 10	Germans occupy Rome
October 13	Italy declares war on Germany
November 6	Kiev liberated
November 9	Creation of United Nations Relief and Rehabilitation Administration
November 28	Teheran Conference

1944

January 22	Anzio landings
January 27	End of the 900-day siege of Leningrad
March 24	Massacre at the Fosse Adreatine, Italy
March 18	Germany occupies Hungary
April 10	Soviets recapture Odessa
June 6	D-Day landings
June 9	Massacre at Tulle, France
June 10	Massacre at Oradour-sur-Glane, France; and Distomo, Greece
June 11	French Resistance rising at Vercors
June 13	V-1 rockets launched against England
July 20	Failed Stauffenberg plot to assassinate Hitler
August 1	Second Warsaw rising
August 15	Landing of Allied troops in southern France

August 21	Dunbarton Oaks Conference, Washington, DC
August 23	Romania agrees armistice with USSR
August 25	Liberation of Paris
August 29	Slovak uprising
August 20	Pétain leaves Vichy
September 4	End of Soviet-Finnish fighting
September 8	First V-2s fired at Britain
September 10	Surrender of Finland
October 5	Soviets reach Hungary
October 7	Start of German withdrawal from Greece
October 9	Start of Moscow Conference
October 20	Start of the liberation of Belgrade
December 24	Massacre at Bande, Belgium

1945

January 17	Soviet armies take Warsaw
January 20	Hungary signs Armistice
January 27	Liberation of Auschwitz
February 4–11	Yalta Conference
February 13	Raid on Dresden
March 4	Finland retrospectively declares war on Germany
March 5	Tito forms new government
March 6	Massacre at De Woeste Hoeve, Holland
March 7	U.S. forces cross the Rhine
March 30	Soviets enter Austria
April 13	Liberation of Vienna
April 23	Red Army enters Berlin
April 28	Death of Mussolini
April 30	Hitler commits suicide/Dachau liberated
May 2	Fall of Berlin
May 7	Germany surrenders
May 8	VE Day

July 17–August 2	Potsdam conference
August 6	Nuclear bomb dropped on Hiroshima
August 9	Nuclear bomb dropped on Nagasaki
August 8	USSR declares war on Japan
August 14	Japanese surrender

THE COLD WAR

1945

February 4–11	Yalta Conference

1946

January 7	Republic of Austria resurrected though divided into four zones of influence (American, British, French, and Soviet)
January 11	People's Republic of Albania established under Enver Hoxha
February 22	Kennan's "Long Telegram"
March 6	Churchill's "Iron Curtain" speech
September 8	Elections in Bulgaria "in favor" of a People's Republic

1947

March 12	Truman Doctrine declared
June 5	Marshall Plan announced

1948

February 26	Communists take over in Czechoslovakia
April 3	Marshall Plan comes into effect
June 24	Beginnings of Berlin Blockade
June 26	Start of the Berlin airlift

1949

January	Founding of Comecon
April 4	NATO formally ratified
May 11–12	End of the Berlin Blockade

May	Communists take charge in Hungary
May 23	Federal Republic of Germany comes into being
August 23	NATO becomes operational
August 29	USSR explodes its first nuclear bomb
October 7	Establishment of the German Democratic Republic
October 16	End of Greek Civil War

1950

| June 25 | Start of Korean war |

1952

| June 30 | End of Marshall Plan |
| October 2 | United Kingdom becomes nuclear power |

1953

March 6	Death of Stalin
June 16–17	Uprisings crushed in GDR
July 27	Armistice concludes Korean War
September 7	Khrushchev head of the Soviet Communist Party
September 8	Creation of South East Asian Treaty Organization (SEATO)

1955

May 9	West Germany joins NATO
May 14	Founding of the Warsaw Pact
May 15	Occupation of Austria ended

1956

April 17	Dissolution of the Cominform
June 29	USSR crushes protests in Poland
October 23	Hungarian Uprising
October 29	Suez Crisis begins

1957

March 25	Signing of the Treaty of Rome
October 4	Launch of Sputnik satellite

1959

January 1	Castro takes charge of Cuba

1960

February 13	France acquires nuclear weapons

1961

April 17	Bay of Pigs invasion
August 13	Berlin border sealed
August 17	Erection of the Berlin Wall

1962

October 15–28	Cuban missile crisis

1964

October 14	Khrushchev replaced by Brezhnev

1966

March 10	France withdraws from NATO Command structure

1967

June 5	Arab-Israeli war (Six-Day War)

1968

January 30	Tet Offensive
June 8	End of Tet Offensive
August 20	Warsaw Pact forces invade Czechoslovakia to crush Prague Spring

1972

May 26   Signing of Strategic Arms Limitation Treaty (SALT)

1973

October 6   Arab-Israeli Yom Kippur War

1975

April 17   North Vietnam overcomes the South

August 1   Helsinki Agreement on Human Rights

1977

June 30   End of SEATO

1979

June 18   SALT II signed

December 24   USSR invades Afghanistan

1980

March 21   United States boycotts Moscow Olympics

August 31   Solidarity movement formed in Poland

1981

December 13   Martial Law imposed in Poland

1982

November 10   Death of Brezhnev, succeeded two days later by Andropov

1984

February 9   Death of Andropov, succeeded on February 13 by Chernenko

1985

March 10   Death of Chernenko who is replaced the next day by Gorbachev

1987

December 8	Signing of Intermediate Nuclear Forces Treaty

1988

May 15	USSR starts withdrawal from Afghanistan

1989

February 11	Independent political parties permitted in Hungary
March 26	Partially free elections conducted in USSR
April 7	Political freedoms permitted in Poland, alongside legalization of Solidarity
June 4	Elections in Poland give majority to Solidarity
September 10	Hungarian border with Austria opened, provoking a flood of East German refugees to the west
October 18	Erich Honnecker resigns as president of the GDR
October 25	Gorbachev announces USSR has no entitlement to interfere in the domestic affairs of its neighbors
November 9	Berlin Wall opened
November 10	Bulgarian Communist Party leader overthrown
December 3	Cold War declared over by leaders of the USSR and United States
December 10	Non-Communist government in Czechoslovakia
December 16–25	Romanian Revolution

1990

January 28	Polish Communist Party dissolved
February 7	Communist Party in the USSR relinquishes "its leading role" in state affairs
29 May	Boris Yeltsin takes charge of Russian Supreme Soviet
October 3	Reunification of Germany
December 9	Lech Walesa elected Polish president

1991

February 25	Warsaw Pact dissolved
August 19	Failed coup in Moscow
August 24	Gorbachev steps down as general secretary of the Communist Party
December 31	USSR gives way to Commonwealth of Independent States

1992

February 1	Formal ending of Cold War

1993

January 1	Czechoslovakia splits into Czech and Slovakian republics

POST-YUGOSLAV WARS

1918

December 1	Kingdom of Serbs, Croats, and Slovenes created and internationally recognized the following year at the Paris Peace Conference

1929

Establishment of the Kingdom of Yugoslavia

1941

Nazi invasion

1945

Founding of the state of Yugoslavia as a federation of six republics and two autonomous provinces

1971

"Croatian Spring," in which Croatian Communist leaders demand greater economic independence, crushed by Tito

1974

Introduction of revised constitution

1980

Death of Tito

1989

September 27   Slovenia declares that it has the right to secede from Yugoslavia

1990

February 1   Serbian forces enter Kosovo

February 17   Founding of SDS in Croatia

April   Elections in Slovenia

April 20   End of state of emergency in Kosovo

May   Elections in Croatia lead to nationalist victory

May 26   SDA created in Bosnia-Herzegovina

June   Slovenia declares sovereignty

July   Establishment of Bosnian SDS and Bosnian HDZ

November   First multiparty elections held in Bosnia-Herzegovina

December   Milošević elected president

December 23   Overwhelming majority vote for independence in Slovenian plebiscite

1991

February 20   Slovenia votes to allow local legislation superiority over federal laws

May 19   Majority of Croatian voters reject the option of their republic remaining part of federal Yugoslavia in a loose confederation

June 25   Croatia and Slovenia announce their independence

June 26   Yugoslav army attacks Slovenia, sparking 10-Day War. Full-scale armed insurrection by the Serb minority in Croatia begins. JNA intervenes on behalf of the insurgents as do volunteer units from Serbia and Montenegro.

July 8   Yugoslav government agrees to the EEC Brioni Agreement, ending the fighting in Slovenia

September 8	Macedonia votes for independence
September 25	UN Security Council introduces an arms embargo on all Yugoslav states
October 7	Yugoslav air strike on Zagreb
December 19	Rebel Serbs declare independence in Krajina (Croatia)

1992

January 9	Serbs inside Bosnia-Herzegovina announce creation of a separate Serb Republic
January 15	EC recognizes Croatia and Slovenia as independent states
February 21	Establishment of UNPROFOR
February 29	Bosnia-Herzegovina declares independence, while Bosnian Serbs declare separate state
March 27	Bosnian Serbs proclaim own constitution
April	Beginning of Serb siege of Sarajevo
April 6	EC recognizes Bosnia-Herzegovina as an independent state
Mid-April	Serbs occupy much of Bosnia and parts of Croatia
April 27	Serbia and Montenegro declare new Yugoslav state
May 30	UN imposes sanctions on Serbia and Montenegro
July	Bosnian Croats proclaim their own autonomous territory, "Herceg-Bosna"
August	International press release of photos of starving Muslims held in Bosnian-Serb prison camps
October 9	UN Security Council creates no-fly zone over Bosnia

1993

January 2	Proposal, authored by international negotiators David Own and Cyril Vance, on the ethnic division of Bosnia rejected by Bosnian Serbs
March	War between Bosnian Croats and Muslims
March 12	Start of NATO flight ban

April-May	Creation of UN safe areas for Bosnian Muslims: Sarajevo, Tuzla, Bihać, Srebrenica, Goražde and Žepa
May 25	International Criminal Tribunal for Yugoslavia (ICTY) created by UN Security Council
July 30	Ceasefire in Bosnia

1994

January	NATO agrees to air strikes to protect UN peacekeepers
February 5	Serbian mortar attack on Sarajevo
February 28	NATO jets shoot down Serb planes
March 18	Bosnian Croats and Muslims agree to U.S.-negotiated peace

1995

January 1	Former U.S. president Jimmy Carter brokers truce between Bosnian Serbs and Muslims
May 24	Serbs ignore UN ultimatum to remove heavy artillery around Sarajevo, prompting further NATO air strikes and Serb attacks on safe areas
July 11	Serbs attack safe area of Srebrenica
July 25	Serbs attack safe area of Žepa/Karadžić. Mladić indicted by ICTY
August 4	Croatia launches large-scale assault (Operation Storm) on rebel Serbs recapturing Serb-held lands in Croatia
August 30	Intensive NATO air strike on Serbs surrounding Sarajevo
September 8	Agreement to divide Muslim and Croat populations within Bosnia, while keeping Bosnia as one state
October 11	Beginning of 60-day ceasefire
November 1–20	Proximity talks at Wright-Patterson Air Force Base, Dayton, Ohio
December 8–9	Peace Implementation Council formed in London
December 14	Signing of the Dayton Peace Accords
December 20	UNPROFOR transfers authority to NATO-led Implementation Force (IFOR)

ONE

The Daily Life of Civilians in Wartime: Europe's Twentieth-Century Experience

Nicholas Atkin

TOWARDS TOTAL WAR

How may we best gain an understanding of the day-to-day lives of European civilians during wartime? This is not an easy question to answer. There is no single experience of war. The ways in which a conflict might impact a civilian are influenced by a set of circumstances unique to an individual: age, gender, race, language, religious beliefs, occupation, social class, and personal psychology, among others. There are several other variables that also have a bearing: grand strategy; the proximity and intensity of the fighting; the discipline of an army; the effects battle has on national and local economies; and the decisions of governments, to name but a few. Most important is the manner in which the nature of warfare itself has changed over time. As a general rule of thumb it may be said that, in the European theater of conflict, the more recent the war the more likely it has been to have interrupted the tempo of daily life.

During the early modern period, Europe's wars were increasingly encroaching upon civilians, something recognized and frequently deplored by contemporaries.[1] Conflicts were becoming ever more frequent and longer in duration, and were fought over a wider geographical area; armies were growing in size, as were navies, and land forces were increasingly mobile; the technology of killing was more deadly, especially since the widespread use of gunpowder since the fifteenth century; and the financial demands of campaigning forced governments to overhaul their administrative structures and increase taxes, leading to the rise of what some historians have contentiously called "fiscal-military" states.[2] Yet in this preindustrial age, unless the fighting was close at hand, civilians could still put war aside and almost out of mind. Unlucky were those local populations that discovered an army camped nearby, all too ready to live off the land and requisition whatever goods, foodstuffs and animals it required.

The French Revolutionary and Napoleonic Wars (1792–1815) ushered in a new type of conflict characterized by the emergence of centralized states, the use of conscription armies, the acquisition of territory on a hitherto undreamed-of scale, the pursuit of ideological goals, a willingness to fight to the bitter end, and attempts to expunge other political systems.[3] In the course of the nineteenth century, such warfare came to be underpinned by the technology of the industrial revolution, whose capacity to facilitate destruction was vividly demonstrated in the Italian and German Wars of Unification of the 1860s and the Franco-Prussian War (1870–71), a struggle in which the railways notably made their mark.[4] For some historians, these encounters already constituted "total wars," implying conflicts "to the last, intent on destroying the enemy's military might, its political system or even its culture."[5]

Whether these hostilities were truly "total" is an ongoing subject of debate, complicated by the theoretical use of the term.[6] Roger Chickering has recently warned against "the master narrative approach," which sees an inexorable march towards totality, a line of interpretation that ignores the particular characteristics of nineteenth-century conflicts.[7] While there is little doubt that the struggles of the 1860s impinged on daily life to a far greater extent than those of the early modern period, they were not all-encompassing. Despite the widespread use of conscription, military planners still had a limited conception of just how many soldiers could be mobilized and still thought in terms of short wars.[8] In the actual fighting itself, the home and fighting fronts were separate and, geographically, the latter remained relatively localized. If the novelist Emile Zola's vivid account of the Franco-Prussian war, *La Débâcle* (1892), is to be believed, the frontier regions of France were indeed devastated by the war, and the soldiers exhausted, starved, and disillusioned. As to the civilians, one critic of the story observes that the war appears as "a tiresome interruption of their normal lives," which they carried on regardless, though not without losing an opportunity to take advantage "of the misfortunes of others."[9] Admittedly it was a standard literary technique, deployed by such novelists as Tolstoy and Stendhal, "to shift focus from the battlefield to the home front and back again" so as "to dramatize the differences between the two," yet the picture they drew largely conveyed the reality.[10]

At the start of World War One (1914–18), it was anticipated by the high commands that this would be a short conflict won by a series of decisive battles, in essence a struggle not so dissimilar to the European campaigns of the 1860s. Generals knew of the destructive powers of new weaponry, in particular machine-guns, barbed wire, and heavy artillery—they had witnessed these new technologies close at hand in their war games, and had studied the lessons of the American Civil War (1861–65) and the Second Boer War (1899–1902). Yet they had not reckoned on the capacity of soldiers to withstand such firepower.[11] Though civilians knew little about the realities of modern warfare, they listened to what the generals, politicians, and newspapers were saying and shared in the hope that the fighting would be over by Christmas.

In the event, such hopes proved misplaced. On the eastern front, huge armies locked horns in a series of gigantic battles, producing millions of refugees in the process, yet it proved impossible to deliver a decisive knockout blow.[12] In the west, the initial failure of the so-called war of movement resulted in a fixed line of trenches stretching from Swiss border to the North Sea.[13] This immobilism also meant that, in contrast to the eastern front, it generally remained possible for civilians to escape the bloodiness of battle, at least during the early months of the conflict. Recalling his time as a young officer, the English novelist Robert Graves remarked on how some 20 miles from the trenches, normal life started to return.[14] In December 1914, as the troops dug in, the London-based travel agent Thomas Cook was offering British holiday makers a choice of a wide range of hotels on the French and Italian Riviera.[15]

Something fundamental, however, had changed, something that would become increasingly evident as the war dragged on. Whereas in previous conflicts, the populace had managed to put the fighting out of mind,[16] in World War One civilians came to *know* that they were at war. This was evidenced in the appearance of food and material shortages, the extensive mobilization of labor forces (women as well as men), the exhortations of government propaganda, the encroachments of the state into every nook and cranny of daily life, and the threat of death, made increasingly possible through long-range shelling, aerial bombardment, and arbitrary violence and reprisals. As the historian David Stevenson writes, World War One was "the prototype for a new model of conflict."[17] Another historian, Richard Overy, elaborates:

The war turned into a conflict of vast mass armies and the mobilization of whole societies, soldier and civilian alike. General Ludendorff, the mastermind behind Germany's war effort between 1916 and 1918, christened the new kind of warfare "total war" for it called on the material, moral and psychological resources of the whole nation. Such a war could only be prosecuted in cooperation with civilian authorities and with the goodwill of the civil population.[18]

Henceforward, concludes Overy, wars would no longer be the sole property of the armed forces and high commands which, it was recognized, could not bring victory on their own. It was equally important for states to marshal their economies and for the civilian population to rally wholeheartedly behind the war effort.

World War One was described at the time as "the war to end all wars," yet sadly conflict remained an ever-present characteristic of Europe's twentieth century. These wars came in all shapes and sizes: civil wars (Russia and Spain); global conflict (World War Two); a war which was not really a war, but what has been described as "a peace" (the Cold War); and a return to what have been termed "little wars" (the post-Yugoslav wars). Aside from the Cold War, whose ambivalent characteristics are discussed later, these displayed obvious elements of totality to a much greater degree than their nineteenth-century forebears: all were of a long duration; all were infused with ideology; all witnessed a blurring of fighting and domestic fronts; all required a gigantic mobilization of economies and resources; all led to material and food shortages; all uprooted populations on an alarming degree; and all brought with them a savagery made deadlier by advances in military technology.

Such characteristics were evident in the Russian Civil War (1917–22). By definition, a civil war is always partly ideological, bringing with it the encroachment of politics into civilian life, yet there have been few ideologies as unforgiving or as ruthless as Bolshevism. Russia's new leaders strained every sinew to preserve the 1917 Revolution and maintain the Red Army in its fight against the many-headed forces of counter-revolution, something evidenced in summer 1918 when the Supreme Council for National Economy hastily devised a brutal economic policy known as War Communism. This entailed an obligatory labor draft of the unemployed, the state takeover of industries, the introduction of strict rationing, and the imposition of severe penalties for alleged slackers. War Communism was also accompanied by an enthusiastic propaganda campaign, though this won few hearts and minds. In the countryside, peasants responded to the forceful requisitioning of their foodstuffs by slaughtering their livestock, hoarding supplies, and killing requisitioning agents. Though the intrusions of War Communism were dependent on the level of Bolshevik military control, there is no question that overall the Civil War itself was hugely disruptive. Through the fighting, which was accompanied by famine, disease, material deprivation, and arbitrary violence, anywhere between 7 million and 8 million civilians and soldiers lost their lives, and approximately 6 million were turned into refugees.[19] It is small wonder that, having defeated their enemies, the Bolsheviks temporarily retreated from communist ideals by permitting a mixed market through the New Economic Policy (NEP).[20]

The lessons of World War One and its aftermath were also observed by Hitler, who believed that Germany had lost the conflict because of alleged Jewish and left-wing subversion of the war effort on the home front. The upshot, in the words of Overy, was that "no state so actively worked to prepare its economy for war as Germany did in the 1930s," though those preparations were far from complete in 1939.[21] In this regard, it is sometimes said that Hitler used the Spanish Civil War (1936–39) as a test-bed for the greater struggle he launched in 1939, yet this was only partially true. The extent to which Nazi Germany, Fascist Italy, and Stalin's Russia provided military equipment to the Nationalists and Republicans has been exaggerated, as has the level of military experimentation.[22] As George Orwell reported, the fighting was not so dissimilar from the western front in World War One, a "stationary" conflict in which soldiers longed for "three things": "a battle, more cigarettes, and a week's leave."[23] Nonetheless, the Spanish Civil War again displayed aspects of totality, most obviously in the attempted ideological mobilization of the people, the prosecution of violence against civilians, and the intervention of the great powers. In this respect, it was widely acknowledged to have become the epicenter of world affairs, as fascism battled against communism and socialism, and liberal democracy watched from the sidelines.

As the Spanish Civil War petered to a close, World War Two (1939–45) began. This was a conflict unprecedented in its scale, encroaching upon every aspect of civilian life. In the words of one historian, it "was truly a 'world' war," a total war eventually involving 61 states.[24] Populations were uprooted to a frightening degree, creating millions of refugees in the process; because of advances in military technology, there was not a sole fighting front, in a traditional sense, but several, with the result that civilians were frequently caught up in the violence, especially that perpetrated from the skies; the extent of Nazi hegemony meant that populations confronted a series of uncomfortable dilemmas about their responses to the occupier; material shortages, notably of food, clothes, and fuel, were felt through all levels of society; in order to remain in the fight, states routinely interfered in the lives of their citizens and had little hesitation in telling people what to do, something as true of the liberal democracies as it was the authoritarian regimes; and the inhumanity that was Nazism and Stalinism brought terror, deportation, and genocide. There was virtually no respite for Europeans, except for those located in neutral countries (Portugal, Spain, Eire, Sweden, Switzerland, Turkey, and the Vatican City), and even here the effects of war reverberated. Otherwise, writes the literary critic Frederick Harris, populations "were immersed in the fighting as deeply and often deeper than the soldiers themselves."[25] The historian Tony Judt has gone as far as saying, "World War two was *primarily* [his italics] a civilian experience."[26]

After 1945, the legacy of war was ever-present. Everyone had a memory of World War Two, especially those groups and individuals subject to the horrors of the Holocaust and Stalinist persecution.[27] There was also the prospect of further conflict as the superpowers, in the shape of the United States and the Soviet Union, stood up to one another in the Cold War. This was a multisided conflict. Among other things, it was a propaganda war; it was an economic war; it was a struggle to establish different spheres of influence in Europe and across the globe; it was an intelligence war; it was a culture war; and it was an arms race. In the words of one historian, it was even a kind of "total war," albeit one very different from what had been experienced in 1939–45. This time there would be no need for the massive mobilization of populations, whether on the fighting front or the home front. Instead the use of nuclear weapons "promised total annihilation in a matter of hours."[28]

Given the enormity of what was at stake, it was inevitable that the Cold War impacted the day-to-day lives of Europeans. In the words of Jeremy Isaacs and Taylor Downing, it "touched many aspects of life— ideology and science, culture and sport. It influenced the images we saw, the songs we sang, and the very language we used for nearly half a century. It helped fix the standard of living in East and West."[29] Nonetheless, such parallels between the Cold War and the "hot wars" of the twentieth century should not be overstated. Though tensions between the United States and the Soviet Union often threatened to spill out into open conflict, especially during the crises "over Berlin and Cuba in the period 1958–1962,"[30] and though both powers fought wars by proxy in Africa, Asia, and elsewhere, the fact remains that a general war between the superpowers was avoided as they feared nuclear catastrophe. The result was that that Europe enjoyed the most sustained period of peace in the twentieth century. This has led one historian to describe the Cold War not as a war but as "the long peace."[31] Viewed from this perspective, it becomes difficult to be precise as to the ways in which this period of tension affected the lives of citizens, other than to say it created a climate of fear and mistrust. By the time of the collapse of communism in 1989–90, most Europeans, whether they lived in East or West, had no direct experience of war beyond what they saw on in their front rooms on "the television screen."[32]

Those television screens were soon to relay the terrible images of the post-Yugoslav wars. Complex in their origins, the ending of the Cold War and the breakup of the Soviet Union in 1989–90 undeniably played a part. Described by historians as a return to small or localized wars, the fighting in former Yugoslavia bore all the nastiness of those internecine conflicts in Russia and Spain. And once again civilians were at the sharp end, subject to bombings, indiscriminate violence, rapes, material shortages, and genocide. It is calculated that, by 1995, the post-Yugoslav wars had produced over 4 million refugees, nearly an eighth of whom had taken refuge in Germany, Sweden, and other parts of Europe,[33] and it is possible that 130,000 people had been killed. In 2007, the International Red Cross reported that at least 17,000 civilians were still unaccounted for.[34]

WHOSE LIVES?

In view of the ways in which war has disrupted the existence of Europeans, it is remarkable that, in the case of the twentieth century, there are relatively few studies of daily life during wartime. Though matters are slowly beginning to change, especially in the case of World War Two,[35] and partially through the efforts of this particular Greenwood series, why this general neglect?

Part of the answer might lie with the questions articulated at the very start of this essay. Whose lives are we writing about? Reflecting in this volume about the experiences of the Russian Civil War, Sam Johnson observes that, "For those caught in the maelstrom, there was no single civilian type, no single victim, no single experience, and, as a result, there is no single narrative that can describe these events."[36] In their pioneering study of daily life during World War Two, Robert Gildea and his team address the very same question, asking whether daily life can ever be a meaningful concept for historians:

> Is it purely private life with the politics left out? Is it history "from the bottom up" rather than that of high politics and great men? Does it deal with the silent majority, the grey mass of autonomous, ordinary people who are the victims of events but do not influence them? Is it habit or routine, a material culture outside the sweep of historical trends? Is it essentially local rather than national or global, or *petite histoire,* anecdotal and descriptive, defying meaningful analysis?[37]

The authors go on to provide an illuminating account of the historiography of daily life and how this has evolved in France, Britain, and Germany, but it does not escape their attention that such approaches have not always been applied to the experiences of wartime.

Another reason for this oversight may have to do with the catholic traditions of military history writing, which for a long time was dominated by former senior officers. As the British author John Keegan reflected in 1976, "military history is many things," among them: "the study of generals and generalship"; "the study of weapons and weapon systems"; "the study of institutions, general staffs, staff colleges, of armies and navies in the round, of the strategic doctrines by which they fight and of the ethos by which they are informed"; and the study of economies at war.[38] Frequently this older sort of military history has been lampooned for the narrowness of its concerns, a type of badges-and-buttons history. According to one writer, "[I]t connotes traditional drum and trumpet operational history with heroic, often panegyric coverage of the past."[39] In the words of Michael Neiberg, it is a top-down type of narrative in which militaries operate "as if they are separate from civilian societies."[40]

Recognizing the deficiencies of this kind of approach, Keegan himself took military history an important step forward by looking at the actual "face of battle," paying particular heed to the psychological and emotional strains of those engaged in combat, drawing on the experiences of soldiers at Agincourt, Waterloo, and the Somme. It is a dimension taken further still by the work of Joanna Bourke, who reminds us that "the characteristic act of men at war is not dying, it is killing."[41] While generals, politicians, and military planners might think of conflict in terms of the pursuit of national and political goals, for those on active service it involves "the lawful killing of other people."[42]

Other historians have also recognized the inadequacies of traditional approaches to warfare and, from the 1980s onwards, forged ahead with what has been called a "new military history." This at last scrutinized the relationship between war and society.[43] As Neiberg puts it, "The practitioners of the war and society approach examine such subjects as the relationships between home fronts and fighting fronts; the differences between history (what happened) and memory (a socially constructed and generally accepted version of that history); tensions between localism and nationalism; and the interactions between war, class, gender and race."[44] Inevitably civilians have figured in this new line of enquiry, but the coverage of daily life still remains uneven, at least for the twentieth century. Economies, institutions, social groups, and communities, and the recollection of the past, prevail over the manner in which war was experienced on the ground.[45] As Frank Tallett observes in this volume, the most innovative military history, what he terms the "newest military history," is that which situates the context of war within an extremely broad societal context, and which does not forget the actual fighting.

Political factors might further explain why historians have shied away from studying daily life in wartime. This is a task fraught with all kinds of dangers, a point also made by Gildea and his team.[46] The intensity of the twentieth-century struggles, their fratricidal nature, their ambiguous moral underpinning, the uncomfortable choices they posed civilians, and the legacies of guilt they bequeathed on the collective psyche, have meant that they have always had the capacity to intrude on the present and disrupt political and social stability. This potential is something that states of all political hues have readily understood, liberal-democratic governments as well as Franco's Spain or Stalin's Russia. The result, in the words of Harold Marcuse, has been that those "who controlled public discourse" have "recollected interpretations of the past that bore little resemblance to what had actually happened."[47] This was especially true in the case of post-1945 Germany, for example. Here, both the Federal and Democratic Republics had to confront the daunting task of reconstruction and, in the emerging Cold War, were eager to prove the superiority of their respective political and economic systems. In this situation, neither had any desire to revisit the daily behavior of Germans under Hitler. Their governments instead constructed a memory in which the German peoples were victims of Nazism, a picture which, in the case of West Germany, only changed through the efforts of historians writing in the 1960s and 1970s. A similar process of "collective amnesia," cultivated by the establishments, overtook Italy and France, with the result that, for a long time, the history of World War Two was either avoided altogether or was written principally as the history of resistance.[48] As General de Gaulle, the undisputed leader of the French resistance overseas, proclaimed in August 1944, "[T]he Republic has never ceased to exist . . .Vichy was and is null and void."[49] It was a view that largely prevailed in France until de Gaulle's retirement from public life in 1969 and the advent of a new generation of historians less troubled by the sensibilities of the past.[50]

Though the study of collective memory remains in its early stages, and lacks a shared methodology,[51] it has been pointed out that it frequently requires regime change, generational change, and change exerted by particular interest groups, most commonly victims' organizations (for instance Jews, resisters, and Communists), before different perspectives of the past can establish a foothold.[52] All these factors have considerably shaped the ways in which writers have approached the Spanish Civil War, one of the most contested fields of historiography, where "even younger historians sometimes cannot resist the combative tone, the propensity to condemn and exculpate, of an earlier period."[53] The passing of time has also been an important factor, though it has not necessarily been a good healer. The French historian Henry Rousso researching in the late 1970s into the Nazi occupation of France thought that a "sufficient period had elapsed" to allow him "to wield his scalpel" only to discover that "the corpse was still warm."[54] It is an experience shared by other historians who have broached the Nazi Occupation, whether of Holland, Denmark, Norway, or Belgium. It is also an experience all too familiar to anyone who has attempted to tackle the recent conflicts in the Balkans, an area that still has to come to terms with the legacies of both World Wars.[55]

The lingering political sensitivity of Europe's wars, and their ability to disrupt the present, has meant that the availability of primary sources released by governments has frequently been uneven, another factor which has discouraged research into *la vie quotidienne*. For a long time working on Franco's Spain, Pétain's France, Stalin's Russia, or Mussolini's Italy was no easy matter, thanks to both official and unofficial censorship. The exception came to be Hitler's Germany, ironic given the earlier reluctance of historians to dig too deeply into the country's past. Having exhausted the ins-and-outs of Nazi foreign policy and having plotted the "twisted road to Auschwitz," in the 1970s historians increasingly took advantage of the release of materials to undertake studies of *Alltagsgeschichte* (literally "the study of daily life"), what was also termed *Geschichte von unten*, "history from below."[56] Ironically, the other exception is proving to be the Soviet Union, which was once obsessively secretive about its past. As Rodric Braithwaite observes, traditional Russian accounts of the famed Great Patriotic War were "overlaid and distorted by decades of pious legend, by the political correctness of officially approved historiography and by the desire of the authorities to emphasize the heroic achievements of the Soviet Union for their own political purposes."[57] The collapse of the USSR in 1989–90, however, precipitated a steady release of hitherto classified material that has facilitated a very different look at Soviet society, both in 1939–45 and in 1917–22.[58]

Even with the steady release of documentation, historians have not been altogether been comfortable of their ground. There remained a sense that they were all too often viewing events through the "filter of the official mind," through the prism of the local commissar or prefect.[59] This unevenness of sources has meant that historians of daily lives have resorted to unusual and imaginative materials to seek out the significance of events. In his groundbreaking studies of the French Resistance, the British historian Roderick Kedward made extensive use of oral testimony. This, he observed, "even fifty years after the event, suggests hypotheses, provides personal details, reveals local colour, facilitates insights, and preserves individuality in a way that historians of an under-documented area of history cannot easily afford to ignore."[60] In his account of Mussolini's Italy, Richard Bosworth was equally innovative, employing a bewildering array of materials, frequently court reports, to understand the "little fascists of the regions, towns and suburbs," alongside "those Italians who sought to get on with their lives, doing their best to ignore the dictatorship."[61]

Inevitably studies of daily life have frequently concentrated on a specific area or region, as opposed to a whole country, so as to eke out particular nuances and ambiguities, a trend especially true of Italy, Spain, and France where there exist rich traditions of local history.[62] Commenting on the appearance of one of the first local studies of occupied France, Kedward observed that this "told us more about life in Vichy France than a dozen books of apparently wider scope."[63] When, in the 1990s, Gildea undertook his extensive study of life in France under the German heel, he was convinced that the true story "lay in the departmental, municipal and Church archives of provincial France."[64] So it is his study begins with one small town in *la France profonde*, Chinon, close to Tours, before branching out to look further afield.

DAILY LIFE AND THE PEOPLE'S WARS

The purpose of this present volume is to attempt to fill some of the gaps in our understanding of daily life during Europe's twentieth-century wars: the two global conflicts; the Russian and Spanish Civil Wars; the post-Yugoslav Wars; and the Cold War. The focus is very definitely not on why these conflicts erupted; nor is it on their operational history. Instead the following essays seek to rescue civilians from obscurity and to place their experiences at the foreground. Drawing on the latest research, each one of the authors is aware of the problems writing about daily life—whose life are they writing about? In pursuing this question, the contributors are sensitive to the many variables that determined the civilian experience, factors over which local populations rarely had control. The authors are also alive to the ways in which societies mutated under the pressure of war and how the vestiges of civil society held firm even under the most extreme of conditions, notably during the Russian Civil War. What is striking is that in the midst of death, privation, hunger, and general disruption, men, women, and children frequently attempted to hold onto the familiar, though they were painfully aware that they were living through the most extraordinary of times. In this way, the wars of the twentieth century could be described as *peoples' wars*, a term usually reserved for the British experience of World War Two.[65]

World War One

Chapter 2, by François Cochet, treats World War One, and stresses the ways in which this conflict was very different from those in the past—in effect Europe's first experience of total war, though he acknowledges that no war can ever be entirely total.[66] Concentrating primarily on Britain, Belgium, France, and Germany, Cochet begins by exploring the complicated relationship between the fighting front and the home front. In a world in which travel and communications were still limited, at least by twenty-first century standards, civilians had scant idea about what life in the trenches was actually like, which might explain why in August 1914 the outbreak of war was so readily accepted. Yet contrary to what is occasionally thought, there was little enthusiasm for the fight, even at the very beginning; instead, populations accepted that the war had to be fought and had to be won. And initially the peoples of Europe stood firm. This togetherness persisted into autumn 1914 as civilians still had little knowledge of a soldier's combat experience. Restricted press reporting and the preparedness of newspapers to make up jingoistic stories, alongside postal censorship and the unwillingness of frontline troops to frighten their families by revealing the horrors of their existence, meant that the true face of battle was kept from view. It was only those civilians living close to the fronts, in occupied territories, or in receiving areas for the wounded and prisoners of war who came to know what modern hostilities really involved. Before long, however, others learned. Rapidly developing military technology meant that towns could be shelled from long distances and increasingly from the air, though the scale of slaughter unleashed from the skies was as nothing compared to that meted out in World War Two.

Such pressures inevitably created domestic tensions and, in the second part of his essay, Cochet examines the social and economic environment. Very few plans had been put in place for the mobilization of either industry or agriculture. Only as the war became a drawn-out affair did governments became more interventionist. Civilians suffered as inflation, food requisitioning, and rationing kicked in, with the result that governments also had to become ever more resourceful to stave off social unrest, which manifested itself in strikes and a hike in trade-union membership. Finally, Cochet addresses the psychological and cultural consequences of the conflict, notably the ways in which families coped with mass death and the anxieties of the ruling elites who feared they were witnessing a breakdown of traditional societal structures. Strikingly Cochet concludes that it was the liberal-democratic societies of France and Britain, rather than the authoritarian ones of Germany and Austria-Hungary, that proved more adept at coping with the demands of a war of attrition, something also true of Britain in 1939–45.

The Russian Civil War

Given Cochet's chosen emphasis on western and central Europe, he has little to say about the Russian experience, though this forms the basis of the next essay by Sam Johnson. Russia paid a heavy price for its involvement in World War One. The demands of wide-scale fighting, which led to "strikes, food riots and a deluge of returning wounded and deserting conscripts," toppled the tsar in February 1917 and facilitated the Bolshevik takeover of October that year.[67] Lenin knew that the revolution's survival hinged on taking Russia out of World War One, something achieved at the Treaty of Brest-Litovsk in March 1918; thereafter, the Red Army could concentrate on tackling its many internal enemies, which coalesced around the tsarist forces of the Whites. Caught in the midst of this vast and ever-moving conflict were Russia's complex ethnic populations, which were forced to make choices. These decisions were made in the most exacting of circumstances. First to suffer was the urban populace, which was engaged in a daily struggle for survival. Food, fuel, and keeping warm were uppermost in people's minds. It was not long before the countryside was also affected. Here, too, food was critical. Many peasants who had initially welcomed Lenin's call for them to seize the land deliberately held on to their grain, hoping to gain the best prices, precipitating town-country antagonisms reminiscent of the nineteenth century. They had not reckoned on the brutality with which both the Reds and Whites would search out their goods. Everyone came under suspicion as the battle lines ebbed back and forth, precipitating huge numbers of refugees in the process. This population movement was in part orchestrated by the Bolsheviks in their attempts to build a new society, yet many chose to leave their homes in the search for employment, food, and safety. Previously thriving cities were left barren, as fear, pestilence, crime, and famine stalked the land.

The Spanish Civil War

The Spanish Civil War (1936–39) was another fratricidal conflict in which communities were pitched against one another. Here, again, ideology impinged on civilian life as the Nationalist and Republican forces strove to capture the nation, both in a physical and cultural sense. As Michael Richards demonstrates, the Republicans had to balance their commitment to building a new society with the demands of fighting the war. Their Nationalist opponents were less fettered by such considerations, and ultimately the Republicans themselves placed the needs of the war effort before social revolution. As Richards continues, ideology was never far away. Civil wars, he argues, are usually more driven by dogma than are interstate conflicts, and Spain was no exception. On the government side, Republican values crept into everyday life with the promotion of secular schooling, attacks on the Catholic Church, and the production of left-wing imagery that was designed to create a war consciousness. The Nationalists countered with the celebration of a counter-revolutionary Catholic culture. Frequently it was women who were caught between these worldviews. These cultural clashes were also so intense that they precipitated a surge of violence against civilians, often through reprisals and arbitrary violence. Atrocities were committed by both sides, though the Nationalists had the most blood on their hands, partially because they were backed by military hardware supplied by Nazi Germany and Fascist Italy. Ultimately, for people on the ground, the war was experienced less as an ideological struggle than as a battle to keep warm, to stave off hunger, and to stay alive, something later true of the post-Yugoslav conflicts.

World War Two

The ensuing chapter (chapter 5, by Atkin) examines the dimensions of World War Two, and stresses the ways in which this war dwarfed previous conflicts, including that of 1914–18. Though the magnitude of the fight makes any generalization hazardous, the author identifies a series of key factors that influenced the civilian experience, notably displacement, government, adjustment, and comportment. The outbreak of fighting in 1939 produced an unprecedented number of refugees. This movement of civilians never ceased throughout the war, as both the German and Soviet regimes ruthlessly moved peoples around, while the final defeat of Nazism 1944–45 brought yet further dislocation. Amid this turmoil, people attempted to get on with their lives as best they could, but much depended geographically on where they lived. Typically Hitler had no blueprint for the empire he was building, but he was clear in his mind that some peoples were racially superior to others. Such notions governed the pitiless ways in which the Nazis dealt with the peoples of Eastern Europe; yet, ultimately, a ruthlessness was exhibited everywhere, especially after the Wannsee Conference (1941–42), which tidied up the final details in the prosecution of the Holocaust. In all parts of Europe civilians had to undergo the painful lessons of adjustment as they coped with the pressures of wartime. As in earlier conflicts, but once again on a far greater scale, much time was devoted to making do, to finding food, to keeping warm, and to avoiding the attention of the occupying forces. Because of the extent of Nazi hegemony, this was extremely difficult, forcing populations into a series of uncomfortable choices. While many attempted to get on with their lives regardless, a small number chose to collaborate;

some managed to resist, though the meanings of resistance and collaboration were extremely fluid, something appreciated after the war when few
countries had any wish to relive their wartime experiences.

The Cold War

In the aftermath of World War Two, Europe yearned for peace yet had
to confront a new kind of conflict in the shape of the Cold War. On the
Continent itself, this never ignited into a hot war, and it is thus difficult to
be precise about the ways in which it impacted day-to-day life, to distin-
guish between developments that resulted from superpower rivalry and
those that would probably have happened anyway. Drawing on the ways
in which military history has been written and the approaches adopted
by the other authors in this volume, chapter 6 by Frank Tallett tackles this
very difficult task and gives a series of fresh insights into how the Cold
War was lived on the ground. Again, much depended on where in Europe
one lived, and the extent to which the superpowers intervened. On occasion, for instance during the Berlin airlift (1948–49), the Cold War felt as
though it was going to descend into an all-out war. The material divide
between east and west Europe was especially acute as the superpowers
established their own models of social and economic development. In so
doing, the two sides believed that they were bestowing freedoms on civilians, though these freedoms were of a very different sort. Inevitably the
Cold War was lived as a "culture war," a war fought not through bullets,
but through rhetoric, symbols, music, film, and propaganda. And, always
lurking in the background, was fear—an anxiety that the Cold War might
not be contained and would break out into open nuclear conflagration, an
irrational conflict in which no side could possibly hope to win.

The Post-Yugoslav Wars

The process of understanding the irrational and unspeakable is currently
being undertaken by those writers attempting to make sense of the Balkan
wars, which erupted with the collapse of the former Yugoslavia, in a state
of disrepair throughout the 1980s.[68] The collapse of the USSR and the dissolution of the Eastern bloc speeded up this disintegration, even though
Yugoslavia had never been a part of the Soviet orbit. As various of the separate republics vied for autonomy, and Serbia held out for a federal state
under its domination, the first Yugoslav war erupted in Slovenia in 1991,
but lasted for a short period. Thereafter there ensued in Croatia a type of
undeclared war as Serbian militias attempted to create a state within a state
having links to Belgrade. Occasionally referred to by some writers (for instance Tony Judt) as the second Yugoslav war (1991–95), before long a third
had erupted within Bosnia (1992–95), where the Serb minority opposed
Bosnian independence, and where the Croat and Muslim populations
were also at loggerheads, what has been called the fourth Yugoslav War

(1992–95), while in 1995 a fifth was fought over and within Kosovo.[69] Amid this confusion, the international community and the United Nations (UN) appeared helpless to prevent ethnic cleansing, random violence, rape, the wanton destruction of economic infrastructure, and the forced migration of civilians, the largest population movement within Europe since the close of World War Two.[70] That said, international intervention in the shape of the Dayton Agreements in 1995 helped bring the wars to an end, and four years later NATO military intervention was successful in curbing Serbian designs on Kosovo.

Drawing on newspaper accounts, personal letters, documentary film footage, and extensive oral testimonies, the final chapter in this study, by Maja Povrzanović Frykman, focuses not on refugees but on those civilians in Croatia and Bosnia-Herzegovina who, in 1992–95, stayed in their homes, the so-called "forgotten majority." In exploring their lives, she takes issue with the widely accepted notion that ethnic tensions exacerbated the intensity of the conflict, and indeed questions whether the post-Yugoslav wars were truly civil wars driven by ethnic tensions. While politicians and army officers attempted to exploit racial hatreds, she argues that these antagonisms were not necessarily shared by civilians at large, who recognized that they lacked the means to change the course of events. In coping with these circumstances, the author shows how time and place were extremely important to how the war was experienced. Threatened by death on a daily basis, civilians became ever more conscious and sensitive to their physical location, and frequently turned into experts on local geography as they learned how to avoid sniper fire, even if this strategy for survival was felt as a "deep humiliation." They also became increasingly aware of their daily habits: buying bread; washing clothes; watching television; traveling on public transport; taking an evening walk. What they had taken for granted in peacetime was no longer so easy amid the fighting; nonetheless, civilians often strove to recreate the humdrum amid the unfamiliar so as to seal off the war going on around them, a process that has been described as an imitation of life. Death, however, became a constant in the civilian experience; and, before long, it was those who had died naturally that generated curiosity in the media and public mind. What is striking is that the lives of these men, women, and children—those who stayed in their homes and who did not flee Croatia and Bosnia-Herzegovina—are already in danger of being overlooked. It is an achievement of this chapter to rescue them from being forgotten.

THE UNIQUE AND THE UNIVERSAL

It will be recalled that it was a standard literary device for nineteenth-century novelists to keep the fighting and domestic fronts separate so as to emphasize the difference between the two, though that difference also inadvertently reflected something of the reality. For instance, in Stendhal's

An unidentified boy in the frontline Sarajevo neighborhood of Dobrinja decorated a barbed-wire fence enclosing a garden with a teddy bear and other toys and flowers during playtime in 1995. Courtesy of AP Photo/Jacqueline Arzt.

Charterhouse of Parma (1839), his hero (or antihero), a Lombard nobleman named Fabrizio del Dongo, goes in search of the battle of Waterloo, after which he wonders whether he was ever in "a real battle."[71] In the twentieth century, the battle would invariably have come to him, and it is telling that contemporary fiction has again reflected that reality. In Ernest Hemmingway's *Farewell to Arms* (1929), an account of World War One in Italy; in Saint Exupéry's *Flight to Arras* (1942), a pilot's view of the 1940 battle of France; in Vasily Grossman's *Life and Fate* (1959), recounting the history of a family caught in the siege of Stalingrad; in John Le Carré's many novels about the Cold War; and in the recent comic-book treatments of the post-Yugoslav conflicts, the lives of combatants and civilians frequently interlard.

For civilians that encounter was both "universal" and "unique," a point established by David and Jeanne Heidler when writing about the early American experience of war.[72] In the many conflicts under review here, populations underwent near-identical experiences, often marked by displacement, cold, hunger, and fear. These sufferings were not so different from those undergone by civilians in earlier conflicts; yet they were different in scale and intensity, a process partially to be explained by the "totalization" of warfare. These experiences were also lived through in a unique fashion. Small wonder that it has been questioned whether it is possible for historians to write about daily life in wartime. To be sure, it cannot be pretended such lives were normal, however much civil society proved resilient in the most extreme of circumstances. Yet that does not discount the subject. As the following essays demonstrate, the struggles, sufferings, and sacrifices of civilians in wartime must never be forgotten. Otherwise the history of warfare is in danger of being reduced to the history of strategies or the history of economies or, at its very worst, it becomes the plaything of governments and establishments with a vested interest in forgetting and in putting across their own version of events.

NOTES

1. See especially the work of the seventeenth-century Dutch philosopher Hugo Grotius, *De iure belli ac pacis libri tres* (Paris: Buon, 1625), available in translation as *On the Law of War and Peace* (Oxford: Oxford University Press, 1925). For other early modern critics, see Jean Chagniot, *Guerre et société à l'époque moderne* (Paris: Presses Universitaires de France, 2001), pp. 161–65.

2. See especially, John Brewer, *The Sinews of Power: War, Money and the English State, 1688–1783* (New York: Knopf, 1989); and Jan Glete, *War and the State in Early Modern Europe: Spain, the Dutch Republic and Sweden as Fiscal-Military States* (London: Routledge, 2001). Among the many studies on the early modern period more generally, see Frank Tallett, *War and Society in Early Modern Europe, 1485–1715* (London: Routledge, 1997 ed.), and Geoffrey Parker, *The Military Revolution: Military Innovation and the Rise of the West* (Cambridge: Cambridge University Press, 1989 ed.). See too the companion volume in this series, Linda S. Frey and Martha L. Frey, *Daily Lives of Civilians in Wartime Europe, 1618–1900* (Westport, Conn.: Greenwood, 2007).

3. See David Andress, *Civil War in the French Revolution* (London: Little Brown, 2005).

4. See Daniel Pick, *War Machine: The Rationalisation of Slaughter in the Modern Age* (New Haven, Conn.: Yale University Press, 1993).

5. Bertrand Taithe, *Citizenship and Wars: France in Turmoil, 1870–1871* (London: Routledge, 2001), p. 22. See also S. Förster and J. Nagler, eds., *On the Road to Total War: The American Civil War and the German Wars of Unification, 1861–1871* (Cambridge: Cambridge University Press, 1997).

6. On total war, see Hugh Strachan, "Total War in the Twentieth Century," in *Total War and Historical Change: Europe 1914–1955,* ed. Arthur Marwick, Clive Emsley, and W. Simpson (Buckingham: Open University Press, 2001), pp. 255–83; his essay "On Total War and Modern War," *International History Review* 22, no. 2 (2000): 341–70; and William J. Philpott, "Total War," in *Modern Military History,* ed. Matthew Hughes and William Philpott (Basingstoke: Palgrave Macmillan, 2006), p. 133.

7. See Roger Chickering's introductory essay in Manfred F. Boemeke, Roger Chickering, and Stig Förster, eds., *Anticipating Total War? The German and American Experiences, 1871–1914* (Cambridge: Cambridge University Press, 1999).

8. This point is made in Philpott, "Total War," p. 135.

9. Leonard Tancock writing in the introduction to Emile Zola, *La Débâcle* (Harmondsworth: Penguin, 1972 ed.), p. 16.

10. Frederick J. Harris, *Encounters with Darkness: French and German Writers on World War II* (Oxford: Oxford University Press, 1983), p. 8.

11. See Joanne Bourke, *Dismembering the Male: Men's Bodies, Britain and the Great War* (London and Chicago: Reaktion Books, 1997), for the experience of soldiers at the front. Also Tim Travers, *The Killing Ground: The British Army, the Western Front and the Emergence of Modern Warfare, 1914–18* (London: Allen and Unwin, 1987).

12. The most authoritative account remains Norman Stone, *The Eastern Front, 1914–1917* (London: Harmondsworth, 1975).

13. Roger Chickering and Stig Förster, eds., *Great War, Total War: Combat and Mobilisation on the Western Front, 1914–1918* (Cambridge: Cambridge University Press, 2000).

14. Robert Graves, *Good bye to All That* (London: Jonathan Cape, 1929).

15. *The Traveller's Gazette,* December 1914, p. 4. This journal, which appeared usually on a weekly basis, then served as the principal advertising organ for Cook's.

16. See Eric Hobsbawn, *The Age of Revolution, 1789–1848* (London: Abacus, 1977), p. 88, who draws attention to the novels of Jane Austen where the protagonists display little awareness of the Napoleonic wars.

17. David Stevenson, *1914–1918: The History of the First World War* (Harmondsworth: Penguin, 2004), p. xix.

18. Richard Overy, "Warfare in Europe since 1918," in *The Oxford Illustrated History of Modern Europe,* ed. T.C.W. Blanning (Oxford: Oxford University Press, 1996), p. 211. See too the essay by Hew Strachan in the same volume, "Military Modernization, 1789–1918," pp. 69–93.

19. Peter Gatrell, "World Wars and Population Displacement in Europe in the Twentieth Century," *Contemporary European History* 16, no. 4 (2007): 418.

20. See Orlando Figes, *A People's Tragedy: The Russian Revolution, 1891–1924* (London: Penguin, 1998).

21. Richard Overy, *Why the Allies Won,* 2nd ed. (London: Pimlico, 2006), p. 243.

22. Among the many works on the Spanish Civil War, see Anthony Beevor, *The Battle for Spain: The Spanish Civil War, 1936–1939* (Harmondsworth: Penguin, 2006). See, too, Roger Chickering and Stig Förster, eds., *The Shadows of Total War: Europe, East Asia and the United States, 1919–1939* (Cambridge: Cambridge University Press, 2003).

23. George Orwell, *Homage to Catalonia* (London: Penguin, 1989 ed.), p. 50.

24. Joanna Bourke, *The Second World War: A People's History* (Oxford: Oxford University Press, 2001), p. 2. See too Roger Chickering and Stig Förster, "Are We There Yet? World War and the Theory of Total War," in *A World at Total War: Global Conflict and the Politics of Destruction, 1937–1945,* ed. Roger Chickering, Stig Förster, and Bernd Greiner (Cambridge: Cambridge University Press, 2005), pp. 1–18.

25. Harris, *Encounters with Darkness,* p. 9.

26. Tony Judt, *Postwar: A History of Europe since 1945* (London: William Heinemann, 2005), p. 13.

27. See Richard Bosworth, *Explaining Auschwitz and Hiroshima: History Writing and the Second World War* (London: Routledge, 1994).

28. Overy, "Warfare in Europe since 1918," p. 224.

29. Jeremy Isaacs and Taylor Downing, *Cold War* (London: Transworld Publishing, 1998), p. ix.

30. John W. Mason, *The Cold War, 1945–1991* (London: Routledge, 1995), p. 75.

31. See John Lewis Gaddis, *The Long Peace: Inquiries into the History of the Cold War* (Oxford: Oxford University Press, 1987). See, too, his *We Now Know: Rethinking Cold War History* (Oxford: Clarendon Press, 1997).

32. Overy, "Warfare in Europe since 1918," p. 230.

33. Carl-Ulrik Schierup, "Former Yugoslavia: Long Waves of International Migration," in *The Cambridge Survey of World Migration*, ed. Robin Cohen (Cambridge: Cambridge University Press, 1995), p. 288. See too the essay by Maja Povrzanović Frykman in this volume. For the experience of refugees more generally, see Michael Marrus, *The Unwanted: European Refugees in the Twentieth Century* (New York: Oxford University Press, 1978).

34. *New York Times*, August 30, 2007.

35. See Robert Gildea, Olivier Wieviorka, and Anette Warring, eds., *Surviving Hitler and Mussolini: Daily Life in Occupied Europe* (Oxford: Berg, 2006), the first of six volumes devoted to this theme, and Jeremy Noakes, ed., *The Civilian in War: The Home Front in Europe, Japan and the USA in World War* (Exeter: University of Exeter Press, 1992). Among older studies, see Gordon Wright, *The Ordeal of Total War* (London: Corgi, 1968); Peter Calvocoressi and Guy Wint, *Total War: Causes and Consequences of the Second World War* (London: Allen Lane, 1972); and Werner Rings, *Life with the Enemy* (New York: Doubleday, 1982). On the century as a whole, see John Bourne, Peter Liddle, and Ian Whitehead, eds., *The Great World War*, vol. 1, *Lightning Strikes Twice* (London: Harper Collins, 2000).

36. See the essay by Sam Johnson, "The Daily Life of Civilians in the Russian Civil War," in this volume.

37. Gildea and team, introduction to Gildea, Wieviorka, and Warrin, *Surviving Hitler and Mussolini*, p. 5.

38. John Keegan, *The Face of Battle: A Study of Agincourt, Waterloo and the Somme* (London: Jonathan Cape, 1976), pp. 25–28. See too George Kasimeris, ed., *Warrior's Dishonour: Barbarity, Morality and Torture in Modern Warfare* (Aldershot: Ashgate, 2006).

39. Benjamin Cooling, quoted in Joanna Bourke, "New Military History," in Hughes and Philpott, *Modern Military History*, p. 259.

40. Michael S. Neiberg, "War and Society," in Hughes and Philpott, *Modern Military History*, p. 48.

41. Joanna Bourke, *An Intimate History of Killing: Face-to-Face Killing in Twentieth-Century Warfare* (London: Granta, 1999), p. 1.

42. Bourke, *An Intimate History of Killing*, p. 1.

43. See especially Geoffrey Best, *War and Society in Revolutionary Europe, 1770–1870* (London: Fontana, 1986); and Brian Bond, *War and Society in Europe, 1870–1970* (London: Fontana, 1984). Among more recent studies see Geoffrey Wawro, *Warfare and Society in Europe, 1792–1914* (London: Routledge, 2000); and Michael Neiberg, *Warfare and Society in Europe, 1898 to the Present Day* (London: Routledge, 2004).

44. Neiberg, "War and Society," p. 42.

45. See Gildea and team, introduction to Gildea, Wieviorka, and Warring, *Surviving Hitler and Mussolini*, p. 5. It was the French historian Fernand Braudel who did much to pioneer the study of everyday life. See his *Civilization and Capitalism 15th–18th Century* (London: Collins, 1981–83), 3 vols.

46. See Gildea and team, introduction to *Surviving Hitler and Mussolini*, p. 5.

47. Harold Marcuse, "Memories of World II and the Holocaust in Europe," in *A Companion to Europe, 1900–1945,* ed. Gordon Martel (Oxford: Blackwell, 2006), p. 500, pp. 487–503, and for much that follows here.

48. It is perhaps France that has been most extensively studied. See, especially, Richard J. Golsan, *Vichy's Afterlife: History and Counterhistory in Postwar France* (Lincoln: University of Nebraska Press, 2000).

49. Quoted in Henry Rousso, *The Vichy Syndrome: History and Memory in France since 1944* (Cambridge, Mass.: Harvard University Press, 1991), p. 17.

50. Much has been written on the historiography of the Vichy years. A good overview is provided in Julian Jackson, *The Dark Years: France 1940–1944* (Oxford: Oxford University Press, 2002).

51. See especially Jay Winter and Emmanuel Sivan, eds., *War and Remembrance in the Twentieth Century* (New York: Cambridge University Press, 1999).

52. Marcuse, "Memories of World War II," pp. 500–501.

53. Wayne Thorpe, "Verdicts of History: The Left in the Spanish Civil War," *Canadian Journal of History* (December 1994): 545.

54. Rousso, *Vichy Syndrome*, p. 1.

55. See Stevan K. Pavlowitch, "Bosnia and Herzegovina in the Second World War," *English Historical Review* 121 (2006): 965–66.

56. On *Alltagsgeschichte* see Geoff Eley, "Labor History, Social History, *Alltagsgeschichte:* Experience, Culture, and the Politics of the Everyday. A New Direction for German Social History," *Journal of Modern History* 61, no. 2 (June 1989): 297–343; and Ian Kershaw, *The Nazi Dictatorship: Problems and Perspectives of Interpretation* (London: Arnold, 1985 ed.). On World War Two see Kershaw's own *Popular Opinion and Political Dissent in the Third Reich* (Oxford: Oxford University Press, 1983); Richard Bessel, ed., *Daily Life in the Third Reich* (Oxford: Blackwell, 1987); Martin Broszat, ed., *Bayern in der N-S Zeit* (Munich-Vienna: Oldenbourg, 1977–83); and Detlev Peukert, *Inside Nazi Germany: Conformity, Opposition and Racism in Everyday Life* (London: Batsford, 1989).

57. Rodric Braithwaite, *Moscow 1941: A City and Its People at War* (London: Profile Books, 2006), p. 400.

58. See Chris Bellamy, *Absolute War: Soviet Russia in the Second World War* (London: Macmillan, 2007).

59. The words belong to Robert Gildea, *Marianne in Chains: In Search of the German Occupation, 1940–45* (London: Macmillan, 2002), p. 9.

60. H. R. Kedward, *In Search of the Maquis: Resistance in Rural France, 1942–44* (Oxford: Oxford University Press, 1993), p. vii.

61. Richard J. B. Bosworth, *Mussolini's Italy: Life under the Dictatorship* (London: Allen Lane, 2005), p. 7.

62. Among many studies on Italy, see especially Camilla Cederna, Martina Lombardi, and Marilea Somaré, eds., *Milano in guerra* (Milan: Feltrinelli, 1979).

63. Roderick Kedward, "The Maquis and the Culture of the Outlaw," in *Vichy France and the Resistance: Culture and Ideology,* ed. Roderick Kedward and Roger Austin (London: Croom Helm, 1985), p. 233. The book under consideration was Pierre Laborie, *Résistants, Vichyssois et autres: L'évolution de l'opinion et des comportements dans le Lot de 1939 à 1944* (Paris: CNRS, 1980).

64. Gildea, *Marianne in Chains*, p. 8.

65. Juliet Gardner, *Wartime: Britain 1939–1945* (London: Headview, 2004), p. xiii. See too Angus Calder, *The People's War* (London: Jonathan Cape, 1969).

66. This is a point made by Bond, *War and Society,* p. 168, in response to Peter Calvocoressi and Guy Wint, *Total War: Causes and Courses of the Second World War* (Harmondsworth: Allen Lane, 1972).

67. Paul Preston, "The Great Civil War, European Politics, 1914–1945," in Blanning, *Oxford History,* p. 151.

68. The periodization of these wars comes from Judt, *Postwar,* p. 674, though not all histories of the former Yugoslavia date the conflicts thus.

69. See Stef Jansen, "The Violence of Memories: Local Narratives of the Past after Ethnic Cleansing in Croatia," *Rethinking History* 6, no. 1 (April 2002): 77–93.

70. See Stef Jansen, "National Numbers in Context: Maps and Stats in Representations of the Post-Yugoslav Wars," *Identities* 12, no. 1 (March 2005): 45–68.

71. See Harris, *Encounters with Darkness,* pp. 9–10, who discusses Stendhal's novel, alongside several other war-based novels.

72. These are the terms used by David S. Heidler and Jeanne T. Heidler, eds., *Daily Lives of Civilians in Wartime Early America* (Westport, Conn.: Greenwood, 2007).

TWO

World War One, 1914–18: Daily Life in Western Societies

François Cochet

World War One broke out for reasons that people in the twenty-first century find difficult to understand. The assassination of Archduke Ferdinand in Sarajevo was merely the trigger for subsequent developments. It was followed by a month of intense negotiations—ones that the chancelleries of Europe pursued with relative optimism, until events began spiraling out of control at the end of July 1914. There is no shortage of explanations as to why war erupted: the badly thought-out and risky strategies of the Central Powers; the clashes between the different types of nationalism that had taken root in the nineteenth century, *the* century of nation building; and the diplomatic negligence of France and Britain. Whatever the cause, a large part of Europe quickly found itself at war. Apart from the principal belligerents of July 1914 (Britain, France, Belgium, Russia, Serbia, Austria-Hungary, and Germany), we can add Turkey in November 1914, Italy in May 1915, Romania in August 1916, the United States and many Latin American countries in April 1917, and Greece in June 1917. Almost the entire world was involved, especially since the European powers had mobilized their colonies in support of a conflict whose length surprised everyone.

The war involved millions of combatants who quickly became trapped in static trench warfare, at least on the western front. Yet the fighting concerned not only combatants. From now on, war would have an impact on society right across the board. Civilians on the home front were especially affected, though admittedly in ways that differed from the frontlines.

Europe on the eve of War 1914.

The purpose of this chapter is to explore the complex relationship between the home front and the war. This is better understood if we relinquish our present notions about warfare. A century of cultural upheavals
has gone by since World War One. Culturally, psychologically, and technologically, that conflict took place in a very different world from our own.

People's horizons between 1914 and 1918 were much more limited than nowadays. They did not usually travel, especially not abroad. Often they lived and died in the same village in which they were born. Sources of information (for example, the press) were not as powerful as they are today. In a world only beginning to be dominated by speed, the present did not yet reign supreme. These various limitations meant that time, as lived on the frontlines, was not the same as time was for civilians back home. The pace of life for civilians rarely coincided with that of the soldiers. These factors thus make it difficult for the historian to assess the ways in which the war was seen by the home front. What did contemporaries imagine the fighting to be like?

There remains another vital factor in exploring the home front. Notwithstanding the differences between countries, societies had to adapt to war, and develop their economies to cope with the ever-growing armaments industry, while at the same time keeping civilians supplied with necessities, for civilians remained by far the largest sector of the population. The world of work went through a process of far-reaching change, involving an unprecedented feminization of the labor force. Though different countries adapted to the demands of war in different ways, in each and every case the belligerent nations learned how to steer or manage their economies, often breaking with the liberal economic theories in fashion at the time.

The final aspect of this study will focus on human suffering. On the part of civilian populations, these miseries were broadly the same. The unprecedented death tolls led to new forms of grieving, including the custom of issuing death notices by the family concerned. The physical separation of soldiers from their families on the home front was another form of psychological anguish. Arrangements for leave were only slowly put in place and were thoroughly unsatisfactory; they did not allow families to see "their" soldier very often.

The war, which took hold little by little, soon became an all-out war, a "total war," which shook the countries involved to their very foundations. Its scale also meant that it would occupy an important place in the memory of Europeans for many years afterwards. It is thus impossible to comprehend its full impact on civilians. The following chapter can only glimpse the full picture, drawing heavily on the French experience.

HOME AND FIGHTING FRONTS AT THE START OF THE WAR: A COMPLICATED AND AMBIGUOUS RELATIONSHIP

Apart from exceptional cases, civilians did not take an active part in the fighting. The picture of the war that they drew for themselves was, therefore, secondhand. At the start of the conflict, civilians also struggled to imagine what the drama of war would mean for them on the home front.

Before fighting first broke out, and in an increasingly fraught international context, the French socialist leader Jean Jaurès wrote in *L'Humanité*, on July 13, 1914, that "the greatest danger currently lies not, if I can say this, in the events themselves. It does not even lie in the steps taken by the diplomats, as guilty as they might be; it lies not in the real intentions of the people, but in sudden impulsive actions that are born of fear, raw uncertainty and prolonged anxiety. It is possible for crowds to give in to these mad panics, and it is by no means certain that governments will resist them either." Jaurès thus understood the essence of the tragic sequences of events that opened the war. Fear of the unknown, the feeling of being attacked and of having to defend oneself: these are what made the people of Europe accept the worst. In the early days of the fighting, governments on both sides took the line that they had been forced into war by the enemy. On August 4, 1914, Kaiser Wilhelm II declared that, "driven to our own legitimate defence, we draw the sword with an unstained conscience and unstained hands." The same day, René Viviani, president of the French Council of Ministers, said to members of the National Assembly: "A nation armed, fighting for its own life and the independence of Europe: such is the spectacle that we are proud to offer the witnesses of this tremendous battle. We have nothing to reproach ourselves with, and we are not afraid."

From Images of War to the Reality of War

The war, as the home front imagined it to be, bore little resemblance to real conditions on the ground. This gap between what civilians imagined the war to be like and what it was in reality remained a constant. No one could have anticipated this. In 1914, all the groups and organizations concerned—political and military leaders, soldiers and ordinary citizens—thought the war was going to be short. Bearing in mind the advances in weaponry, none of the belligerents could have imagined that the war might last beyond the end of 1914. Rather it was expected that the clash would be nasty, but of short duration. The fact that everyone was totally convinced of this broadly explains why so few people were opposed to the war.

With the benefit of hindsight, it is known that the enthusiasm that accompanied the outbreak of fighting, and which was witnessed in several capital cities, needs to be qualified. There were certainly scenes of rejoicing in a few large cities. Around major railway stations, through which enlisted men necessarily had to pass, there were also scenes of enthusiasm that have been compared to a collective hysteria. All the necessary ingredients were there: the atmosphere of the crowd, the excitement of civilians who were accompanying the soldiers, and frequently the presence of alcohol. The press exacerbated the situation by glorifying the combatants. Recalling initial mobilization, *L'Echo de Paris* stated on November 14, 1914, that "as for us, the non-combatants, Frenchmen of a lesser kind, we will die happy to have seen such glory." Even at this time, however, the war's disappointments were already very real. Moreover, scenes of enthusiasm were restricted to large cities. In smaller towns, and especially in the countryside, the mood was largely one of sadness and resignation. In France, mobilization was made known by the *tocsin,* the ringing of church bells that usually announced bad news. In Germany, the enthusiastic scenes witnessed in Berlin were not replicated in working-class towns, such as Bremen. Among minorities, for example the Poles, Alsatians, and Slavs in the German empire, there was no enthusiasm whatsoever, even if this did not translate into actual rejection of the war.

Although cracks in public opinion soon manifested themselves, it is difficult to account for the spirit of togetherness that accompanied the outbreak of war. The French example is revealing in this regard. Coercive measures were drawn up in France to combat pacifist demonstrations. The government feared that conscription evasion would be especially common, and that many young Frenchmen would refuse to go to war. The infamous *Carnet B* contained the names of nearly two thousand people to be arrested as a preventative measure in France for when mobilization was announced. In the event, such steps were unnecessary. Although the military high command had been anticipating a draft-dodge rate of close to 10 percent, in the event it was little more than 1.5 percent. What had happened? Part of the answer lies in the failure of the Second International, the international organization of socialist parties, to achieve unanimous opposition to the war. The working-class conscience was still ruled by national considerations. In the Reichstag, German socialists voted for war credits, just like their French counterparts in the National Assembly. At the headquarters of the Socialist International in Brussels, German socialists rejected the idea of initiating a general strike, which, it was believed, would leave Germany at the mercy of what they considered to be Russian savagery.

What Did the Home Front Know about the Real War?

In answering this question, it should be recalled that soldiers could only communicate with their families by mail. Postal networks were quickly set up for the armies. Since provisions for letter censorship were established by all the belligerent nations, and today such correspondence makes an excellent research tool for the historian. But were soldiers able to tell their families the real truth about the war? Nothing is less certain. Letters to family were a lifeline, but the combatants sought to reassure their families, rather than worry them. In these cases, some things were better left unsaid. This author has personally had the opportunity to compare letters sent by a soldier to his wife with the private diary of another combatant, both written at one of the high points of the Battle of Verdun (1916). Both men were in the same squad, and effectively they lived only yards away from each other. When the former wrote to his wife and said that everything was fine, the latter discreetly noted in his diary that the situation was unbearable, and that the Germans were shelling French lines heavily. Thus the home front rarely learned the whole truth about the fighting through private correspondence. Civilians discovered even less from the news circulated by the press, the only media outlet at the time.

News was very strictly regulated by fiendishly elaborate censorship mechanisms, even if these differed from country to country. In France, the public was not properly told about the setbacks of August 1914 until the very start of 1915, several months after the events had taken place. Newspapers developed a system of complete disinformation. In Germany, news was wholly controlled by General Headquarters. Until the end of 1914, reporters in France were not allowed to go into the militarized zones. So they made up the stories that they did not have. This gave rise to an unusual process, known as *bourrage de crâne* (literally "stuffing of heads," usually with misinformation). This was seen especially at the beginning of the war. On August 19, *Le Journal* claimed that 80 percent of German shells failed to explode. On September 15, *Le Matin* suggested that shrapnel only caused superficial wounds. The same newspaper in August had also claimed that the wounded "laugh, joke and ask to be sent back to the front." As one author reflects, "newspapers (apart from the pacifist ones) described for the most part a war waged entirely with heroism, a willingness to accept dangerous missions, a deep love for country, and a bitter perseverance with victory in mind. The soldier wanted neither to disappoint nor frighten his old father and mother. So he toned down and softened his letters, making them believe in the bright colours of the sky blues, while he himself was reduced to a hollow wreck covered in mud."[1] From spring 1915 onwards, *bourrage de crâne* diminished without stopping altogether.

The wounded were the only part of the real war that the home front ever saw. In Limoges alone, 10 temporary hospitals were opened. This location was not chosen by chance. Far from the trench warfare of Champagne, Argonne, and the Somme, the town was an excellent place to assemble and recuperate the seriously injured. On August 31, 1915, the minister Julien Godart spoke to the *Courrier du Centre*. Limoges, in his own words, was "an important centre where it is possible to admit wounded from all the military hospitals in the Central region where they will receive appropriate treatment coordinated by medical specialists well known in their fields." Two French military districts, the 12th (Limoges) and the 18th (Bordeaux), looked after about half the French wounded between them.

In rural regions, all that was seen of the enemy were prisoners of war. Used as farm laborers from summer 1915 onwards, they were initially looked upon with suspicion, at least until farmers realized they had a cheap labor force at their disposal. What little else was known of the war remained relatively abstract, creating patterns of behavior that are revealing of how the French saw themselves and the conflict. For instance, in Paris a lively atmosphere persisted in which different groups of citizens campaigned for victory. During winter 1914–15, Parisian women sported fashion items inspired by the military style, with braid and stylish cuts akin to military jackets. This was but a parody of patriotism, although it has led some historians into thinking that state propaganda might be an expression of society's feelings, and not just a top-down process whereby governments attempt to control the thoughts of their citizens.

As they advanced through Belgium, the Germans committed dreadful atrocities against the local populations, which they then repeated in northern France and the Ardennes.[2] It is known that 4,421 Belgian civilians and 725 French were murdered during the German advance. This savagery was the result of German officers being unable to control their men in the face of unexpected Belgian resistance. Above all, it showed that the myth of *Franctireurkrieg* was widespread. The German press, civil authorities, and soldiers were all convinced that these civilian uprisings were part of the military preparations to resist the invasion of Belgium, as they had been in 1870–71 at the time of the Franco-Prussian war. The torching of towns and villages and mass executions of civilians thus became commonplace.

One million Belgian refugees, such as these from Antwerp, fled the country. George Grantham Bain Collection. Courtesy of Library of Congress.

Civilians in occupied areas found themselves in the middle of the fighting. On August 20, 1914, the Germans entered Brussels. Out of a total population of 7.5 million, 1 million Belgians took flight. A German military government was set up. This government deported many burgomasters to Germany, and dispensed with existing administrative units such as the regional councils. At the beginning of 1915, the Belgian civilian population was struck by genuine famine. Signs of a demographic disaster were growing more numerous. The Belgian birth rate plunged by three-quarters while the mortality rate doubled. The black market had a field day (food prices during German occupation rose by 1,200 percent) and only essentials were available (bread, potatoes), though there was not enough to go round. On leaving Belgium, the Germans dismantled what they could of the Belgian industrial sector in order to transport it back to Germany. They destroyed what was left. Twenty-six blast furnaces were torn down, a reminder that the war was an industrial one.

Those who managed to flee Belgium joined a band of refugees who were not welcome everywhere. From August 1914, the authorities in Rheims became wary of new arrivals. In October 1914, Le Havre's local council said the town had reached saturation point and claimed no more refugees could be accommodated.[3] Refugees from the Ardennes arrived in Limoges on September 1, 1914, and then came families from the Pas-de-Calais who had been evacuated provisionally to Normandy and La Rochelle. About 6,000 civilians had to be sheltered temporarily in the town circus at Limoges, and in various requisitioned premises.

Even if at the start of the war the technology did not exist to carry out long-distance bombing raids, certain towns suffered artillery shelling. Belgrade was the first major city bombarded during the war. In the eyes of the world, Rheims became a martyred town. Located only a few miles from the frontlines, it suffered 1,051 days of artillery bombardments, which left nearly 800 of its inhabitants dead. Its civilian population, numbering about 100,000 at the start of the war, was reduced to less than 20,000 by 1915; those who could, fled in the early days of the war. The civilians who remained behind were made into heroes by national propaganda.[4]

As the war persisted, the technology to inflict damage at a long range was steadily developed. The Germans launched bombing raids on England with airships. Civilian casualties caused by these Zeppelin air raids totaled 1,400 deaths and 3,400 injured. The British did not stand idly by. In the second half of the war they launched reprisal attacks with aeroplanes. In 1918 alone, the British organized 350 raids against Germany, involving 2,319 planes. In total, 700 German civilians were killed and 1,800 injured. It should not be forgotten, however, that for each day of combat, the ground war cost the lives of 1,200 German soldiers and 900 French ones.

Some civilians were also directly affected by internment policies. At the start of the war, every country rounded up members of enemy nationalities. Civilians were imprisoned in camps where living conditions were often poor, especially in Germany, which was affected by food shortages early on. Throughout the war, there was a tense atmosphere of spy mania. People saw spies everywhere. On August 7, 1914, the *Courrier du Centre* in Limoges, miles away from any fighting, reported that the salesman for the food manufacturer Kub, which was thought to be German, had been arrested and thrown into the local prison (*la prison des Bénédictins*).

All in all, the civilians' experiences of the war were very different, depending on how near to, or far from, the fighting they were, and more generally, whether they saw any of the direct effects of the war. The cases we have just mentioned should not make us forget the main point. In most instances, civilians on the home front had no direct experience of the war. They were forced to imagine what the war was like through soldiers' letters, government propaganda, press reports, and word of mouth.

Intellectuals and the War: A "War Culture"?

Opinion was carefully watched and subtly guided during the war. In France, news from the frontlines passed through a central office, headed by Paul Reboux, within the propaganda department of the French Foreign Office.[5]

The war, as imagined and celebrated by civilian writers on the home front, was nothing like the real war. Those present-day scholars (all of whom incidentally are French) who believe they can discern a "war culture" in these writings have misunderstood the nature of such commentaries. The American author Jay M. Winter, on the other hand, clearly appreciates what lay behind the violent language used by the home front authors. "In fact [they] were proclaiming their allegiance to a romantic war, the seductive force of which the intellectuals could not resist."[6] Writers who made pompous patriotism into a specialty were often mocked by the public. One such was Henry Lavedan, a member of the Académie Française, almost completely forgotten today but famous at the time. In *L'Illustration* on April 28, 1917, on the eve of the Chemin des Dames offensive, he eulogized that, "for the soldier, an attack is a sublime moment in the war, a grand manoeuvre, the most solemn and sacred of all, during which, and even more than usual, he no longer thinks about himself but gives of himself entirely."

In the religious domain, France was different from elsewhere. The official separation of the churches from the state had been proclaimed less than 10 years before the war began. Here, more than in other countries, the churches, and especially the Catholic Church, which included 90 percent of all worshipers, had to carry the banner of aggressive patriotism to show that its followers belonged to the national community. On August 6, 1914, the bishop of Tulle celebrated a mass for men leaving for the front. For the first time since 1905, the prefect was in attendance. The "children's crusade," launched by the French Catholic Church in the southwest, also provides a good example of how Catholics rallied behind the war effort. The children went on pilgrimage, wearing the sign of the Sacred Heart and placing themselves under the patronage of Joan of Arc and the Virgin Mary.[7] So it was, in becoming accepted as part of the nation, that the churches helped overcome any reticence about taking up arms and taking life. Even if the consequences of the separation of the churches and the state were specific to France, similar warmongering was seen elsewhere. Threatened by an atmosphere of de-Christianization, the churches across Europe were determined that the war would be an opportunity to rebuild a Christian consensus. This involved religious leaders in proving that God was on the side of their country. The problem was that all sides enjoyed divine approbation. To the German *Gott mitt uns* (God is with us), the French reply was, "France, eldest daughter of the Church." Later in the war, the Americans would say, "In God we trust."

The sermon delivered by English Bishop Arthur Winnington-Ingram is often quoted to illustrate this phenomenon, though somewhat unfairly, it must be said. With our twenty-first-century notions, and knowing what has happened since the end of World War One, it is impossible for us not to be scandalized by what he stated. If, however, we take the trouble to contextualize it—and do the basic job of any historian—it becomes easier to understand.

The sermon was given when the international community had just heard about events in Turkey (the Armenian genocide). Its discourse of hatred against the Germans is, consequently, easier to put into context, as it was the Germans who were thought to have made the genocide possible. "First, we saw Belgium knifed in the back and devastated," pronounced Winnington-Ingram, "then Poland, then Serbia, and then the Armenian nation killed—at least 500,000 Armenians have been killed. So, to save the world's freedom, to save freedom itself, to save the honour of women and the innocence of children, all that is noblest in Europe and all who love freedom and honour, all those of us who place their principles above life itself, have joined forces together in a great crusade—it cannot be denied—to kill the Germans: to kill them not for the pleasure of killing, but to save the world, killing the good and the wicked, the young and the old."[8] In a similar vein, though using less brutal language, on September 8, 1914, the parish priest of St. Etienne du Mont, a church in the Place du Panthéon in the fifth arrondissement of Paris, published a booklet attributing the victory at the Marne to the miraculous intervention of St. Geneviève, protector of Paris.

So it was on the home front that several civilians and agencies felt obliged to trumpet an ultrapatriotic discourse, both to prosecute the war and to show a sense of solidarity with those on the fighting front. There was no wish to appear more fortunate than the troops in the trenches. Otherwise, the families of such men would have immediately accused such civilians of having cushy postings that enabled them to avoid the real dangers of

"*Pro Patria*"

Le Bon Évêque de Meaux

Monseigneur MARBEAU accueillant les blessés qu'il garde sous sa protection.

Translation: "For the country. The good bishop of Meaux." This 1914 poster shows the bishop of Meaux with nurses and a member of the clergy, welcoming some wounded soldiers. Artist: P. Loubere. Courtesy of Library of Congress.

combat. A war culture thus became a distinguishing feature of the home front. Talk made up for inactivity. It was a way of misappropriating or hijacking a true patriotic defense of one's native soil, and one which was frequently expressed in the early days of mobilization. Newspapers on all sides were always ready to brandish their patriotism and foster a hatred of the enemy that was not necessarily shared by those in the trenches. They thus had a big hand in demonizing the enemy in ways that were surprising or even grotesque. In Germany, any French names for professions were Germanized. *Coiffeur* (hairdresser) became *Haarkünsler,* and the adjective *grand* was banned from display on the fronts of public establishments, restaurants, or hotels. In France, the names of some roses were changed, and theoretically *bergers allemand* (German Shepherds) had to be referred to as *bergers alsaciens* (Alsatians).[9] Most examples of this pseudo-war culture had no effect beyond Paris and barely touched the actual daily lives of civilians on the home front. But they made it possible for a patriotic consciousness to be formed at little expense. Actresses who were desperate for headlines loudly declaimed their patriotic feelings, which were all the more ardent for being of little consequence. In May 1916, the aging Sarah Bernhardt told a French newspaper: "I do not know what fear is. Fear is a product 'Made in Germany.'"

Consequently, it is unfortunate that some French historians have thought it right to construct an entire theory about the unanimity of patriotic discourse which, they say, led to an "eschatological millenarianism."[10] Wishing at any price to inject some modernity into a historical discourse, these authors have used semantic oversimplifications that interest the present-day media, which prefers caricatures to historical complexities.

THE ECONOMIC AND SOCIAL DIMENSIONS OF THE WAR

In the eyes of most civilians, the most tangible reality of the war consisted in how it disrupted ordinary living conditions.

Work Disrupted and Redistributed

At the beginning of the conflict, there were no plans for mobilizing industry. As we have seen, everyone, both in Germany and in France, believed that the war would be short. That said, mobilization disrupted productivity, especially in the countryside. In Charente, 20,000 farmworkers were called up. In Haute-Vienne, out of 54,000 conscripted men, 35,000 were *paysans* (peasants).[11] Industry in towns was also disrupted by mobilization, and initially there were many layoffs. In August 1914, 52 percent of French companies were closed temporarily due to mobilization. In rural areas, the heavy summer work was disrupted not only because men were being called up, but also because the tractors of the period, namely horses, were requisitioned. At least six horses were needed, for example, to haul a piece of light artillery. Thus, in the early months of the war, in all the belligerent countries, improvisation was the order of the day. New industrial regions sometimes emerged. Such was the case in France where the industrial *départements* in the northeast were quickly occupied by the Germans. This gave the country a new industrial map. Central and southwestern areas mainly benefited from these regional changes. In the center of the country, the porcelain industry, the great specialty of Limoges, was able to redevelop itself. Toy producers, in particular, quickly appreciated that the bulk of dolls' heads came from Germany. The Lanternier Company seized the gap in the market and started making them. For its part, the Michelaud Company gave up producing porcelain in order to manufacture isolators and sparkplugs for engines. Faure, an engineering company, began manufacturing shells in November 1914. They made 50 times as many shells in December 1916 than in November 1914. This factory is interesting in other ways. It provides a perfect example of the difficulties felt by the business world at the time of mobilization. At the beginning of August 1914, only 4 out of the factory's 200 workers were exempt from conscription. By March 1917, the labor force had risen again to 130, working night and day by shifts. Seventy of these were women.

In all the belligerent nations, solutions had to be found to lessen the effects of labor shortage. In Germany, 1,200,000 soldiers benefited from exemption from military duty, and thus escaped the trenches. On December 5, 1915, an attempt was made to channel the young and elderly into work by means of a law concerning "auxiliary service." Elizabeth Luders became head of the Women's Labor Office. In France, in spring 1915, the Dalbiez

Translation: "War industries. Exhibition organized by the Charity for Disabled Soldiers." This poster shows an interior view of a factory. Artist: H. Chachoin, 1918. Courtesy of Library of Congress.

Law provided for "special appointments," essentially protected professions. Qualified workers were withdrawn from the frontlines to work in armament factories. Female workers were in demand everywhere. In both France and Great Britain, labor was drafted in from the colonies. Prisoners of war were also put to work.

The war industries sucked in any spare members of the labor force. For instance, weapons manufacturers at Tulle welcomed workers from villages in the surrounding rural areas, refugees from Belgium, French refugees from the Ardennes, and those from the north generally. Women, too, came to appear on the factory floor in industries that had traditionally been dominated by men.

The big names in industry from the pre-1914 period were still around. Schneiders in France and Krupp in Germany increased their wealth thanks to war-related manufacturing. Others made a name for themselves in the course of the war. Louis Renault, whose company was founded in 1898, became a dazzling success by diversifying production to include not only cars but also aircraft engines and, by the end of the war, tanks.

Material Difficulties and Wartime Profiteers

Civilians suffered most due to prices and the difficulty of obtaining certain goods during the war, although this situation differed from country to country and among social classes.

Between July 28 (Madrid) and July 31 (London), 1914, the stock markets closed. At around the same time in France, the price of bank notes was set at a fixed rate and silver pieces (five-franc coins) disappeared. Shops with multiple branches (Félix Potin or Damoy) refused to sell certain goods rather than be obliged to give out small change. The growing shortage of coins in precious metal, which were often hoarded, contributed to price rises in all the belligerent nations.

Quickly and tangibly, war-driven inflation rose. In February 1918, the French labor minister unveiled statistics showing that prices in the country had risen disproportionately. In Paris, in July 1914, the 13 base products making up the retail price index stood at 1,075, but reached 1,982 in October 1917. Inflation also affected countries other than France. In Berlin, retail prices increased by 89 percent between July 1914 and January 1916. On July 21 that year, the prefect of Corrèze reported violent clashes at the Tulle market between female shoppers and female stall owners after the latter came to an agreement to hike up prices even higher than usual. Considerable mistrust evolved between social classes, denting any notions that nations were at one in their patriotism. "The town's shopkeepers blame the country people and the country people suspect the town's shopkeepers," reported the prefect.[12]

Faced with austerity and growing social discontent on the home fronts, the belligerent nations bought social peace in a variety of ways.

In Germany, General Headquarters, which had considerable influence over the ways in which industry was run, encouraged high salary structures. In France, the state dug into its own pockets. A system of war benefits was created at the very outbreak of the fighting. Wives or parents of enlisted men received 1.25 francs per day, and half a franc for each child. These benefits were paid from the end of August 1914 onwards, although such amounts were not enough to live on. In urban centers, for example, they did not compensate for the loss of the salary of a worker who had been called up. On the other hand, in some rural areas, where the lot of farm workers was exceedingly tough, these benefits were a real boon when compared with the situation before the war.

The war also disrupted the usual commercial distribution networks. Belligerent countries soon noticed things that had not been measured before. Thus, in Germany, the authorities woke up to the percentage of foodstuffs consumed before the war that came from abroad. In June 1916, a government office was created to limit such imports as much as possible.

During the war, economies experienced declining productivity, especially in the agricultural sector. Having lost men due to enlistment, rural regions could no longer ensure national self-sufficiency in wartime. In Germany, the 1916 harvest was particularly bad. Official rations covered hardly half of what was needed. The black market exploded. In summer 1918, real food shortages occurred. France and Britain were better off in this regard. They were not affected by blockades, and could buy in bulk—though at the cost of mounting foreign debt—from the United States, Australia, and Argentina.

Rationing was established in a variety of ways and at different moments in the course of the war. Because of naval blockades, rationing in Germany and Austria-Hungry was more dramatic than in England or France. In France, restrictions came late and were limited. By a decree of April 14, 1917, the sale of meat was forbidden two days a week, and a sugar rationing card was introduced on January 1, 1917. Bread was rationed in April 1917, but the bread rationing card was not really used until May 1918.

Despite the best efforts of governments, such hardships did threaten the civil peace. The first strikes, since the beginning of the war, took place in Germany at the Sarre colliery in May 1916. They did not focus on any political issue, and simply revolved around material questions. The workers called for salary increases to counter the inflation that was whittling down their meager buying power. The same process occurred in France, where strikes erupted in 1916. In spring the following year, the "strike of the dressmakers' apprentices" involved 18,000 women, but they did not make any political demands. In Britain, trade union leaders made appeals for a social truce at the beginning of the war. Such appeals did not prevent maverick strikes—outside of union control—during the second half of the war. In 1917–18, even London policemen went on strike.

World War One thus led to material inequalities among civilians. Generally speaking, it was salaried social groups who were much more affected by inflation than those who lived off private incomes. Salaries lagged further behind prices than commercial incomes, which were often boosted as a consequence of the war.

Profiteers reigned supreme, and in France were nicknamed the *nouveaux-riches*, yet anyone who provided goods for the military did extremely well for themselves. The armies in rural areas needed more than arms and munitions. They needed clothing, fodder for animals, food rations. Horses, too, were greatly in demand and the nations at war paid dearly for them. In Normandy, for example, some *paysans* disguised colts as adult horses so as to exact a better price from the army.

The notion of "war profiteer" can be transferred to the international level. In 1915, the British began a blockade against the Central Powers, but at the same time they increased exports to neutral countries (Switzerland or the Low Countries) who, everyone knew, often re-exported goods to Germany. The entry of the United States into the war in 1917 certainly lends support to the idea that the war was a crusade for democracy, yet its involvement had been precipitated by the all-out submarine war ordered by the German admiralty in February. This seriously harmed American economic interests, which to that point had benefited enormously from the fall in European manufacturing and the demands for goods "made in the USA."

The Central Powers Learn Interventionist Economics

Given the urgency of the situation, governments were forced to intervene directly in their economies, notably with respect to planning the manufacture of war-related goods. Usually they did this slowly and reticently, except for Germany, where many initiatives sprang from the private industrial sector and were taken up by government. Early on a Raw Materials Division was formed within the Ministry of War, but the idea had originally stemmed from a private company, Allgemeine Elektrizitäts-Gesellschaft (AEG), and its president, Walter Rathenau. On August 8, 1914, the two most powerful business associations in the steel industry formed the German Industry War Committee, which shared out the orders made by the Reich. Across in France, similar developments were taking place. On September 20, 1914, in Bordeaux, French Minister of War Alexandre Millerand met a number of major industrialists, notably from the steel sector. The French state was greatly reliant on manufacturing undertaken by private companies because national arsenals were not capable of meeting targets for arms and munitions. Monthly meetings were then held in Paris between the ministries concerned and industrialists organized into regional groups, who divided the orders between them. The Ironworks Committee, a powerful business association at the time, played an important role in sharing out the commissions.

Even in Britain, the country where free trade was first practiced, interventionist tendencies became the norm. The law of August 8, 1914, the Defence of the Realm Act (or DORA), led the government to regulate the use of raw materials. One 1916 law (the Corn Product Act) made it illegal to leave land fallow.

From the end of 1915, the reasons for developing a war economy became wholly apparent. From now on, the front was stabilized to the west. Moreover, the Artois and Champagne offensives had shown the Allies that the artillery had to be considerably strengthened in order to breach the German defense network. The war thus entered an industrial phase. Henceforward, governments increasingly understood that victory awaited the best mobilized. At the same time, governments appreciated that civilian goods had still to be produced for civilians on the home front.

Difficulties were especially mounting for the Central Powers, due to the blockade, which was beginning to have its effect. Food supplies, but also raw materials like cotton and nonferrous metals, became ever scarce in Germany and Austria-Hungry, leading to strategies for the manufacture of substitute *ersatz* products. In 1915, the German government created the Wartime Cereal Company, which had a commercial monopoly on cereals on national soil. Nevertheless, food rationing became necessary in Germany in 1915. The following year even greater restrictions were imposed, and German civilians were entitled to only 9 ounces of meat per week and 7 ounces of bread a day. With the invasion and occupation of nine of its *départements*, which between them represented 14 percent of the country's industrial capacity, France faced problems of a different magnitude. Coal especially was in short supply. Through the submarine campaign waged by the Germans, Britain too was affected, though less so than its chief ally.

Countries at war now started to legislate on matters that had escaped their notice before 1914. In France, for example, laws issued on February 2 and 9, 1916, created in each rural municipality a permanent farming board to organize agricultural work, to find means to exploit uncultivated land, and to improve yields from the rest. Regional coal offices also appeared. They were to act as the intermediaries between industrialists and wholesalers.

Governments started the requisitioning of goods, imposing levies on products and raw materials at state-fixed prices that were below the market rate. It is, therefore, easy to see why such practices led to protests, and even to deception. It was in this environment that the mayor's office at the town of Frère-Champenoise (Marne) refused to hand over 267 quintals (565,800 pounds) of wheat to the military authorities, and did a deal with a miller who would pay a better price for the grain. On June 2, 1917, the prefect of Loir-et-Cher ordered searches of surrounding farms, and found 138,000 tons of wheat hidden across 25 communes in his *département*.

As to the financing of the war, governments took increasingly interventionist measures. Treasury advances, or those from central banks, were the first steps in this direction, especially in 1914–15 when everyone was convinced the war would be brief. Afterwards, several methods of financing the conflict were combined, though this happened differently in every country. Artificially increasing money supply by printing paper currency (inflation) was a tactic adopted by all governments, but it was the preferred means in France and Italy. Domestic and foreign loans were, however, the most common methods. In France, for example, the state made a consolidated loan from its citizens for each year of the war. Germany more or less copied this move. French and German civilians readily signed up to these loans. They emptied their piggybanks and paid for state bonds, not only out of a sense of patriotism but through the knowledge that such loans yielded a good return for the period (nearly 5 percent interest, at a time when inflation was not measured precisely). Yet these subsidies to government were insufficient to finance the war. Foreign loans increasingly became the norm, especially those offered by the United States. In this respect, the Americans treated the belligerents differently. From 1915 onwards, American banks barely loaned anything to Germany, yet granted larger and larger sums to the British and the French. This indicated the extent to which the U.S. government had already taken sides. It was not a matter of being philanthropic, but of betting on who was most likely to win the war.

Tax revenue was the final means by which states could finance the war. In this regard, national attitudes were key. The British government made greater recourse to taxation than did its German and French counterparts. Over the four years of the war, income tax in Britain, traditionally low, rose by 40 percent. In France, there had been talk of a possible income tax since the end of the nineteenth century, but it was finally introduced in 1914 and applied to income earned in 1915. It was not collected until 1916. It raised little money. In Germany, under pressure from trade unions, special taxes on war profits (*Kriegsteur*) were voted for. Ultimately, however, fiscal revenues were of minor importance in financing the war.

THE PSYCHOLOGICAL AND CULTURAL CONSEQUENCES OF THE WAR

World War One caused most upheaval in terms of cultural and psychological patterns of behavior.

Societal Changes

In spite of the private tragedy endured by families who had lost a father, a son, or a husband, civilians on the home fronts still adapted to the war. Normal pastimes continued, often providing a surreal quality to their lives. On May 17, 1915, the Prefect of Corrèze fumed about the fact that "some innkeepers and licensees continue to organize public dances in their

World War One, 1914–18   41

establishments, in spite of the difficult times we are in." In 1922, the French state's welfare department published a booklet giving statistics regarding the war.[13] The historian who reads this document closely can accurately measure a number of societal changes. The statistics clearly indicate, for example, that cases of venereal disease (VD) rose in France between 1916 and 1919, especially in the nonmilitarized regions (85 percent of cases). Does this mean that for French men and women, World War One had been a period of permissiveness? In truth, the spread of VD is not hard to explain. Soldiers were far away from their wives, and lived for the moment; the injunction to live life to the full undoubtedly diluted the strict moral codes of the day; and the financial lot of many women, deprived of their husband's or partner's wage, meant that they were occasionally forced to work as prostitutes, with all the dangers that involved. It might be added that these figures also show that the authorities had become more skilled in measuring sexually transmitted diseases. Whatever the case, the elites within society were certainly agitated by a moral decline. A hike in illegitimate births further stoked these fears. In France they accounted for 8.4 percent of births in 1913, but amounted to 14.2 percent by 1917.[14] Both rural and urban areas were affected, but especially the latter where soldiers were on leave or were passing through on their way to or from the frontlines. Unquestionably, the pressures of wartime led to a relaxation in sexual behavior.

Petty crime also rose sharply, especially theft. Women were in charge of families, and the absence of paternal authority, important in patriarchal societies, sometimes had discernible consequences. A rash of child crime frequently broke out, again usually in the major cities where organized gangs were much in evidence.[15]

Social disintegration led people to explore ways of getting out of the war. Once again, such behavior suggests that the commitment to the war effort, seen as important by some historians, does not bear too much close scrutiny. Patriotic talk was often only a veneer, and more often than not a kind of conformism. As is usually the case with human nature, how people behaved in private mattered far more than what they said for effect in public, especially when it was a question of self-preservation.

Several French examples may be cited, not so as to stigmatize a country that paid a high price for its involvement in the war, but simply to describe the variety of ways in which people avoided the war, techniques undoubtedly copied elsewhere. By 1916, the French military faced a manpower crisis, created by the astounding casualties incurred early on in the war. The French army had lost 100,000 men per month (killed, wounded, taken prisoner) between the months of August and December 1914, a casualty rate much higher than that suffered by its British ally. Accordingly, the recruitment boards in the *départements,* which decided whether a young man was fit for service in the army or not, became less and less selective. It was a question of finding as many soldiers as possible. At the same time, the number of volunteers remained steady, and even grew. Some historians have again concluded that this is a proof of a deeply rooted patriotism. It is only when we remember that the act of volunteering enabled a soldier to choose which branch of the armed services he would serve that it becomes clear that this was really a way of avoiding the war. By enlisting, before being called up, a soldier could choose to join a heavy artillery regiment where he would be in infinitely less danger of death than in the infantry, in which most combatants served, and which suffered the heaviest losses. Elsewhere, some civil servants self-issued certificates giving them exemption from military service, while anarchist groups, who were against the war, forged such documents. In 1915, a network of doctors selling military discharge certificates (at a high price) was uncovered.

It should also be said that members of the French parliament were not conspicuous for their heroism. Though they initially responded well to the nation's call, in November 1914 they secured the right to choose between either their military post or their seat in the chamber. Out of the 220 parliamentarians of military age, only 20 chose to stay in the army. At this time, 200 British Members of Parliament (MPs) were involved in combat. This suggests that even among the elites, civilians endured the war more than they supported it, and did not subscribe to the propaganda churned out by their respective governments.

The moral suffering of civilians was undeniably considerable. It was characterized by the obvious absence of young or mature adult men. The armies' conscription structures affected men aged between 20 and 45. Only the eldest and the youngest were left behind. The remaining male adults on the home fronts were those unfit for combat, the wounded, or those who had been demobbed. Such absences caused all the more suffering for those who did not know what had happened to their loved ones. It was only at the end of 1914 that French soldiers, taken prisoner during the Battle of the Marne, could let their families know that they were still alive. Meanwhile, their families suffered months of unspeakable anguish. How could they know, moreover, whether a combatant had not been killed between the day when he wrote a letter to his family and the day that they received it? It is impossible to quantify all these anxieties. All that may be safely said is that they affected millions of families in Europe, regardless of the uniform worn by the soldier whose homecoming was awaited.

In these circumstances, how could families attempt to empathize, be it only in a small way, with the lot of a son, brother, or father who was fighting so far away? The home front adopted a series of practices through which it could take some solace. Comfort was found in symbolic objects that made civilians feel close to their loved ones. There was a roaring trade in brass shell tips, in cigarette lighters made by soldiers from rifle cartridges. This was more than a junk-shop patriotism; it was rather a means of sharing in the ordeals of the fighting front, without actually being there. Societies at war were thus societies in movement, destabilized by war, and subject to violent forces pulling them apart, even if many people attempted to hide their anxieties within the privacy of the home.

These movements also took place in a geographical sense. At the end of August 1914, a large proportion of the civilian population left Paris before the battle of the Marne turned in France's favor. Those who had the financial means found refuge provisionally far from the noise of the guns. A similar exodus of the wealthy took place in spring 1918 when long-range German guns bombarded the capital. Civilians streamed away from the combat zones, foreshadowing the larger movements of people at the end of the war. Inhabitants of those territories, which later became Czechoslovakia and Yugoslavia, arrived in Hungary. Millions of Russians fled from civil war and Bolshevism, while 2 million Poles, from various countries of Europe, returned to their newly reestablished homeland. It has been calculated that nearly 10 million exiles were wandering about Eastern Europe in 1920.[16]

Within the intellectual domain, there was also much movement. Ideological combat did not cease during the war. Within France, the political parties agreed to bury the hatchet for the duration of the war in what was called the *Union sacrée.* Yet this truce was always fragile. The proof lies in the very stormy debates that shook Limoges at the beginning of 1915. At the beginning of the twentieth century, this town had been at the sharp end of the anticlerical battles that raged within France. The crisis calmed down after mobilization in 1914, but was far from being forgotten. *Le Populaire du Centre* (socialist) and the *Croix de Limoges* (Catholic) waged merciless press campaigns, each accusing the other of duping the poor by doling out subscription items and gifts. In this town, at least, there was little unanimity in the face of war.

Societies in Constant Mourning

The most obvious dimension of World War One was mass death. France lost as many people during the 1914–18 conflict as it did in all the Revolutionary and Napoleonic campaigns combined (1792–1815). For the whole of Europe, it has been calculated that around 8 million lost their lives, a figure that would be much higher if we were to add the numbers who died in the Spanish Flu epidemic that accompanied the end of the war, and those killed in the Russian Civil War. Never had any previous war been so devastating. These losses were found to be in the younger age brackets of the Europe populations. Essentially, the mortalities were young men aged 20 to 35.

France and Germany were the countries most affected, losing approximately 10 percent of their "active" population. Approximately 1.375 million French were killed, and the drop in birthrate as a result of this slaughter amounted to over 2 million babies who were never conceived. Germany suffered military losses of 1.9 million. Also in Germany, 737,000 civilians died, and the accompanying drop in the birth rate amounted to a loss of 3 million. Out of 6 million men called up in Britain, 744,000 were killed. The drop in the birth rate is calculated at around 750,000. Russia lost 1.7 million soldiers, Italy 750,000, and Austria-Hungary 1.5 million.

To lend substance to these otherwise abstract figures, a series of local examples may be given. On the eve of the war, Tulle in France had 20,000 inhabitants. By 1918, the town had lost 532 men, 94 of whom were farmers. Of the 173 local primary schoolteachers called up, 95 lost their lives. Out of its population of 310,000, the *département* of Corrèze suffered 14,053 mortalities. On the basis of this particular example, from the center of France, it is possible to extrapolate the full extent of the losses. The mortality rate had overtaken the birth rate. In 1915, at Tulle, there were 308 births and 480 deaths. In 1916, there were 272 births, and 408 deaths listed in the civil registers.

The war did not distribute death very evenly. Since workers had been withdrawn from the frontlines to keep the wheels of industry turning, losses were usually more severe among agricultural workers than blue-collar workers. For France, the losses in the farming sector amounted to 10.2 percent of those conscripted, against 9 percent of all other categories of workers.

Military deaths signaled a complete break with cultural trends in the early twentieth century. Hitherto death had been ritualized in a human group within villages and urban communities—the deceased was surrounded by his nearest relatives. Henceforward, a death took place hundreds of miles away on the frontlines. Moreover, many bodies were never found. This was the case for about a third of those who died fighting for the French army. It was thus impossible for the families of lost ones to grieve over the body of the deceased. Mourning accordingly became more of a private occasion throughout all European societies in the 1920s and 1930s. Even so, national observances sometimes brought mourning onto a wider stage. In Britain, the Kitchener recruitment campaign had led to the unusual trend of the Pals' Battalions, in which entire groups of friends, neighbors, or work colleagues enlisted. By the end of the war, whole districts in towns or entire villages were affected by mass bereavement. Central London lost more than 5,000 men.[17] Ought the remains of the dead to be brought back to the soil of the homeland? This question very quickly arose after the war. In the course of the campaigning itself, soldiers were buried in mass graves in the place where they had fallen. Depending on the cultures of the different countries, different practices were adopted. Germany and Britain chose to leave the bodies where they had been killed, or where they had been buried for the first time. The United States decided to repatriate its dead. The French state at first forbade the bodies to be moved; it then gave permission for families to bring back the remains of those soldiers who had been identified.

When talking about human casualties of the war, we should not forget those caused afterwards by Spanish flu, a disease that affected every area of Europe, and an epidemic reminiscent of the Black Death of 1348–52. In the month of September 1918, in Marseilles, 50 percent of all deaths were due to this plague. In one month, the small town of Troyes suffered 140 deaths. Wholly perplexed, people blamed the disease on tinned food imported from Spain, hence its popular name, though its origins lay in Asia.[18]

Traumatized Societies

High death rates among young men caused major social upheavals. In France, for example, which was especially affected because its population was stagnant even before the war, an aging of the population was already visible. By 1918, those in their sixties represented 13.6 percent of the population, whereas in 1916 they only amounted to 12.6 percent.

Emerging out of the war, there were some 6.5 million invalids in Europe, of whom 100,000 were completely handicapped, poor human wrecks left behind by the fighting. In France, they were nicknamed the *Gueules cassées* (especially, but not exclusively, those with severe facial injuries). Europe-wide, there were also 4.2 million widows and about 8 million orphans. In France alone, the war begat 680,000 widows and 1 million orphans. The social importance of these categories in societies in the 1920s and 1930s was considerable. Veteran organizations became a major force.[19] The consequences of the war were seen daily both in town and country. In the towns, there were many widows, who were sometimes known as the "fiancées of 1914." Social pressure forced them into endless mourning. In the countryside young women, whose fathers had been killed, often stayed in the family home with their mother, and became known as the "spinsters of '14." Orphans were the focus of charity relief programs and public welfare schemes, and special group status was claimed for them, especially in France.[20]

In view of these losses, it is not difficult to understand why at the end of the war an immense sense of relief spread everywhere, in the camps of both the victorious and the defeated powers. But this relief was tempered by tears of immeasurable loss.

CONCLUSIONS

By 1918, the differences between the Central Powers and the Allies were more marked than ever. The former had not known how, or had not been able, to pursue the war and, at the same time, preserve standards of living among its civilians. By contrast, the main western Allies (France and England)—the world's two richest nations, as heirs of the nineteenth-century industrial revolution—amazingly succeeded in maintaining those standards of living, while spending more and more on the war, even if this meant that they were in debt to the United States.

This was a war that had brought about major social upheavals, as important as those geopolitical changes effected at the Paris Peace Settlement. Indeed, for Europe, World War One represents a major dividing

Europe post–World War One.

line. In part a product of nineteenth-century cultural reflexes, it pushed the young twentieth century into a human tragedy. It also prefigured later developments. Through the conflict, humanity entered into a phase of total war, which would culminate in a second worldwide conflict. Henceforth, war involved not only soldiers but also civilians, including women and children, on a scale unimagined in the nineteenth century. However, we must not fall into muddled classifications. Not all social classes were affected in the same way. A whole series of concentric circles lie between those directly involved in the war itself (soldiers, bombed or occupied civilians) and those only affected by its material and psychological consequences. Some people even made a living from the war, and not only those who were manufacturing armaments, as the pacifist propaganda of the 1920s and 1930s would have had us believe. It was thus never entirely a total war, and historians must constantly remind themselves that World War One, like every human drama, was a complex and frequently contradictory phenomenon.

NOTES

Translated from the original French by Brian Sudlow.

1. Jean-Baptiste Duroselle, *La Grande Guerre des Français* (Paris: Perrin, 1994), p. 426.

2. John Horne and Alan Kramer, "German 'Atrocities' and Franco-German Opinion in 1914: The Evidence of German Soldiers' Diaries," *Journal of Modern History* 66, no. 1 (1994): 1–33. See too their *German Atrocities: A History of Denial* (New Haven, Conn., and London: Yale University Press, 2001).

3. Philippe Nivet, *Les Réfugiés français de la grande guerre: Les "Boches du Nord"* (Paris: Economica/Hautes Etudes Militaires, 2004), p. 91.

4. François Cochet, *Rémois en guerre, 1914–1918: L'héroïsation au quotidien* (Nancy: Presses Universitaire de Nancy, 1993).

5. Jay M. Winter, *La première guerre mondiale* (Paris: France Loisirs, 1992), p. 157.

6. Winter, *La première guerre mondiale,* p. 143.

7. Stéphane Audoin-Rouzeau, *La Guerre des enfants 1914–19: Essai d'histoire culturelle* (Paris: Armand Colin, 1993).

8. Quoted in Winter, *La première guerre mondiale,* p. 147.

9. Pierre Darmon, *Vivre à Paris pendant la Grande Guerre* (Paris: Fayard, 2002), p. 141.

10. Stéphane Audoin-Rouzeau and Annette Becker, "Violence et consentement: La *culture de guerre* du premier conflit mondial," in *Pour une histoire culturelle,* ed. Jean-Pierre Rioux et Jean-François Sirinelli (Paris: Editions du Seuil, 1997), pp. 251–271.

11. See Nicolas Bidault, *L'Utilisation des prisonniers de guerre ennemis comme main d'œuvre en Charente et Haute-Vienne,* Mémoire de Maîtrise, Université de Limoges, 2003.

12. Archives départementales de Corrèze, 1 M 66.

13. Archives de l'Assistance publique, 338 Per 14.

14. Duroselle, *La Grande Guerre*, p. 430.

15. See Yves Pourcher, *Les jours de guerre: La vie des Français au jour le jour entre 1914 et 1918* (Paris: Plon, 1994).

16. Michael Marrus, *Les exclus: Les réfugiés européens au XXe siècle* (Paris: Calmann-Lévy, 1986).

17. See Jay M. Winter, *Sites of Memory, Sites of Mourning: The Great War in European Cultural History* (Cambridge: Cambridge University Press, 1995).

18. Darmon, *Vivre à Paris*, p. 391.

19. Antoine Prost, *Les anciens combattants et la société française* (Paris: Presses Nationales de la Fondation des Sciences Politiques, 1977).

20. Olivier Faron, *Les Enfants du deuil: Orphelins et pupilles de la nation de la Première Guerre mondiale, 1914–1941* (Paris: La Découverte, 2001).

THREE

The Daily Lives of Civilians in the Russian Civil War

Sam Johnson

The Russian Civil War was a devastating event. It was fought over huge swathes of territory, on three fronts and across 11 time zones, in a land occupied by many national, linguistic, ethnic, and religious groups, among them Orthodox Russians, Catholic Poles, Ukrainians, Jews, Georgians, and Muslims. Lasting for just three years, it was a savage and brutal conflict, and cast a bitter shadow over the Soviet Union into the 1920s and beyond.

The first question to be addressed by this chapter is who exactly were the civilians of this war? The answer is not straightforward. Civilians occasionally became combatants, willingly or unwillingly, and thanks to the vast ethnic tapestry of the former tsarist empire, it is not easy to decide which groups of civilians should demand attention. For the Russian Civil War was not simply a case of Russians versus Russians. It was, as in every other civil war, a case of brothers ranked against brothers, but also Whites against Reds, Greens versus Reds, Russians against Ukrainians, Poles, Belorussians, and Latvians, the proletariat against the bourgeoisie, the old versus the new—the list could go on. For those caught in the maelstrom, there was no single civilian type, no single victim, no single experience, and, as a result, there is no single narrative that can describe these events.

The Russian Civil War is further complicated by the fact that this was not the only harsh encounter faced by the peoples of the former Russian empire in the aftermath of the Bolshevik takeover. In the course of 1917–21, the Russian peoples experienced social and political revolution,

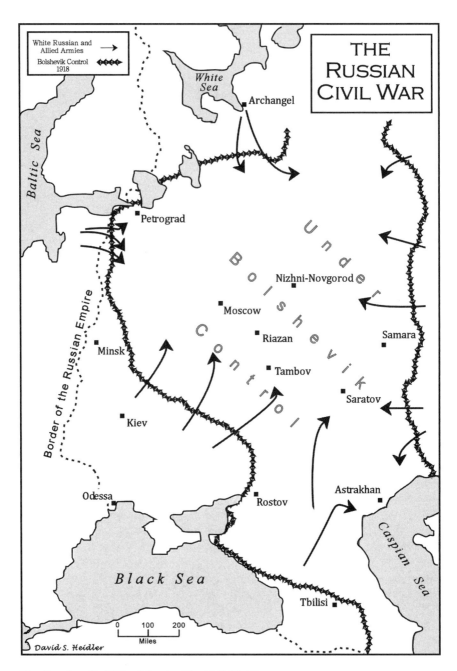

The Russian Civil War. Map by David S. Heidler.

famine, War Communism, and the so-called Red Terror, all of which fore-shadowed the experiences to be endured under Stalin. In the words of one historian, the Civil War, and its associated hardships, was merely one ele-ment in "a people's tragedy."[1] Another notes that the Civil War and Revo-lution should not be divorced from preceding experiences, but viewed as a "continuum of crisis."[2] It was yet another terrible convulsion, following on from Russia's disastrous part in World War One, the February Revolu-tion (which ousted the tsarist regime), and the Bolshevik takeover of Oc-tober 1917 (which toppled the Provisional Government). The three-year Civil War resulted in the deaths of between 7 million and 8 million people, both military personnel and civilians; the destruction of industry and ag-riculture; and the beginnings of Russia's diplomatic isolation.[3]

Given the complexities of the Civil War, historians have generally fo-cused on the broader aspects of the military campaign. Politics, the Bolshe-vik Party, Lenin, Trotsky, and the foreign interventions by Britain, France, the United States, and Czechoslovakia, thus dominate the historiography.[4] The everyday experiences of civilians have been given little thought, and merely form a backdrop to the revolution itself. Consequently, delineating the lives of ordinary people in the Civil War is no easy task. Aware of this challenge, this chapter nonetheless dwells on the diversity of the war: its urban and rural manifestations, the impact of the famine and, finally, the routing of the Volunteer Army, which prompted mass evacuation and an international refugee crisis.

THE ORIGINS OF THE WAR

The Russian Civil War began in late 1917, in the wake of the October Bol-shevik takeover. Although shots were not fired until the end of the year, the coming-to-power of Lenin and the Russian Social Democratic Labor Party ensured that the severe divisions in Russian political life could not be healed in the immediate future. Ostensibly, the Bolsheviks were de-fenders of Russia's proletariat, its urban working class. In 1917, however, they played on rural loyalties by inciting the peasantry to sequester land. In addition, they were modernizers, with clear ideological goals about the kind of society they wished to achieve. The old ways would be destroyed, and a communist state would arise from the ashes. The Civil War thus seemed a certainty from the beginning, especially when we recall Russia's simmering social and ethnic tensions. Nonetheless the conflict was not immediately ignited by the Bolshevik takeover. Lenin and his followers sought a breathing space in which to deal with domestic issues.

As the Russian writer Alexsei Tolstoi famously remarked, under the Bol-sheviks, "Everything was cancelled. Ranks, honours, pensions, officers' epaulettes, the thirtieth letter of the alphabet, God, private property, and even the right to live as one wishes—all were cancelled."[5] Some of these things, for instance the abolition of military rank, had already occurred in the wake of the February Revolution. But the rest was set in train by the Bolsheviks. In late 1917, Lenin's government marked its growing ascendancy by banning opposition newspapers and closing down the recently elected Constituent Assembly (parliament). This initiative drew the wrath of all the other political parties of every hue, notably the Socialist Revolutionaries and Kadets (Constitutional Democrats). In addition, the apparatus of state security (political police), the Cheka, was set up. A forerunner of the KGB, the Cheka proved ruthless during the Civil War. During the Red Terror of 1918, it was responsible for the murder of thousands of people, who were deemed to be "bourgeois" and "enemies of the revolution." Social divisions in Russia were further emphasized by the introduction, in 1918, of food rationing on a strict class basis. Manual workers topped this hierarchy, while aristocrats and the middle classes were at the bottom. Class warfare was actively encouraged and pursued by the Bolsheviks.

Finally, in March 1918, the Bolsheviks extracted Russia from World War One by signing a punitive peace settlement with imperial Germany. This treaty, which involved handing over a large part of Russia's western provinces to Berlin, ensured the explosion of various ethnic animosities.[6] Though the Bolsheviks themselves liked to present the Civil War as a class war, nationalist tensions were ever present. Ukrainians and Georgians wanted independence. Similarly Poland, which had once been partially ruled by the tsar, was eager to reclaim its historic territories. Much of the Bolsheviks' time would be spent resisting nationalist pretensions, with the result that the war was fought on many fronts.

In December 1917, the anti-Bolshevik Volunteer Army was formed. Drawn largely from the ranks of Cossacks, it was led by former tsarist generals. Subsequently, it developed into a wider movement, known as the Whites, and attracted the support of other political groupings, especially the Kadets. United in their aim of ousting the Bolsheviks, in loose terms the Whites represented the old order, though as a movement it was marked more by diversity than homogeneity, and drew on peasants, workers, and former soldiers, as well as aristocrats, civil servants, and the cream of tsarist society. By contrast, the Reds were recruited from Russia's urban workers, and were depicted as a proletariat army fighting for Bolshevism. But here too, social composition was not clear-cut. In 1918, the Bolsheviks recruited former tsarist officers to their cause. The blanket terms Red and White conceal, therefore, a multitude of differences.

The Red and White armies did not meet in battle until late 1917. In campaigning terms, the war was fought on three fronts: to the north and west, in the south, and, far away in the east, in Siberia. Essentially, the Reds fought to hold the center of Russia, while the Whites battled on the peripheries, occasionally alongside the allied interventionist armies. Red victory has often been attributed to geographical and strategic factors.[7] At the height of the war, around 3.75 million men were involved in the fighting, around 3 million for the Reds.[8] Massive recruitment from Russia's

reservoir of war-weary men and women was perhaps the greatest achievement of the Commissar for War, Leon Trotsky. As a propagandist, Trotsky
was inspired; as a military strategist, he was cold-blooded. The success of
the Reds was due in no small part to him. For ordinary Russian citizens,
however, the pursuit of civil war marked continued hardships, the questioning of allegiances, and a daily battle for survival.

URBAN LIFE

By 1917, life in Russia had reached a crisis point sufficient to precipitate
revolution. Politics mattered, of course, but living and working conditions
had a hand in the downfall of the Romanov regime in February, not least
the intermittent food supply. For one historian, the Russian revolution
began "in the bread queue."[9] From the everyday perspective, the early
months of the Civil War presented few new challenges. The same daily
fight for survival existed, with the search for foodstuffs a pressing problem, particularly for those living in the former imperial capital Petrograd
(St. Petersburg until 1914). Throughout the Civil War, citizens of Petrograd
and other cities waged "an almost zoological" struggle to fill their bellies.[10]
A popular slogan of the day went: "Down with Lenin and horsemeat, give
us the tsar and pork."[11] Every day of the week, people queued for hour
upon hour to purchase meager scraps of food. Sometimes they queued in
order to obtain a ticket that would allow them to queue the next day.[12]

The outside lines of supply to Petrograd and other cities were, at best, intermittent and at worst, nonexistent. World War One was to blame for this.
To begin with, it dislocated the nation's transport system, which had been
mobilized to convey troops and munitions. Next, the economic impact
of the fighting on the countryside encouraged the peasantry to withhold
grain for its own purposes, since it was no longer worthwhile to sell this
for the low prices fixed by the Russian state. The urban peoples of Russia
were utterly dependent on supplies from the outside world. Petrograd
suffered more than most. Its northerly position made it more vulnerable,
since it was further from those parts of Russia that continued to produce
food in the immediate postrevolution period, such as the Volga basin and
Western Siberia. The supply lines increasingly narrowed, and in the case
of Petrograd were eventually severed.

Before 1917–18, Petersburg was the equal of London, Paris, and Berlin.
Much of the city was electrified; it had an integrated transport system of
trains, buses, and trams; elegant shops, department stores, and cinemas
bedecked its main boulevard, *Nevskii Prospekt*. It was home to government workers, civil servants, and the imperial court. However, it was not
only occupied by the middle and upper classes, and its economy was not
entirely given over to professional life. Petersburg was an important industrial center, and was noted for its metal production. It had, therefore, a
sizeable working class, many of whom were highly skilled, literate, and politicized. This proletariat included an army of metal workers, upon whom

Pushcart merchants in suburbs selling small garden products, Petrograd, Russia, 1918. Conditions had not deteriorated as drastically as they would. Courtesy of Library of Congress.

the Bolsheviks relied during their attempts to gain power in 1917. During World War One, the imperial capital had also played an important role in the manufacture of munitions and armaments. By 1920, this jewel of the Russian Empire, one of Europe's most beautiful and sophisticated cities, was a sorrowful shadow of its former self.

For one observer, Emma Goldman, a Russian Anarchist who had emigrated to the United States before World War One, a visit to the former imperial capital in the early years of the Civil War was a dispiriting experience:

It was almost in ruins, as if a hurricane had swept over it. The houses looked like broken old tombs upon neglected and forgotten cemeteries. The streets were dirty and deserted; all life had gone from them. The population of Petrograd before the war was almost two millions; in 1920 it had dwindled to five hundred thousand. The people walked about like living corpses; the shortage of food and fuel was slowly sapping the city; grim death was clutching at its heart. Emaciated and frostbitten men, women and children, were being whipped by the common lash, the search for a piece of bread or a stick of wood. It was a heart-rending sight by day, an oppressive weight by night. The utter stillness of the large city was paralysing. It fairly haunted me, this awful oppressive silence broken only by occasional shots.[13]

Petrograd was the crucible of revolution and, as such, it was inevitable that its people would bear the brunt of the ensuing difficulties and upheavals. Many of these harsh experiences are evident in Goldman's reflections. One feature of the Civil War, for instance, was the mass movement and displacement of population.[14] As this visitor noted all too readily, Petrograd was a ghost town.

Milk line in Petrograd (St. Petersburg). George Grantham Bain Collection. Courtesy of Library of Congress.

The statistics of Russia's rapid urban depopulation are stark. In 1917, partly as a result of an in-migration to Petrograd's factories and workshops during World War One, its population stood at 2.5 million. By 1920, the figure had shriveled to 722,000.[15] In part, this was the product of the Bolsheviks moving their capital to Moscow in February 1918, which forced a whole army of bureaucrats, apparatchiks, and soldiers to up their bags. In addition, the breakdown of industry meant that factory workers became unemployed and idle, with no means of support. By late 1918, the metalworkers of Petrograd, who had once numbered 250,000, were reduced to 50,000. Left to fend for themselves, they inevitably departed in droves, in search of better lives and, more importantly, sustenance in the countryside, or in lands further south. The ebb and flow of refugees was a constant feature of the Civil War, particularly in the south. It was not only workers that left. People of all classes deserted Petrograd, from the lowliest worker to nobles, teachers, and doctors. All abandoned their city to its fate. As W. Bruce Lincoln observed, "seven out of every ten men and women who had lived there in 1917 no longer remained in the summer of 1920."[16]

The dislocation of the civilians led to some extraordinary demographic shifts. Many cities in the north and west witnessed massive depopulation, with Kiev (the capital of Ukraine), for instance, reduced to around 140,000 people. Moscow lost around 300,000 of its citizens. The cities of the south soaked up the recurrent floods of refugees. Samara and Tbilisi, for example, almost doubled in size. In Saratov, located south of Moscow on the banks of the Volga river, statistics show that the population decreased by a mere 10,000 between 1920,[17] yet these figures disguise an ever-changing population, one that ebbed and flowed as refugees came and went. This was especially the case in 1919, when its strategic position led to a prolonged siege by the Whites. War, blockade, disease, and famine meant that Saratov's population shrank by 25 percent in the period 1915–22.

For most people food, rather than politics, was the central focus of their tenuous existence, and hunger usually prompted mass migration. Other civilians were fleeing from battle. In Saratov province, from 1918 onwards the authorities found it increasingly difficult to manage the thousands of refugees that arrived from all directions. Among them were former prisoners of war who had been in German or Austrian camps, workers from northern cities, victims of the front line in the west, and "all sorts of vagrants, pick-pockets, fortune tellers, singers, people with talking parrots promising happiness, petty tradesmen, Chinese, etc."[18] As welfare or private charity systems barely functioned, refugees and migrants had to fend for themselves. The result was that criminality of all kinds increased dramatically during the war.

As a response to the food crisis, an alternative economy developed in Russia. This had its origins in the latter part of World War One, but continued in the early months of the Civil War. The absence of reliable supply lines meant that urban folk were dependent on the interventions of resourceful individuals who were known as bagmen.[19] There was a shortage of all goods, whether comestibles, clothes, or fuel, which was accompanied by massive inflation of essential commodities. In 1918, Alexei Babine, a Russian-born American citizen who worked at a school in Saratov, traveled from the city to Riazan, where he observed another resourceful seller in the Civil War, the bread peddler:

I was at last on a train to Riazan. The train was very crowded, and it took me some time to secure a seat in the passageway. At Atkarsk and Rtishchevo bread peddlers appeared, selling four and five pound loaves for 12–14 rubles, the same loaves that usually had sold for 20–25 kopecks. Many passengers took advantage of this: "A loaf this size costs no less than 50 rubles in Moscow," they explained.[20]

The gaps in supply were serviced by the bagmen, who formed a crucial connection to town and country. Thousands of men, and sometimes women, traveled repeatedly from the cities to the countryside, bringing with them small quantities of goods, such as penknives, cigarette lighters, candlesticks.[21] These items would be bartered, exchanged, or sold for foodstuffs supplied by the peasantry, whereupon the bagman would return to the city and sell his wares at inflated and impossible prices. The smallest, most insignificant amount of food could stave off the clutches of death. In a city where the daily intake had been reduced to "a pitiful" 306 calories, an egg, a spoonful of sugar or flour, might make a difference to one's prospects of survival.[22] For the same reason, the consumption of "civil war sausage" (horsemeat) and domestic pets became the norm, at least when there was a sufficient supply of animals to be eaten.[23]

The black market was a crucial part of everyday life in the Civil War. This was the case for all social classes, though class lines were increasingly blurred. The revolution had by design and default blurred social distinctions, and the disintegration of normal economic life ensured the devaluing of paper money and savings. Eventually, the Bolsheviks nationalized the banks and confiscated their savings and gold deposits for their own ends. The possession of money and former wealth or status now meant nothing. Whether previously princesses, generals, factory workers, cab drivers, housewives, or teachers—everyone now faced the same daily search for sustenance. For the so-called members of the "former classes," as the middle and upper classes were deemed henceforward by the Bolsheviks, the official distribution of food via the rationing system was inequitable.[24] The population was classified according to occupation, with those at the top receiving the largest rations:

1. Those engaged in heavy physical labor.
2. Those in less heavy manual labor and white-collar employees.
3. Members of intelligentsia and free professions.
4. House owners, stall owners, and so forth, the "bourgeois" category.[25]

Because of their former positions, aristocrats and the bourgeoisie were bottom of the heap. It was not, therefore, an uncommon sight to see such people selling their worldly goods on Petrograd's streets. Sometimes these possessions were pitiful. A British journalist, who traveled through Russia in 1919, observed the daily struggle of civilian life in Moscow. On street corners he saw:

Men and women [selling] little slices of sweetmeats and rolls. Soldiers, too, stood there with two or three lumps of sugar in the lid of a cardboard box as their sole stock in trade. [. . .] One could tell that some of these poor devils were well-educated people to whom the Revolution and its consequences had meant ruin and misery.[26]

Necessity found many people begging, sweeping snow, selling newspapers or cigarettes or turning to prostitution.[27] One study has estimated that there were 30,000 prostitutes in Petrograd in late 1918, around 42 percent of whom were drawn from the middle and upper classes.[28]

Other shortages, besides those of food, created problems. Fuel was second on the list. The search for fuel accounted, in part, for the dilapidation of Petrograd described by Goldman in 1920. Petrograders burnt anything they could to keep themselves warm. Keeping warm was a challenge even in ordinary times, but the winter of 1917–18 was particularly harsh. Fuel supplies from outside the city had all but vanished. People resorted to dismantling wooden buildings, removing door and window frames, and burning furniture, paper, and books. Many of these materials were stripped from grand buildings, which were once private property, but which now belonged to the state. The Bolsheviks confiscated all private apartments and houses. Working-class families moved into these properties alongside aristocrats and bourgeois tenants. The story was repeated all over Russia. "The well-to-do people," recorded Babine, "are being expelled from their residences to unsanitary basements and to hovels on the outskirts of the city, while the poor are encouraged to occupy the rich men's 'palaces.' "[29] And, lest the former classes tried to take what was no longer theirs, houses and apartments were regularly searched by the occupying armies, whether White or Red. In 1918 Saratov, ruled by the Bolsheviks, the apartment of Babine's landlady was searched:

Our house was searched for provisions yesterday afternoon—quite leniently, according to our landlady's statement. She declared some 100 lbs. of flour in her possession, and had her bread tickets [i.e. ration card] clipped in consequence, to keep her from getting more than her share of the Bolshevik bounty.[30]

Hunger and cold were not the only life-threatening matters to be dealt with. As Goldman's observations intimate, Petrograd was a dangerous city on a number of levels. Violence became an everyday occurrence. As one historian has noted, "[N]ever had Russian workers had so many weapons in their hands; never before had so many been trained to use them."[31] Retribution of all kinds was distributed on a daily basis, with robbery and murder commonplace. The Bolsheviks encouraged the proletariat to extort what was truly theirs from the bourgeoisie. The Bolshevik slogan "death to the bourgeoisie" was implemented literally. Hostages were routinely rounded up, imprisoned, and shot. Individuals were attacked and beaten in the street, and sometimes stripped of every belonging and item of clothing. Few would venture outdoors at night. Just as the social system was swept away, so too was the legal and moral order. Fear governed the thoughts of many ordinary Russians, and grew more intense during the period known as the Red Terror.

The Red Terror occurred in the wake of the assassination of the chief of the Petrograd Cheka, Moses Uritskii, and the attempted assassination on Lenin in August 1918. It instigated the further pursuit of class warfare, since the would-be assassin was revealed to be a counter-revolutionary bourgeois. In reality, Fanny Kaplan was a disgruntled socialist, unhappy with the manner in which the Bolsheviks were ruling. Nevertheless, his actions unleashed a whirlwind of violence and murder throughout Russia, led by the Cheka. Directed by Felix Dzerzhinskii, the Cheka arrested, beat up, tortured, and shot thousands of people, ostensibly as punishment for their part in purported counter-revolutionary plots. There are no precise figures for numbers killed, but most were innocent of any crimes against the Bolsheviks.[32] Most people were shot with a single bullet to the back of the head. Others were tortured in horrific and unimaginable ways. Such violence happened throughout Russia and was inflicted on all kinds of people, from all walks of life: "Landowners, priests, physicians, rich merchants, and businessmen are daily reported shot in cold blood and without even a semblance of a trial."[33]

The Terror, inevitably, added to the climate of fear in Russia, particularly as arrests and shootings were so arbitrary. Rumor and counter-rumor abounded; denunciations of neighbors, relatives, friends, and strangers were common. Babine observed, "[B]oth our, and everybody else's, pervading problem is to keep alive and to outlast the Bolsheviks."[34] The terrifying atmosphere, the constant search for food and other supplies, ensured that everybody in Russia was solely focused on his or her own welfare. This accounts, in part, for the large numbers of orphaned children who populated the nooks and crannies of Russia's broken towns and cities. By 1922, anywhere between 7 million and 9 million children were living on the streets, either abandoned or orphaned.[35] They survived by roaming around in gangs, by stealing, begging, and picking pockets.[36] Some were rounded up and put in orphanages, but most were left to fend for themselves by whatever means were at their disposal.

Death had thus to be staved off from all directions. Disease loomed as readily as starvation, especially typhus and cholera. Babine recorded the dangers of participating in the daily bread-queue: "Constant standing in bread and other lines has resulted in my clothes being so filled with lice that I have to take off my undershirt every night and institute a thorough hunt before going to bed, without being able to exterminate them entirely."[37] The spread of disease was, in part, the result of the breakdown of urban infrastructure. Donald J. Raleigh vividly describes the position in Saratov:

Bad nutrition, lack of heat, soap and water, physical exhaustion and stress, serious over-crowding, and interaction with hordes of refugees transformed Saratov into a natural breeding ground for illness and infectious disease, giving rise to one of the most cataclysmic public health crises in modern history. Chronic scarcities of medicines, bandages, and vaccines aggravated the situation.[38]

In Saratov the infectious disease rate doubled between 1918 and 1919. Treatment was further hampered by the drastic decline in medical personnel, through death and their enlistment into the ranks of the Red Army. In addition, the constant waves of refugees that traveled to Saratov and other cities brought with them fresh epidemics.[39] Typhus was a particular problem. A British military observer reported the effect of this disease in the town of Novonikolaevsk, in the south:

There were 37,000 typhus cases in that town. Fifty doctors had died in that town alone during the space of one month and a half and more than 20,000 corpses lay unburied outside the town. . . . The linen and the clothes of the patients were never changed, and most of them lay in a most filthy condition in their everyday clothes on the floor. They were never washed, and the male attendants waited for the periodical attacks of unconsciousness which are characteristic of typhus in order to steal from the patients, their rings, jewellery, watches and even their food.[40]

In Petrograd, the sewage system ceased functioning, so rubbish was left to rot in the canals and on the streets, as were the corpses of both humans and animals. Little wonder that the death rate here shot up. In 1917, it was around 23:1,000. By 1919, it was 70:1,000.[41] In 1918, the writer Maxsim Gorkii wrote to his mistress, "Petrograd is a dying city. Everyone is leaving it, by foot, by horse, by train. Dead horses lie in the street. The city is unbelievably dirty. The Moika and Fontanka [canals] are full of rubbish. This is the death of Russia."[42]

The Civil War precipitated a complete transformation of urban life in Russia. The abolition of class distinctions meant that everybody, from child to woman to soldier, encountered the same daily difficulties. The result was that a degree of homogeneity was evident in Russian urban society by 1921. Describing life in Moscow, a British observer noted that every citizen, regardless of his or her former status, lived and looked the same as everyone else. Everybody was reduced to the same materially impoverished level. What is more, they lived in a city that had become as dilapidated as their lives:

The general appearance of Moscow is rather horrible for anyone who remembers it as it was in the old days. The streets are almost empty, and the people one sees in them are ragged and haggard. The buildings are in as bad a repair as the people and their clothes. Many of them are a wilderness of broken windows, broken doors, broken roofs and broken gutters. Very, very few of them look any longer like dwelling-houses. Neglect and impoverishment have broken them as completely as an earthquake or a bombardment could have done.[43]

A return to the old ways was impossible. The manner in which a town or city had once been ordered, socially, politically, economically, and culturally, was totally shattered in the civil war. The urban infrastructure was destroyed, including hospitals and schools, as were the mechanisms for disposing of rubbish and sewage, alongside the provision of transport and electricity. Russia's urban landscape was thus wholly transformed. As for the urban population itself, ordinary life became brutalized. As Raleigh has noted, the Civil War "transformed individuals [of all social classes and political outlooks] into migrants, refugees, class enemies, the diseased, the hungry and the malnourished."[44] The conflict also stripped away moral boundaries, bred violence, sowed mistrust, and ensured that day-to-day life was one of primitive struggle. To all intents and purposes, twentieth-century men and women had been turned into prehistoric hunter-gatherers.

THE COUNTRYSIDE

For many observers, both Russian and non-Russian, writing at the turn of the nineteenth and early twentieth centuries, the embodiment of Russia was its peasantry. The simple life of the peasant, his superstitious outlook, his naiveté and loyalty to the tsar, symbolized Russia. The land on which the peasant lived and toiled also appeared unchanged and untouched by those new developments in agriculture that were commonplace in Europe. Many commentators thus believed the Russian peasant was incapable of engaging with politics, let alone partaking in revolution.

Events before and during the Civil War proved that the Russian peasant was anything but an apolitical individual. He was more than capable of engaging in revolution, something reflected at the local level. While the cities, especially Petrograd, hosted and fed the revolution, the countryside played its own part. In late 1917 and 1918, for instance, the peasantry responded with gusto to the Bolshevik's October 1917 Decree on Land, and their exhortation to seize and divide noble property. The peasantry pursued, therefore, its own agenda in the countryside. As the traditional patterns of order and authority collapsed and shriveled away, the peasantry instigated its own form of rule. It set up its own institutions, managed its own affairs without outside intrusion, and learned to live without the towns.[45] The revolution granted the peasantry a free hand. Throughout Russia, especially in 1917–18, peasants seized noble land, destroyed the aristocracy's houses, and took their livestock, seed, pasture, and forests.[46] As the both the Red and White armies discovered, the free hand granted the peasants by the revolution ensured that they were unwilling to relinquish any political and material gains.

What was daily life like in the countryside prior to the Civil War? Even without the interventions of World War One, which was fought over large parts of Russia's western provinces, rural life in Russia was far from enviable. It was tough, untouched by the sophistications of the city, and the tsarist state had often interfered in rural affairs. Most peasant families occupied a single building, the *izba*, usually constructed from wood, with a mud floor. It was often shared with animals, especially in winter. The *izba* was effectively an extended family. Parents-in-law often lived with their offspring, alongside their grandchildren. Three or four generations might live in the same house. Peasant families farmed their own piece of land, on which they grew oats, hemp, or wheat. This produce was sometimes sold, but more commonly the peasant retained such produce for his own purposes. The women of the household usually looked after the animals, such as cows and chickens, maintained the kitchen garden, and were responsible for child care.

Before the revolution, a degree of self-sufficiency was discernible in the Russian countryside, though rural life was not, by any means, free from outside intervention. In their early years, many peasant children attended schools, staffed by teachers trained in towns.[47] Villages were also the home to a range of officials, including policemen, priests, tax collectors, the local noble, and his family. While peasant life was self-regulated via the commune, it was never free from external supervision and regulation, most obviously through the imposition and collection of taxes.

To what extent did the Civil War affect everyday life in the countryside? In the immediate term, much depended on where geographically peasants lived. Given that the western provinces were at the heart of battle for much of World War One, in these regions the rural population had already suffered in similar ways to the northern and western cities. For example, the search for food was almost as intense as in Petrograd and other cities. Never self-sufficient, peasant men and women depended on the outside world for their survival, and once again the role of bagman proved important. In the southern provinces, the peasantry was much better off. Here, at least in 1917, there were grain surpluses. In general, however, the countryside lacked the goods that the towns had normally provided in peacetime. Russia's industry had been entirely given over to the production of war materiel, and the breakdown in the transportation system separated town and countryside. Household items, once produced in urban factories, now had to be fashioned and improvised by the peasantry.[48]

Slowly but surely the countryside became increasingly self-sufficient, and there developed a widespread belief that the towns were deliberately withholding vital products, such as kerosene, tobacco, tea, and cotton. The upshot was that the peasantry became resentful of urban centers and, when urban refugees arrived in rural villages, they were often greeted with hostility or turned away.[49] For their part, townspeople remained reliant on the countryside for foodstuffs, but the peasantry was reluctant to relinquish its precious produce.

Much of European Russian was overrun many times by both Reds and Whites in the course of the Civil War. Indeed, the peasants experienced a change of occupiers more than the urban population. Moscow and Petrograd were, for instance, only ever occupied by the Bolsheviks. But the vast lands in between and beyond exchanged hands frequently. Rural loyalty was, therefore, constantly in question. Peasants found themselves accused by both sides of espionage, counter-revolution, and hoarding grain. Individual peasants, and their families, often paid the price for these accusations, and untold numbers were summarily executed. At the heart of Red and White anxiety about the countryside lay the issue of food. The countryside was, after all, the breadbasket that supplied the towns, workers, and soldiers. In the Bolshevik worldview, the proletariat headed the social hierarchy, and their day-to-day survival was of the utmost priority. It followed that if grain was withheld by peasantry, then the rural population was guilty of betraying the revolution. As for the Whites, the withholding of foodstuffs indicated a pro-Bolshevik family or village. Unwillingly, therefore, the peasantry was at the heart of the Civil War, geographically and ideologically. This was to the obvious discomfort of the peasants who were reluctant to engage with the Bolshevik or White agenda, even if the revolution offered them opportunity to improve their lot in other ways.

Such reluctance was demonstrated in many ways. In the course of World War One, the peasantry had already shown that it was far from being a passive, inert mass. It would not heed the bidding of the authorities, unless there were obvious gains. While the cities of the north starved through want of grain, the peasantry refused to sell its produce for the fixed prices imposed by the state. It preferred to hold onto any surplus, which it used to fatten up its cattle and to make illegal alcohol, known as *samogon*.[50] By mid-1917, the Provisional Government instigated a system of forcible grain requisitioning in the countryside. Small bands of troops were sent to search out hoarded grain, an action that caused inevitable resentment. It was a practice continued in the Civil War and, in part, was responsible for fostering of both anti-Red and anti-White sentiment in the countryside.

Most significantly, from the perspective of the rural populace the Bolsheviks introduced in May 1918 a state grain monopoly and launched a "ruthless and terrorist war" against the grain-hoarding peasant.[51] All surplus grain was now the property of the state and the Bolsheviks subsequently waged an unrelenting campaign to ensure that it relinquished every last ounce. In particular, the Reds aimed their venom towards the supposed wealthier peasant, the *kulak*, who was accused of counter-revolution. The period of total self-reliance for the countryside came to an end from mid-1918 onwards. Henceforth, the Civil War encroached on peasant life in dramatic fashion

In particular, the countryside came into contact with thousands of Bolshevik foot soldiers, from its army of "food brigades," who were sent to find hidden grain and punish those responsible for hiding it.[52] Additionally, these brigades set about organizing the village along class lines and attempted to instigate open warfare between poorer and richer peasants. The outcome of this local incitement was expressed by a peasant in Samara, who made the following appeal to the local Bolshevik authorities:

I, a working peasant, working only with my family and my own callused hands, had one of my two horses confiscated, leaving me with only one horse, and they also took 15 *funt* of wool, all without payment.

I ask you, comrade representatives, to defend my rights as you should defend the interests of all working peasants, and I ask you to consider why the comrade leaders took my horse and wool, and when I have only two horses, and whether

I can really be a *kulak* with only two horses, and whether I can exploit the labour of others when I do not have enough animals and tools for myself. Surely my interests, the interests of a working peasant, will be defended by Comrade Lenin, surely I will be defended by you, representatives of the higher authorities.[53]

There was a widespread failure, however, to ignite wholesale class resentment, and villagers remained obstinately unwilling to embrace the kind of class-consciousness advocated by the Bolsheviks. While peasants were willing to take action against the local nobility, they were less inclined to act against their own kind. Moreover, in response to the attempt to requisition grain, peasants proved their obduracy. They often concealed their produce, fed it to livestock, or sold it elsewhere. But the Bolsheviks were not to be fooled so easily, and their war on the villages worsened as the years of civil war dragged out. Efforts to extort grain increased in violence. Threats, beatings, and shootings become a regular part of everyday existence.

In many ways, life in the countryside was characterized by violence. This had already been true, to some extent, of peasant life in general, but the Civil War intensified the elemental rivalries and forces in the village, as well as bringing in new ones from the outside. This was particularly the case during the period of War Communism, which was an effort by the Bolshevik regime to place the entire economy on a war footing. Introduced in summer 1918, War Communism meant that all agricultural produce became the property of the state. Grain requisitioning only intensified peasant resentment. Once the Bolshevik food brigades began to take away seed grain (which was essential for the following year's crop), the threat of famine loomed, and a period of outright resistance began. There were, from now on, concerted attempts to resist requisitioning and outside interference. Peasant uprisings occurred throughout Russia and took several forms. Sometimes the village united and forced out Bolshevik officials. On other occasions, entire provinces rose up against conscription into the Red Army. Violence inevitably typified these "peasant wars."[54]

Violence towards the countryside further resulted from the different patterns of occupation imposed by the Reds and Whites on the western provinces. As these territories frequently changed hands, the occupying authorities suspected all manner of collaborationist behavior. The complexity of the Civil War in European Russia ensured that loyalty was questioned on many levels, not just social, but ethnic and national. In Ukraine and Poland, all kinds of political groupings emerged, from anarchists to nationalists.[55] As one historian has noted, "[N]o other region of the Russian Empire witnessed more violence, more destruction, and more unvarnished cruelty" during the Civil War than Ukraine.[56] One of the most violent aspects of the conflict in Ukraine, which impacted the daily life of one significant ethnic group, were anti-Jewish pogroms, or massacres, which took place in late 1919.

Pogroms

The pogroms took place during a period of White occupation in Ukraine, under the leadership of General Antonin Denikin. In tsarist times, this part of the Russian Empire was home to the majority of its Jews, legally confined within the boundaries of an area known as the Pale of Settlement. During World War One, the Jewish population of Ukraine, just like the rural populace, found itself in the midst of battle. All kinds of accusations were leveled at the empire's Jews during this time, including allegations that they were pro-German, that they shirked their military obligations, and that they were exploiting the war for financial ends. They had also been subject to deportation orders—thousands were ordered to pack up and leave their homes at a moment's notice.[57] The Civil War found Jewish loyalties further questioned.

The questioning of Jewish loyalty was undoubtedly bound up with the widespread belief on the part of the Whites that Bolshevism was a Jewish conspiracy. After all, did not the Bolsheviks possess prominent numbers of Jews in their ranks? Such a conspiracy was, of course, entirely false, but it had grievous repercussions for ordinary Jews under White occupation.[58] Life was already difficult for Jews in Ukraine. Poverty was an age-old problem and, as for everyone else in Russia, the Civil War exacerbated the material situation. But Jewish life was made worse by the recurrent waves of violence perpetrated throughout 1919. Once again, loyalties were questioned, in an arena of battle that was fraught with numerous nationalist questions. Rural animosity also played its part, and peasants, alongside Cossacks from the Volunteer Army, were responsible for unleashing horrific terrors against Ukrainian Jews.[59] During 1919, countless Jewish homes were raided, property was set alight, belongings were destroyed and ransacked, and synagogues desecrated. Many thousand Jews were beaten, tortured, raped, and murdered. Daily life for the Jews of the former Russian Empire thus became even more desperate during the Civil War.[60]

EVACUATION, REFUGEES, AND FAMINE

In the final military engagements of the Civil War in 1920 and 1921, fresh "enemies" appeared to aggravate the conditions of life in Russia. In particular, two events hastened the worsening violence. First, the final routing of the Volunteer Army in the south of Russia precipitated another refugee crisis. Second, the catastrophic famine in the Volga region increased the number of refugees in Russia, and cost the lives of millions. By the time of the final Bolshevik victory in late 1921, Russia was left exhausted, emaciated, and broken, its people demoralized, starving, and afraid.

The ultimate military engagements took place in the south of Russia, as the Red Army inexorably pushed the Whites towards the Crimea. Accompanying the soldiers of the Volunteer Army were a mass of civilians,

A Russian woman and children get ready to flee from
their famine-stricken home near Perozecse, in the Russian Federation. September 12, 1921. Courtesy of AP
Photo.

comprising wives, children, and families of the troops, but also numerous
individuals who knew they would not survive in Lenin's Russia. By 1920,
anybody of *bourgeois* or aristocratic extraction was wise to try and escape,
since only death awaited them at the hands of the Cheka.[61] The denoue-
ment of the Civil War saw thousands of panic-stricken people pushed
onto the Crimean peninsula with no means of escape except via the sea.
In late 1920, ships from the British and French navies rescued thousands,
and evacuated them to Constantinople in Turkey. One British military observer reported the evacuation to his superiors:

Following the collapse of General Wrangel's [leader of the Whites] army in the
Crimea, large numbers of refugees poured into Constantinople during the latter
part of November. No one whoever witnessed the plight of these 140,000 Russians can ever forget it. Some 60 to 70 transports crowded beyond description—
homeless, hungry, thirsty, sick men, women and children rightly described as a

seething mass of humanity. Many of these wretched people had been standing on the deck for nine days.[62]

As one commentator remarked, at some point in the Civil War, almost every individual was turned into a refugee. From those who fled the cities of the north in search of food, to the Jews of Ukraine chased from their villages by pogromists, and to the peasants fleeing the famine regions of 1921, the chief impact of the war on ordinary life had been to render millions homeless. Ultimately, the White army itself became a refugee, too, with its defeated troops scattered to the winds.[63] Those who fled alongside Wrangel's routed army, carrying their entire worldly wealth on their person, were displaced far beyond Russia. They formed a part of a Russian emigration, estimated at between 2 million and 3 million people.

   In the Civil War, most of these people, who originated from a range of social backgrounds, endured food shortages, disease, and fear. Many lost not only their worldly wealth and position in life, but also their families. After leaving Russia, they were herded into camps in Turkey, Greece, and Bulgaria. Their future was uncertain and they subsisted on the rations made available by the Red Cross and other charities. The same problems they encountered in the fighting itself inevitably dogged their lives as refugees. Describing a camp in Greece, a U.S. colonel in the medical corps referred to the appalling conditions in which the refugees lived and concluded that "a large proportion of them show evidence of under-nourishment which further pre-disposes them to disease." In a hospital where the total numbered 458, he discovered those with various diseases numbered:

Typhus fever 37; suspected typhus 68; recurrent fever 16; malaria 84; dysentery (bacillary) 89; measles 4; influenza 53; pneumonia 25; miscellaneous and unclassified 82. . . . During the 24 hours covered by this report there were 18 deaths, only 5 of which were in hospital. Of this 13 deaths in barracks, 9 were children under 3 years of age. Two of the adults died of pneumonia. [Sanitary conditions] are about as bad as can be imagined. The overcrowding in most of the barracks is extreme. Clothing is woefully inadequate; many of the refugees are clad only in rags. The water supply has been improved during the past two weeks but it is still insufficient. The food is inadequate in quantity and variety and is prepared and served in a most unsanitary way.[64]

The evacuation and the flood of refugees that deluged parts of southeast Europe brought about the intervention of the outside world. Another event, one that took place inside Russia, also attracted aid from Western European and American institutions. The famine of 1921–22, although seemingly not a part of the Civil War, since it took hold after the White defeat, was nevertheless bound up in the disasters that had preceded it.

   The famine, like so much of the early period of Bolshevik rule, foreshadowed events during Stalin's rule. And, akin to the disastrous famine in Ukraine in the 1930s, the crisis that hit the provinces of the Volga (south

of Moscow) was in part man-made.[65] In essence, it was the result of ac-
cumulated factors, beginning with World War One, which drew men to
battle and away from the fields. In addition, the food policies of the tsarist
regime, the Provisional Government, and the Bolsheviks had disincentiv-
ized the peasant. For many years afterwards, he only planted enough seed
to give him produce for his own needs. We have already seen how peasant
practices altered in the Civil War and how the situation was made worse
by the food brigades, which often confiscated seed grain. This situation
was further aggravated by natural circumstances, namely drought. In
1920 and 1921 the crops failed.[66]

The famine of 1921–22 was the most devastating one ever confronted by
Russia, a land well accustomed to natural disasters.[67] It affected around
35 million people, who were reduced to scavenging for food and sustenance in any way they could. Many thousands fled their dry, dusty villages, and wandered on foot in search of food elsewhere. Once again,
Russia endured a refugee problem. And, just as in the Crimean evacuation, outside forces were mobilized to assist and alleviate the situation,
including the Red Cross and the American Relief Association. A British
writer who visited the famine-struck province of Samara described the
wretched condition of refugees he encountered:

The conditions under which they are living are appalling. Their only shelter
consists of strips of rags stretched from poles to the sides of carts in which they
have transported themselves and their belongings into the town. Usually there is
no protection from the sky whatever. In these uncouth tents the whole family is
herded together—old men with emaciated bodies and eyes that scarcely are to be
seen in their death's-heads of faces, women hardly able to step from one side of
the shelter to the other, and children, innumerable children, sitting listlessly on the
ground, too exhausted to move, to talk or to play.

 There is one story common to all these hundreds of people. All through the
summer they have watched their soil harden to stone under the rays of a terrible
sun, and the few scattered shoots which had pushed their heads through it blacken
and perish. They have been living on the tiny remnants of the last year's harvest—
which also, it must be remembered, was a failure—eked out with all kinds of
surrogates—acorns, bark, lime-tree leaves, pigweed, clay, insects beaten-up into
a paste, even animals' droppings—anything that will hold a modicum of flour
together and cheat them into imagining that they are eating something else.[68]

In this part of Russia, there really was nothing left to eat—at least, nothing that was conventionally deemed food. Peasants were left to forage
amongst the forests and the arid, broken fields. Some peasants were driven
to even more desperate measures by the gnawing hunger in their bellies
and they turned to cannibalism.[69]

There are no precise statistics that reveal the total deaths resulting from
the famine of 1921–22. Soviet historians estimated the losses at around
5 million. For the Western visitors who aided in famine relief, the figure

stood at around 10 million.[70] Whatever the truth behind these statistics, the famine represented the final sacrifice of the Russian civilian population during its Civil War.

NOTES

1. Orlando Figes, *A People's Tragedy: The Russian Revolution 1891–1924* (London: Penguin, 1996).

2. Peter Holquist, *Making War, Forging Revolution: Russia's Continuum of Crisis, 1914–1921* (Cambridge, Mass. Harvard University Press, 2002).

3. Evan Mawdsley, *The Russian Civil War* (London: Allen and Unwin, 1987), p. 287. There are no precise numbers on the casualties of the Russian Civil War, though one historian estimates that around 90 percent of its victims were civilians. See Richard Pipes, *Russia under the Bolshevik Regime* (London: Harvill, 1994), pp. 138–139.

4. See Peter Kenez, *Civil War in South Russia, 1919–1920: The Defeat of the Whites* (Berkeley: University of California Press, 1977); Mawdsley, *The Russian Civil War;* Oliver H. Radkey, *The Unknown Civil War in Soviet Russia: A Study of the Green Movement in the Tambov Region, 1920–21* (Stanford, Calif.: Hoover Institution Press, 1976); Betty M. Unterberger, *American Intervention in the Russian Civil War* (Lexington, MA: D. C. Heath, 1969); Michael J. Carley, *Revolution and Intervention: The French Government and the Russian Civil War 1917–1919* (Kingston, Canada: McGill-Queen's University Press, 1983); and George. A. Brinkley, *The Volunteer Army and Allied Intervention in South Russia, 1917–1922: A Study in the Politics and Diplomacy of the Russian Civil War* (Notre Dame, Ind.: University of Notre Dame Press, 1966).

5. Quoted in W. Bruce Lincoln, *Red Victory: A History of the Russian Civil War* (New York: Simon and Schuster, 1989), pp. 52–53.

6. Figes, *A People's Tragedy,* p. 548. As a result of the Treaty of Brest-Litovsk, Russia lost approximately half of its European territories, 54 percent of its heavy industry and 89 percent of its coal mines.

7. Pipes, *Russia under the Bolshevik Regime,* pp. 10–11. For another perspective, see Mawdsley, *The Russian Civil War,* pp. 272–290.

8. Pipes, *Russia Under the Bolshevik Regime,* p. 11.

9. Figes, *A People's Tragedy,* p. 301.

10. Isaac Deutscher, *The Prophet Unarmed: Trotsky, 1921–1929* (New York: Oxford University Press, 1965), p. 7.

11. Mary McAuley, "Bread without the Bourgeoisie," in *Party, State and Society in the Russian Civil War,* ed. Diane P. Koenker, William G. Rosenberg, and Ronald J. Suny), (Bloomington, IN: Indiana University Press, 1989), p. 158.

12. Lincoln, *Red Victory,* p. 57.

13. Emma Goldman, *My Disillusionment with Russia,* 1923, quoted in Figes, *A People's Tragedy,* p. 603.

14. This was also a continuation of events catalyzed by World War One; see Peter Gatrell, *A Whole Empire Walking: Refugees in Russia during World War 1* (Bloomington: Indiana University Press, 1999).

15. Lewis H. Siegelbaum, *Soviet State and Society between Revolutions, 1918–1929* (Cambridge: Cambridge University Press, 1992), pp. 27–28.

16. Lincoln, *Red Victory,* p. 62.

17. A chart of the population changes for the major cities of the former tsarist empire can be found in Diane Koenker, "Urbanization and Deurbanization in the Russian Revolution and Civil War," *Journal of Modern History* 57, no. 3 (Sept. 1985): 424–50. See also Daniel R. Brower, "'The City in Danger': The Civil War and the Russian Urban Population," in *Party, State and Society in the Russian Civil War,* ed. Koenker, Rosenberg, and Suny, pp. 58–80.

18. Donald J. Raleigh, *Experiencing Russia's Civil War: Politics, Society and Revolutionary Culture in Saratov, 1917–1922* (Princeton, N.J.: Princeton University Press, 2002), pp. 64–71, 181, 188.

19. Lars T. Lih, *Bread and Authority in Russia, 1914–1921* (Berkeley: University of California Press, 1990), pp. 76–81; Lincoln, *Red Victory,* p. 71.

20. Donald J. Raleigh, ed., *A Russian Civil War Diary: Alexis Babine in Saratov, 1917–1922* (Durham, N.C.: Duke University Press, 1988), entry for June 24, 1918, pp. 90–91.

21. Figes, *A People's Tragedy,* p. 611.

22. Lincoln, *Red Victory,* pp. 57, 59.

23. Figes, *A People's Tragedy,* p. 604; Raleigh, *Experiencing Russia's Civil War,* p. 392.

24. Lih, *Bread and Authority in Russia,* p. 244.

25. Macauley, "Bread without the Bourgeoisie," p. 163.

26. C. E. Bechhoffer [C.E.B. Roberts], *Through Starving Russia: Being the Record of a Journey to Moscow and the Volga Provinces in August and September 1921* (London: Methuen, 1921), p. 22.

27. Lincoln, *Red Victory,* pp. 51–52.

28. Macauley, "Bread without the Bourgeoisie," p. 43.

29. Raleigh, *A Russian Civil War Diary,* entry for January 15, 1918, p. 56.

30. Raleigh, *A Russian Civil War Diary,* entry for December 1, 1918, p. 54.

31. Lincoln, *Red Victory,* p. 54.

32. Mawdsley, *The Russian Civil War,* p. 83, suggests that the official figure of 6,300 was an "understatement."

33. Raleigh, *A Russian Civil War Diary,* entry for January 15, 1918, p. 56.

34. Raleigh, *A Russian Civil War Diary,* entry for October 21, 1918, p. 113.

35. Pipes, *Russia under the Bolsheviks,* pp. 320–321.

36. See Alan M. Ball, *And Now My Soul is Hardened: Abandoned Children in Soviet Russia, 1918–1930* (Berkeley: University of California Press, 1994).

37. Raleigh, *A Russian Civil War Diary,* entry for February 22, 1920, p. 160.

38. Raleigh, *Experiencing Russia's Civil War,* p. 198.

39. Raleigh, *Experiencing Russia's Civil War,* pp. 199–202.

40. Francis McCullagh, *A Prisoner of the Reds* (London: J. Murray, 1921), pp. 32–33.

41. Catherine Merridale, *Night of Stone: Death and Memory in Russia* (London: Granta, 2000), p. 131.

42. Quoted in Figes, *A People's Tragedy,* p. 603.

43. Bechhoffer, *Through Starving Russia,* pp. 133–34.

44. Raleigh, *Experiencing Russia's Civil War,* p. 207.

45. Figes, *A People's Tragedy,* p. 609.

46. Orlando Figes, *Peasant Russia, Civil War: The Volga Countryside in Revolution, 1917–1921* (London: Weidenfeld and Nicolson, 1991), pp. 47–61.

47. See Ben Eklof, *Russian Peasant Schools: Officialdom, Village Culture and Popular Pedagogy, 1861–1914* (Berkeley: University of California Press, 1987).

48. Figes, *A People's Tragedy*, p. 608.

49. Figes, *Peasant Russia, Civil War,* pp. 142–43.

50. Lincoln, *Red Victory*, pp. 59–60.

51. Figes, *Peasant Russia, Civil War,* p. 185.

52. Figes, *Peasant Russia, Civil War,* pp. 183–84.

53. Quoted in Figes, *Peasant Russia, Civil War,* pp. 360–361. A *funt* was equal to approximately 0.88 pounds.

54. Figes, *Peasant Russia, Civil War,* pp. 321–353; Taisa Osipova, "Peasant Rebellions: Origin, Scope, Dynamics and Consequences," in Vladimir N. Brovkin, *The Bolsheviks in Russian Society: The Revolution and the Civil Wars* (New Haven, Conn.: Yale University Press, 1997), pp. 154–76.

55. Norman Davies, *White Eagle, Red Star: The Polish-Soviet War, 1919–20* (London: Pimlico, 1972).

56. Lincoln, *Red Victory,* p. 302.

57. Eric Lohr, *Nationalizing the Russian Empire: The Campaign Against Enemy Aliens in World War I* (Cambridge, Mass.: Harvard University Press, 2003), pp. 137–50.

58. Though, it must be said, the Reds were also guilty of perpetrating atrocities against Jews, especially during the war against Poland.

59. Peter Kenez, "Pogroms and White Ideology," in *Pogroms: Anti-Jewish Violence in Modern Russian History.* ed. John D. Klier and Shlomo Lambroza (Cambridge: Cambridge University Press, 1992), pp. 293–313.

60. Alexander Victor Prusin, *Nationalizing a Borderland: War, Ethnicity, and Anti-Jewish Violence in East Galicia, 1914–1920* (Tuscaloosa: University of Alabama Press, 2005).

61. The Cheka developed a range of unpleasant and slow ways of killing its victims, ranging from crushing their skulls, sawing them alive, immersing them in boiling water, and stripping off their skin. See Lincoln, *Red Victory,* pp. 382–86.

62. TNA, War Office file 32/51/36, General Harington to British War Office, London, September 22, 1921.

63. Paul Robinson, *The Russian White Army in Exile, 1920–1941* (Oxford: Oxford University Press, 1999).

64. TNA, Foreign Office file 286/276, Memorandum from American Red Cross on the "Refugee Camps at Salonique," March 21, 1921.

65. Robert Conquest, *The Harvest of Sorrows: Soviet Collectivisation and the Terror Famine* (New York: Oxford University Press, 1987).

66. Bertrand M. Patenaude, *The Big Show in Bololand: The American Relief Expedition to Soviet Russia in the Famine of 1921* (Stanford, Calif.: Stanford University Press, 2002), pp. 26–27.

67. Until that point, the most disastrous had been the famine of 1891–92, but it affected far fewer people and swept away far fewer people.

68. Bechhoffer, *Through Starving Russia*, pp. 40–41.

69. Patenaude, *Big Show in Bololand*, pp. 262–70.

70. Patenaude, *Big Show in Bololand*, pp. 196–98.

FOUR

Daily Life in the Spanish Civil War, 1936–39

Michael Richards

As ideological conflicts, civil wars encapsulate a significant incursion of politics into daily life. The struggle to define "the nation" entails the construction and strengthening of state power, as well as the mobilization of ideas and principles that legitimize violence and the consequent sacrifices of the struggle. The war itself requires, in turn, the mobilization of populations to fight and the creation of productive and distributive apparatus for the provision of resources and supplies. This harnessing of power draws on a preexisting social setting and the preexisting conflicts that created the potential for war in the first place. Alongside this structural conditioning, entirely contingent and accidental factors, such as where geographically one happens to be when the conflict begins, play a part in the ways in which civil war is experienced. The invention of founding myths during civil wars, based particularly on defining "the nation," is perpetuated through dissemination by movements which are usually, to varying degrees, revolutionary or which claim to be so.

On several counts, therefore, civil wars can be related to the concept of total war, although this term was devised originally to account for the way in which *interstate* wars affected substantial areas of civilian life and contributed to longer-term change.[1] This chapter takes up these arguments with reference to the Spanish Civil War of 1936–39. It does so by tracing the links between four indispensable areas of analysis in exploring the Spanish conflict and wartime daily life. All of these spheres suggest something of the totalizing effects of civil war: (1) the shape of the state and its relationship to political and economic power, (2) mentalities and ideologies within society, (3) the use, rationale, and significance of coercion and violence, and finally (4) the struggle for resources as an element that determined victory and defeat.

STATE, ECONOMY, AND SOCIETY

The nature of both the initially weakened Republican state and the nascent Nationalist state underwent evolution during the war and this evolution contributed to the changing relationship of state power to society in the zones controlled by the opposing sides. These changes can best be described by delineating three broad phases in the war, before moving on to discuss the economic framework—again, something that changed over time—for an understanding of the daily experience of the conflict.

To begin with, from July 18, 1936, until the change of government in the Loyalist or Republican zone in September 1936 (under the leadership of the left-Socialist Francisco Largo Caballero), it makes sense to talk not of a civil war but of a state of military rebellion against the constituted power. This provoked a popular revolutionary movement, and sparked reprisals carried out by both sides. An important qualification to this summary would be that this particular military coup was backed, in very practical terms and virtually from the first day, by the force of Nazi Germany and Fascist Italy.[2] This aid would be indispensable in transporting the rebels' key forces strategically from place to place. Before long, the troops supplied by Mussolini, and Nazi military hardware, would become extensively involved in the fighting.

The reality in the early stages, however, was one of brutal policing measures, carried out by the military rebels and backed by armed force, and a governmental crisis that was only partially and defectively resolved by arming the masses—rapidly and loosely grouped under the banner of the Milicias Anti-fascistas Obreras y Campesinas (Workers' and Peasants' Anti-Fascist Militia), controlled, significantly, in Catalonia by the bourgeois regional government. A violent collective response to the military coup and the collectivization of property in rural and urban areas then ensued. The military aspects of this popular response were chaotic and there were varying levels of enthusiasm on the part of the populace when volunteering to fight. Many volunteers in Madrid, at this initial stage, left the city for the front every morning, with something to eat packed, and returned to their homes late in the evening. The fighting was real enough, however, and there was more killing still on the home front. Violence against individuals deemed to have organized or supported the rebellion, or thought to have been associated with its interests—the middle classes, property owners, the clergy—was intrinsic to the popular backlash. No region remaining under the formal jurisdiction of the Republican government following the attempted coup in July 1936 escaped revolutionary changes and the violence of revolutionary suppression and transformation. Anticlerical violence was an especially important part of the purge of the old order. Only in the Catholic and socially conservative, but pro-Republican, Basque Country was the revolution relatively marginal to daily life in the immediate aftermath of the coup. All over Spain, therefore, the rule of law was "substituted by the language and the dialectic of arms, disregard for human rights and the cult of violence."[3]

The popular revolution was inchoate, confused, as revolutions usually are, and rested on unsteady foundations; the upheaval was often compared at the time to such natural disasters as hurricanes or earthquakes. For activists of the leftist organizations, especially during the first months, the term *guerra civil* was not used; what was being fought for was *la revolución*. Others, particularly in the rural south, saw things in broadly similar terms, though these civilians were less obviously political. In speaking of the conflict as "the rising of the people against the *señoritos*" they were, however, consciously or unconsciously appropriating the notion of *la rebelión* (revolt, rebellion, rising) which, in its reactionary form, had been claimed by the military conservatives who staged the coup. It was now popularly put to use to make some sense of the revolutionary situation.[4] The symbols of bourgeois and exploitative daily life were overturned: street names were changed and dress codes overhauled (blue overalls and red neckerchiefs and no hats and neckties). Songs, banners, slogans, advertisements, public meetings, theater and music-hall productions: all these forms were used to express the sense of change. Tipping in restaurants, unreasonable rents, and money-lending were the first to go in Barcelona, and it would not be too long before money itself was abolished in many areas of the Republican zone. The sense of the strength of the masses was intoxicating. Doubts were swept away as the people took control of public space.[5]

Amid this developing situation, in September 1936 the anarcho-syndicalist Confederación Nacional del Trabajo (CNT) joined the bourgeois regional government in Catalonia, whose aim was to bring about reform and put fighting the war first before carrying out any kind of social revolution. That the accomplishments of the revolution were overestimated is not surprising. In the cities, largely because of working-class initiatives, public transport continued to run, shops were open, the factories were functioning, and telephone, gas, and water supplies operated, none of them in the interests of profit. The social, economic, and political transformations achieved in the Republican zone were not, however, brought about as a result of heightening class contradictions, as in the classic Marxist formulation, but through political events that had led to a greater awareness of inequalities and possibilities for change. The social revolution, though clearly based on class conflict, was triggered by the military coup in July 1936, following five years of the greatest degree of political liberty and participation ever enjoyed, as a result of the proclamation of the reforming and democratizing Second Republic in 1931. The extent and the depth of these revolutionary achievements during the war, therefore, need to be assessed through historical analysis of the war as popularly experienced.

A second phase in the Civil War can be identified as lasting from around November 1936 until August 1937, a period defined temporally by the failure of the rebel forces to take Madrid and the general realization that the war was going to be a protracted one. It was also a period in which the parties of the left increasingly fell out with one another. Though activists of the communist (Stalinist) Partido Comunista de España (PCE) played a leading role in the Republican Junta de Defensa (Defense Committee) in Madrid and became the dominant political force in the city, they were at odds with the dissident Marxist Partido Obrero de Unificación Marxista (POUM), which campaigned for revolution as a continuous process. The latter believed revolution could only be sustained through the spontaneous actions of the workers, a belief that led to the infamous May Days in Barcelona in 1937, and the subsequent suppression of the POUM and the anarchist movement, the CNT-Federación Anarquista Ibérica (FAI). Internecine clashes additionally arose from the forced conversion of the Republic's fighting forces from a "people in arms" (led by revolutionary trade unionists through the militias) into a People's Army, a more conventional modern force carrying merely a radical label, a transformation that was staunchly resisted by the POUM militias and the CNT-FAI. Exacerbating these divisions were underlying class antagonisms, between middle-class Republicans and smallholding peasants, on the one hand, and the industrial and landless workers on the other.

Aside from this "civil war within the Civil War," by spring 1937 people at large were increasingly conscious of what was going on around them and started to refer to the conflagration simply as *la guerra*. Most people primarily experienced the conflict through hardship, hunger, loss of life, and loss of security and daily equilibrium. This insecurity bred fear that became intertwined with violence in the rearguard, as we will see. Indeed, the social effects of the fighting were beginning to pinch. In many areas, especially urban centers like Madrid, daily life was shaped by the existence of a mass itinerant population that had fled rural areas, especially Toledo and Extremadura, within a few months of the coup. There was now a mass refugee problem. Coping with the social fallout did not necessarily mean that people were oblivious to the wider political conflict, yet the daily struggle for survival was starting to be an overriding concern and affected levels of political solidarity. Political commitment was always filtered and diluted by these daily pressures. It is misleading to believe, as has sometimes been suggested, that ideological commitment, even in times of war, can be measured merely on the basis of the willingness of people to volunteer to fight and be prepared to die.[6]

Backed by aid from Stalin, which came with several political and financial strings attached, the Republican government initiated the necessary process of reconstructing a state and an army fit for the purpose of

Two young girls took refuge in the mouth of a sewer during a fascist raid in Madrid, Spain, February 8, 1937, during the Spanish Civil War. Though weeks of such raids seem to have made them more interested than frightened of the falling bombs, fear was ever-present. Courtesy of AP Photo.

fighting a war rather than merely suppressing a military revolt.[7] With more efficient processes of mobilization in place, the conflict became rhetorically, in both zones, a *Guerra de Liberación Nacional*. This process was further aided by an instinctive realization by Nationalists and Republicans that unity was crucial. It was also marked by the instilling of terror in the civilian population, which had become a *military* objective. This was signaled in the bombing of Guernica in the Basque Country in April 1937. Given the ways in which German and Italian aircraft bombed civilians in Madrid and Barcelona, it is small wonder that the Republican narrative of the war as a national struggle against foreign invasion became highly persuasive.[8]

Aspects of this intermediate stage of the conflict prepared the way for its final phase, which lasted from around August 1937 until Franco's victory at the end of March 1939. In effect, the conflict became a modern total war of attrition as the majority of the civilian population was mobilized, in both the military and economic arenas. For example, the age scale for the call-up in the Republican area of control was extended at both ends of the spectrum, and more and more young and middle-aged men were conscripted. Through a coercive process of forced unity, the Republic was politically stronger than it had been, yet continued to show signs of weakness. Initially the government had been able to make the relief of food shortages a focus of solidarity, yet it could do little to prevent the urban population from suffering extreme hunger by 1938, which led to disease and disillusionment. By this stage, a return to normality became an understandable and obsessive desire, which made the defeat of the Republicans all the more likely.

Land Collectives, the War Economy, and Labor

Curiously, historians still know relatively little about the ways in which the civilian population responded to such wartime economic pressures. These were several: demands for increased production, revolutionary collectivization in Republican areas, the development of a war economy (and thereby economic militarization) in both zones, changing working conditions, and the regulation of the labor-capital relationship.

The most important problems (affecting the revolution in the Loyalist zone and maintenance of the economic system in the rebel zone) were in the allocation of productive resources.[9] The agrarian collectives, formed in the Republican zone as a central element of the wartime revolution, suggest the scale and nature of the challenge. The collectives could rarely aim merely to be self-sufficient, however much their members believed in a loosely federated social organization. They needed to supply urban and industrial centers where food shortages were a constant problem, and they also needed to contribute to feeding men at the front. But problems of exchange were aggravated by the unevenness of the revolutionary process and persistently constrained productive forces. Rule 13 of the anarchist Collective of Salas Altas in Aragón, for example, approved in December 1936, stated that "money available to the Collective will be used only to purchase goods in those regions where money still exists."[10]

Efficiency was not necessarily the priority of the rank-and-file socialists and anarchists who carried out the land seizures in response to the rebellion. Although production levels were not uniformly disastrous, a key aim was to transfer and transform economic power—primarily through ownership of the means of production—which, as activists saw it, constituted a victory in itself and, they argued, was central to the war mobilization of the Republic in the early months of the conflict. One of the founding principles of an Aragón collective insisted that "all trace of exploitation of man by man is abolished and consequently all forms of tenant farming, sharecropping or paid employment." Most collectivization took place during July and August 1936 in the absence of business owners and landowners and their agents, who fled in the face of the revolution. In Catalonia, where Barcelona took the lead in industrial collectivization, the process in agriculture began a little later than elsewhere. In Andalucía, in the south, the timetable varied from place to place, depending on local conditions, and in Castile collectivization was not widespread until summer 1937. Generally speaking, the most radical forms occurred where the process had begun earliest and where the revolutionary impulse had been strongest: in Aragón, for example, in the northeast.

In many areas a weekly wage was guaranteed to each family—the *salario familiar*, which was popular in anarchist collectives. The governing council of collectives also instituted a family rationing system by which daily food consumption was regulated. Clothing was also to be rationed to ensure more equitable distribution. Perhaps inevitably, official Republican currency was undermined and lost its value so that local arrangements using vouchers and coupons for specified goods and bartering flourished, especially where doctrinal considerations were in favor of abolishing money. In practice, a wide range of wages were paid, usually in accord with the financial capacities of each operation. In the end, the agrarian collectives, however radical they might have been, tended to lay bare the inherent contradictions of the cross-class Republican political and social project, which had grown ever weaker since its inception in 1931. The need to debate collectively in this communal environment before decisions could be made, and the undermining of hierarchy insisted upon by anarchist doctrine, hampered production at a time when a more streamlined system would have been more rational. In other words, although some revolutionary measures, such as rationing, were consistent with wartime measures, the socialized moral economy of collectivization conflicted with an efficient war economy. This realization would give added urgency to the Republican state's suppression of the revolution during the war.

The precise extent of land collectivization is not wholly clear, but it is usually estimated that in Aragón, where the anarchist CNT was dominant, there were some 450 collectivities, each one, on average, incorporating some 1,000 members. In Levante (the east coast around Valencia) there were probably around 350, in New Castile (above all in the provinces of Toledo, Guadalajara, Ciudad Real, Madrid, and Cuenca) there were between 200 and 300, largely under the control of the Socialist Union General de Trabajadores (UGT) trade union. In rural Catalonia there were 100 collectivized projects. The spontaneous nature of the process of expropriation often overrode conflicting prewar claims of the various left-wing groups, so that the directive committees in many areas were composed of a variety of political groups, from anarchists to leftist Republicans. Great tracts of land in the latifundista regions of the south—Andalucía, Extremadura, and Murcia—were also collectivized by the landless laborers and here there was greater communalization of land in areas that were previously worked as large estates (latifundia). These areas were also often, coincidentally, closer to the fighting front. In Jaén, to take one province of Andalucía renowned for olive production, 65 percent of cultivated land was expropriated. By August 1938, the Republican Institute of Agrarian Reform calculated that 2,213 collectivized units were operating in the Loyalist zone (without counting Catalonia), involving some 3 million participants. The Nationalists, however, controlled more productive land and, although the level of wheat production is only one indicator of Republican economic performance, the fact that 1937 production in the Loyalist zone was half the rate for the same area in 1932 suggests the scale of the problem.

Outside of agriculture, the Loyalists were blessed with the fact that the key industrial and urban bases (Barcelona, Madrid, Valencia, Asturias, the central coastal area, and the Basque Country) were in their zone, though this state of affairs would change as Franco's Nationalists notched up a series of victories in northern Spain in the latter half of 1937.[11] A year earlier, the Loyalists had been quick to meet the requirements of war through the establishment of a War Industry Commission run by the workers themselves, especially activists of the anarchist CNT. Again, organization conflicted with principles. Anarchist activists could not help but be confused by the situation: "although we were anti-authoritarian, we were suddenly the only authority there," remarked one.[12] Seizure or confiscation implied the appropriation by Republican authorities of a center of production but did not define any necessary future mode of functioning. Collectivization, on the other hand, specified a particular form of operation whereby economic power was seized by the workforce, which took on the responsibility of production.

By October 1936, some 500 factories in Catalonia (mainly in Barcelona) employing 50,000 workers were under the commission's control, though supply problems remained and the requirement of cooperating rationally with the Republican central government complicated matters. Other divisions hindered the process. While anarchist theory could be adapted to more or less self-sufficient agricultural units, utopian anarchism blended uncomfortably with the more reformist, productivist, and rational strand of collectivism that was powerful within the CNT. As Josep Bricall makes clear, "on suppressing certain institutions of contemporary society, such as money or more general means of interchange, the new ordering of the economy in industrial zones was incapacitated because such things as credit and action in the market were fundamental elements."[13] In addition, the socialist Partido Socialista Obrero Español (PSOE), the Unión General de Trabajadores (UGT), and the communist PCE and the Partit Socialista

Unifacat de Catalunya (PSUC) constantly prioritized the centralization of the economy in the interests of victory.

With all of these constraints, it is not surprising that conventional forms of the measurement of performance suggest disappointing results. Production in Catalonia was centered on the metallurgy sector, which demonstrated quite impressive growth until April 1937; however, for a variety of reasons, by 1938 Catalan industrial production, including metallurgy, had fallen drastically below July 1936 levels. In contrast, centralized discipline was guaranteed in the rebel zone where the primary aim of the Nationalist insurgents was to suppress the workers and their trade unions through violence and to militarize industry under the command of the Nationalist Ministry of Defense, resorting at times to penal labor.[14] Unfettered by dreams of building a new society, the rebels thus built up a stronger economic base and always possessed a greater unity in their commitment to counter-revolution, a cause enthusiastically supported by the ruthless soldiers of the colonial army of Africa.

MENTALITIES AND IDEOLOGIES

It is sufficient merely to look at the doctrinal output and its dissemination in political newspapers and posters to indicate that the Spanish war, at least in the Republican zone, was fought over ideas. Such a view would support the contention that civil wars are generally more ideologically motivated than interstate war. Ideology certainly permeated everyday life during the Republic, notably in the promotion of laic education, institutionalized in revolutionary areas in the form of self-consciously rationalist and socialist schools. The intensity of cultural and political activities (beginning with the new regime's democratic and historic electoral victory of April 1931) was thus very real, though certain associated images have endured longer than others. Even allowing for an understandable sense of nostalgia, the often festive atmosphere that pushed for a popularization of the political (and, up to a point, the politicization of the personal) has been recalled in many post-Franco testimonies. For example, there was undoubtedly a growth of women's expectations, as expressed by a woman from Málaga who was in her twenties during the years of the Republic:

The Republic changed customs, people had more open minds, there was a rapid intensification; one could tell in the way people expressed themselves, in communication between people, people simply spoke more and about more things, about politics; when there were informal meetings in the canteen, women went along too.[15]

Once war came, the siege mentality in the Republican zone, the struggle there to secure basic material needs, and internal political arguments, all interacted with ideological commitment in shaping those new patterns of social and cultural practice initiated in 1931.

For conservatives, and many of the middle classes, memories of the Republic were very different and focused largely on the regime's attempts to reform religious practice within a broader program to separate Church and state. In January 1932, a law for the secularization of cemeteries was introduced that established new criteria by which burials might be accompanied by religious ceremony. It was argued that funerals had become opportunities for politically inspired disorder, although the law was applied patchily. Shortly afterwards divorce and civil marriage were legalized, a popular and measured reform. These measures were a prelude to the Law of Confessions and Religious Congregations. Passed in May 1933, this law strictly regulated the holding of public religious devotions, such as Holy Week processions, which provoked the resistance of the middle classes and the Church and motivated the disapproving papal encyclical *Dilectissima Nobis* of June 1933. Probably the most controversial and damaging act was the removal of crucifixes from state schools, begun in January 1932, in pursuance of article 48 of the 1931 Constitution of the Republic.

The resentment produced by these measures would be recalled by Catholics during the Civil War just as, on the other side, the Church's resistance to modernization would also be recalled. This perceived failure to modernize provoked yet further anticlericalism. A Republican civil war decree of August 1936 invoked the article of the 1933 Law of Confessions that allowed for the closure of all establishments belonging to religious orders and congregations when elements of the Church were deemed to be involved in political activity. This included giving any form of allegiance to the insurrectionary generals or "having offered vows or prayers for the triumph of the rebellion." The decree formalized practices that had already begun to be enforced popularly, in the streets, as part of the revolutionary and bloody turning over of power.

Whatever the case, symbols remained vital to both sides during the war, though inevitably the ways in which they were used evolved according to circumstances. The Republican government decreed in 1937, for example, that the anniversary of the proclamation of the Second Republic (April 14), while not to be ignored, should not be celebrated too vigorously because people's thoughts had to be with those in the trenches as an inspiration to a greater effort in the workplace. *El Socialista* declared that "no-one should forget that the war, which is fought out at the front, is won on the home front."[16] The ubiquity of ideological forms generally during the war, not least in the shape of propaganda and the myths that affected aspects of political and social behavior, has led some historians to suggest an overly simplistic picture of popular wartime mentalities. Commitment has been imagined monolithically, as though the population of the Republican zone constituted a single social and political collective living only for the battle. One of the challenges for historians of the war, therefore, is to gauge the extent and manner of the *internalization* of doctrine and the effect of this on wartime mobilization.

At the very onset of the war, the Republicans recognized the need to create a war consciousness, as they were aware that they were not as politically and socially homogenous as their opponents. This initiative took many forms. In the early stages, before Republican conscription worked efficiently, radio broadcasts were made from the battlefront to the home front designed to boost morale, restate the rationale behind the antifascist fight, and boost the numbers of fighting men. Officially, social and leisure activities, for example, were to be sacrificed for the victory or resolutely directed towards it. The Socialist Workers' Federation of Sporting Culture proclaimed in early November 1936 that "these are not moments for throwing the discus or the javelin but the hand grenade and the cartridge of dynamite."[17] War demands often conflicted with revolutionary desire. Moral emancipation was central to living out the freedom that the revolution promised, but legitimate proletarian pleasure had to be curbed by an almost ascetic sense of worker and warrior restraint in the interests of raising morale for the struggle. While an anarchist collective in Aragón was ready to sacrifice coffee in order to save funds to purchase a movie projector (to project Ministry of Culture films produced in the war effort), it could not escape the moral crises presented by internal disputes over property, for instance how to treat smallholders and how to respond to violence and terror.

Women's Roles during the War

Modern ways of thinking could find an appropriate cultural setting more easily in urban centers though, again, the fact of war affected the process, sometimes constraining action and sometimes encouraging greater recklessness. Alongside the legalization of civil marriages there was an opening of the public sphere, particularly, though not exclusively, to women, who had been generally controlled before the years of the Second Republic. Images of the stylized "new woman" and the armed and active *miliciana* as part of the iconography—especially in posters—suggested some level of symbolic redefinition of gender roles. Again, there were important limits to this change. Men on the left politically did not necessarily believe that women faced any special subordination based on their sex, and were protective of their privileged position in the labor force. They often appeared to share some conservatives' views expressed in highly traditional images of femininity. These images were manipulated during the war. Public pictorial and discursive representations of the *miliciana* (the militia-women who had helped build barricades against the insurgents in Barcelona and Madrid in July 1936 and had taken up arms in defense of the government) underwent significant change; the purity of the war heroine oscillated with a picture of the uncontrolled loose woman. In the process, the morality of young female volunteer fighters, whose experiences at the front were largely restricted to washing clothes and cooking, was subjected to fierce scrutiny.[18] Fear of a loss of masculine control meant that the *miliciana,* as a social category, was publicly associated with prostitution and, as such, a threat to the health of the male Republican fighter. This was one area where, up to a point, gender considerations cut across the divisions of war and the politicized Republican "woman as whore" narrative was carried over into the Francoist postwar years. As territory fell to the Nationalist forces, women who had become politicized, particularly those active in rural communities, were likely to be denounced and castigated for shameful behavior and were often punished violently and ritually by both occupiers and members of the community.

In urban areas, punishment extended to women who had provided assistance to refugees, the wounded, children, literacy campaigns, feeding stations, and shelters in the rearguard. Many of these women were also, of course, affiliates of women's political organizations, such as the Agrupación de Mujeres Antifascistas (AMA), linked to the Communist PCE and the anarchist Mujeres Libres (Free Women).[19] The AMA had some 20,000 members during the war, which channeled women's political and social activities through voluntary work in addition to feeding the family and mothering. These groups, as part of their consciously feminist principles, sponsored literacy classes and other educational courses for women, since it was an article of faith that Spanish patriarchy was founded principally on a lack of educational opportunities as a deliberate obstacle to emancipation.

War also meant dramatic changes in extra-domestic work patterns. Although working-class women had long worked outside the home for a necessary wage, they were called upon to stand in for absent men during the war, as many wartime visual images attest, working in the fields, especially, but not only, at harvest time. There was no concerted government policy to bring about revolutionary change in gender relations, although the November 1936 Republican Decree for the Reorganization of Popular Militias emphasized the slogan, "Men to the Front, Women to Work." There was some logic to this in terms of protecting production and initiating reforms, such as the elimination of piecework, but women were paid on average 50 percent less than men, even in the collectivized enterprises of the revolutionary movements.

While women had a greater public profile, this largely projected the female social role as one of mother and spouse, in spite of the work of particular women activists who wrote articles in the anarchist newspaper *Tierra y Libertad* (Land and Freedom) arguing for a different perception of women. In the mainstream press of the Republican zone, supposed letters from the front were regularly published where women, invariably described in relation to men as mothers, sisters, and sweethearts, were comfortingly imagined as spending whole nights or vigils occupied in sewing and knitting. Groups of women had indeed banded together to collect material and war donations and to make winter woolens to send to soldiers, but this was not all that they did. As Mary Nash has concluded, women in the Republican zone participated in public activities in a qualitatively different way than before, but war equally implied a paradoxical intensification of the classically feminine functions, both in real and discursive terms, because it was women who more than ever provided food and the basic necessities of daily survival.[20] The extent of change in family relations, the sexual division of labor, and ways of thinking about male and female morality was ultimately constrained, a limitation that can only partly be explained by the systematic destruction of new gender images by the Nationalist forces as they made military inroads.

Whereas the cause of female emancipation suffered from neglect in the Republic, the Nationalist state oppressively intervened in women's lives, both in the public and private spheres. Censorship that contrasted the Republic's "hedonism" with Catholic "austerity" enabled highly traditional models of femininity and masculinity to be propagated. The activists of the Sección Femenina (SF), the Women's Section of Franco's state party, the Falange, transmitted images of the domestic model of femininity and used them to enforce particular forms of behavior: control of life in the streets (where much of Spanish popular life was traditionally led), even to the extent of regulation of language, expressions, and forms of greeting.[21] These were features of wartime life that would strongly affect the drab, fearful, and resigned moral life of the early 1940s. Although SF activists inevitably benefited from their own public work in aiding Franco's war effort, motherhood was idealized beyond every other female "calling" during the war in the Nationalist zone. Building upon strong prewar Catholic foundations, women's other ambitions were largely prohibited. Pronatalism became a significant part of Nationalist discourse, although in occupied areas and, more generally after the war, it was difficult to reconcile such values with the demands of industry and agriculture and the need for the cheap labor that poor working-class women traditionally provided.[22]

Idealized images of women and the reality never truly overlapped, though this did not stem the flow of propaganda. On the Republican side, the meaning of revolutionary change was portrayed through visual representation, through thousands of poster images that aimed to lodge the slogans, party acronyms, watchwords, and political heroes (both Spanish and foreign, especially Marxist and Soviet) firmly within the consciences of the people. The revolution, the war effort, and some of its victories, were subsequently expressed in a celebratory renaming of streets which, alongside the erection of barricades, the setting up of checkpoints, and the use for humanitarian purposes of churches and other buildings linked in the public mind with the old monarchical power, reshaped the physical landscape.[23] Churches were also put to use for the Popular Courts to administer "revolutionary justice," which was also a channel for the construction of the new order.

Instilling a War Consciousness among Civilians

Though the prescribed slogans and symbols, such as the clenched fist salute, can be seen as primarily ideological, the ways people spoke to each other, using the popular form of address even to strangers, the ways people dressed (fewer hats and ties and a preponderance of gender-neutral overalls and paramilitary uniforms), all recalled and made conscious reference to an existing proletarian culture that was not merely imported or conjunctural. Its dominance was the result of the war and did not mean that everyone living in the government war zone had been ideologically transformed. The need to instill war consciousness in order to supplement (rather than replace) class consciousness (and other forms of identity) was no easy matter and complicates the picture for historians.

In the wake of the May 1937 clashes within the Republican forces, between anarchists and dissident Marxists, on the one hand, and government forces backed by communist agents, on the other, a new government under the socialist Juan Negrín was instituted. Negrín focused on the need to relegitimize the state in order to mobilize for an efficient and effective fight that might keep the Republic alive until a generalized European war began, which was increasingly likely from early 1938 as Hitler's Germany expanded territorially. As part of the strategy of attracting a more benevolent attitude from Britain and France, the revolution was downgraded by the Republican regime, though social transformation remained the priority of masses of ordinary Republican supporters.[24] From the spring of 1937, newspapers in the Republican sphere contained noticeably much less news about the home front and about public politics and the economic and social role of locally rooted groups and organizations. Increasingly the papers came to resemble simple organs of propaganda in favor of a "rational" war effort. The emphasis also shifted towards foreign affairs, not unnaturally, since foreign intervention by the liberal democracies held out the hope of the republic's salvation.

In the process, the Republic managed to antagonize libertarians and other revolutionaries, as well as regional nationalists, especially in Catalonia. Everyday solidarity, based on real social demands, vied with these centrifugal forces and was expressed through the iconography of internationalist communism, symbolized by images of some of the key revolutionaries, such as Josef Stalin and his Spanish acolytes. The symbolism was taken up collectively but was understood in any number of ways. During the siege of Madrid, in November 1936, a demonstration of 200,000 women took place calling for the mobilization of the entire population in defense of the capital along the lines recommended by the PCE leadership. Massive posters of Stalin, Lenin, and Marx were vividly to the fore.

Believing in the symbols was a collective enterprise, but it was also an individual matter; and psychological factors undoubtedly played a part. For women in particular, the need to meet daily needs diluted ideological divisions. Behind the lines women activists of parties of the left appear to have been less combative than their male counterparts.[25]

As in the Republican zone, the daily social practices and moral codes behind the Nationalist lines had strongly ideological connotations. Also, as in the government zone, these practices and codes shaped the nature and objectives of the violence. On the Nationalist home front entrenched customs and values were not so much transformed as resurrected, instrumentalized, and put directly to use to oppose socialism, Marxism, liberalism, laicism, and democratic culture in general. Even leaving aside the political violence for a moment, there can have been little doubt about the effect of political authoritarianism on daily life in conquered areas. To take one example, in early September 1936, an order was issued for the destruction of socialist and communist literature and works likely to offend against the "holy principles of religion and Christian morals."

Coeducation, introduced in the Republican Constitution of 1931, was declared to be criminal, indeed, "a crime against decent women" and "against the health of the people," and officially suppressed.[26] Long lists of schoolteachers punished for their political associations and ideas were printed in the press.[27] Many of those teachers who were confirmed in their positions were among those who had volunteered for the Nationalist front at an early stage of the conflict.[28] The majority of the others were suspended until declaring in writing their "patriotic adhesion to Spain." Loyalty, however, could only be proved in this way provided there was no outstanding denunciation made to the authorities from within the community. The effects of this educational counter-revolution were to be felt for decades after the war.[29]

The community was implicated through public acts of devotion. Within weeks of the rebellion, throughout Nationalist Spain, in such provinces as Seville and Cádiz in the south and elsewhere in Aragón, the placing of crucifixes in schoolrooms, which had been removed by a prewar Republican statute, became the center of processional ceremonies of liberation from the Republican revolution, attended by mayors, military governors, and local ecclesiastical representatives. These acts took place within a context of generalized religiosity and acts of penitence and expiation, like the solemn act of amends dedicated to the Sacred Heart of Jesus in Seville during the first week of September 1936. Further north, the front page of the *Diario de Navarra* showed a picture of a woman teacher in Pamplona kissing a large crucifix in front of the rows of children. The hierarchy of the Church, though a willing participant in the public resurgence of devotion and appreciative of it, found the politicization of the rituals difficult to control.[30] The constraints worked both ways, however. Totalitarian trappings—the raised arm salute, militarist ceremony, and rhetorical glorification of national "essences"—gave a fascistic flavor to daily life, but the modern aspects of this were circumscribed by the heavily Castilian, clerical, and Catholic nature of authority.

Much of the mobilizing effort remained quite strictly military rather than actively political and a careful vigilance was maintained over public order.[31] Public collective mobilizations blended this militarism with Catholic customs and political trappings, provided largely by the Falange, were relatively peripheral. Religion, however, was itself profoundly political in Spain, not least during the years of the Republic when the Church claimed that it had been persecuted. The processions of local invocations of the Virgin Mary were therefore both an expression of popular religiosity and a political ritual. Religious influences also shaped military mobilization, encouraging volunteering and justifying conscription as the Church conferred the status of crusade to the Nationalist military campaign. Catholic tropes abounded also in the cultural and psychological elements of the war. The Virgin Mary was frequently called upon to intercede as a symbol of motherhood to give meaning to the battle; indeed, this was part of the function of the devotional processions. Catholic pamphlets, styled as catechisms, were distributed to Nationalist troops, which compared the Spanish mothers of Nationalist soldiers to the Mother of Christ.[32]

These initiatives have influenced the context for current historical debate about the nature of Nationalist ritual and ceremony. The previously accepted view that the apparent resurgence of religiosity was, in fact, superficial and narrowly political is currently being reassessed. Alongside duress, opportunism, and understandable political conformism, an important collective need for consolation and a genuine faith and search for meaning were also expressed through ritual.[33]

The austerely Catholic soldiers of Carlist Navarre were something of a case apart, because they saw the rebellion as a religious crusade from the very beginning. For them, the war represented a replaying of the Carlist wars against the liberal Spanish state in the nineteenth century and an opportunity for justice (which slipped easily and violently towards revenge). In complaining of the apparent disregard behind the lines for ideals of sacrifice and denial of pleasures and luxuries, they invoked memories of fathers and grandfathers who had fought in these earlier campaigns. The holding of public dances in Pamplona for the local middle class did not reflect the ascetic tone that was fitting for the "Crusade" and gradually, within months, the "Crusade" discourse took hold throughout the Nationalist zone.[34] It is therefore possible to overstate the sense in which the "Crusade" brought into being a new spiritual unity in the entire rebel area. For the propagandists there was doubtless a great deal of value in a discourse that appeared to justify the war and unite the forces of the conservative rebellion. Nonetheless, it is also meaningful to speak about a community of suffering in the Nationalist zone that was perpetuated into the postwar era. Earthly goals and sacred ideology and myths were harmonized in genuinely popular acts of reparation. In Zaragoza, the flags of the Foreign Legionnaires of Africa, a vital part of Franco's fighting forces, were passed through the streets to coincide with the procession of children to the temple of the Virgin of the Pillar in September 1936, in a ceremony organized by the women's section of the Falange. The procession included 500 child affiliates of the Falangist Movement, 2,000 women, and 3,000 adult male Falangists. The children deposited baskets of flowers at the feet of the Virgin, who had become honorary Captain-General of the Spanish army.[35] Such acts were appropriate to, as the *Heraldo de Aragón* put it, "the re-forging of the Hispanic Race." In a similar vein, the Nationalist press made much of the conversion to Christianity of young Moors fighting in the Spanish Legion who, it was claimed, would not leave for battle without receiving baptismal waters. Stories also appeared about Republican working-class prisoners partaking of spiritual assistance from army chaplains before their execution by firing squad.[36] Violence, indeed, was never far from the normality of religious public devotions. In order to "redeem the suffering" of the war, journalistic writings and sermons delivered by priests argued that society needed purification and that sins had to be expiated. Overturning Republican political authority and sanctifying conquered territory were twin processes.

CIVIL WAR AND VIOLENCE

The distinction between battlefront and home front is not a rigid one in civil wars; the conflict erupts within communities. The killing was closely related to social class and religious cleavages, which were embedded in society. Civil wars involve the capture of people, in physical, ideological, and cultural terms, as well as the seizure of territory. An important way of demonstrating loyalty and avoiding imprisonment and other punishment was to participate in political violence, usually by denouncing neighbors or other acquaintances. As Ronald Fraser noted in his classic study of the experience of the war, based on oral interviews, "the zones lacked definite frontiers, front lines; everything was fluid, ambiguous; and yet—who could imagine it?—it was going to be years before the frontiers which were being invisibly created could again be crossed."[37]

DEATH NUMBERS FROM THE CIVIL WAR

Violence became permissible once the rebellious military began to murder those who opposed the coup and the state reciprocated by executing captured rebels. As in other historical cases, a catastrophic event legitimized violence, which was unleashed even within families. There were some 350,000 deaths during the period 1936–39 over and above the predictable rate based on prewar statistics. The prewar norm was 380,000 deaths annually, whereas 413,000 mortalities were recorded officially for 1936, 472,000 in 1937, 485,000 in 1938, and 470,000 in 1939, roughly a 20 percent rise on the 1935 death rate each year during the period 1937–39.[38] Mortality did not return to prewar levels until 1943; with a recorded figure of 484,000, there were as many mortalities in 1941 as there were at the height of the war because of delays in registering deaths; epidemics as a result of a continuation of wartime conditions; and postwar hunger and political repression. Adding these postwar recorded figures (215,000 during 1940–42) to the wartime figure, we can estimate the total human losses on both sides attributable directly or indirectly to the civil war as 565,000. Very few families remained unaffected by intimate loss.

The archival record, always by nature deficient, is particularly fragmented in the area of the numbers killed in the rearguard, especially as so many lost their lives on both sides after being "taken for a ride" (*paseado*), a euphemism for the rounding up of enemies, and their transport in cars or lorries, usually to the outskirts of town, where they were shot and buried in unmarked pits. In wartime Cáceres (the northern region of Extremadura in southeastern Spain), following occupation by the Nationalists, there were many more illegal "paseos" (1,170) than there were executions following the "legal" process of military councils (375), as there were also in Lugo (in Galicia, in the northwest of the peninsula) where there were 168 deaths after summary trials and 416 *muertes irregulares*.[39] After a couple of decades of local and regional research, it is generally accepted that at least 100,000 "Reds" were executed by the Nationalists during the war years, and at least a further 50,000 in the postwar purge. Fewer, approximately 38,000, were killed in the Republican zone, mostly during the first three months, from July to September 1936, in the revolutionary violence and anticlerical purge that followed the military rebellion.[40] About half of the total wartime deaths recorded in one way or another occurred through violence applied away from the field of battle; and some three-quarters of the total war-related deaths in the period 1936–44 were nonbattle fatalities. The vast majority of these, on both sides, were not prisoners who had been captured at the front but individuals rounded up in communities, or taken from city and provincial prison cells, because of alleged political affiliations and allegiances, the allegations often resulting from a denunciation to the authorities.

It makes sense to analyze the violence in each zone in turn, but it is necessary to remember first that the violence was generated particularly in small or relatively small communities where social relations were direct—and where most Spaniards lived—in contrast to large cities where thousands were indeed killed but where social interaction was complex and indirect and where it was possible to evade the public glare. Although there are now many local and regional studies of the civil war violence, not all of these address questions about some of the important analytical variables, though most have something to say about the contribution of prewar social tensions, and many describe the means and opportunities for violence in localities: the availability of arms, for example, the extent of criminality and the nature of the vacuum of political authority following the coup. The data explored thus far suggests that, although the extent of direct combat varied considerably, the highest death rates—in the fighting *and* in the repression combined—were in areas where battlefronts were most actively in flux. Despite the weaknesses of other records, we can still say a little more about the nature of the violence in each zone.

Religion played an important, though highly complex, role in the violence in both zones. It was very common for the violent purge of local society, which accompanied the imposition of Nationalist political power, to be dignified, elevated, and ultimately legitimated through religious rhetoric, symbolism, and rationale. Gender perceptions were also significant.[41] The Navarran town of Lodosa fell early on to the rebels, mainly composed of Carlist militia volunteers, the Requeté, as did the rest of the province.[42] As in the whole of Spain, the "liberation" brought with it a process actively described as "social regeneration," which always involved some level of violence. Regeneration was seen, in a strange amalgam, as "Christian charity" with "terror and panic."[43] On this occasion, the local chief of the Requeté was lauded in the local newspapers as "an exemplary patriot, good Christian and valiant soldier." In Lodosa, "extraordinary, truly astonishing and admirable works of apostleship and redemption were carried out." These included "rigorous punishment" and "convincing with tenderness": "Many old and young women who have had long tongues (been 'gossips'), and have created uproar amongst the communist crowd, have had their hair completely cut off and been made to walk through the streets followed by the people and the gibberish (*algarabía*, literally Arabic) of that infantile flock was forcibly replaced by cries of 'Viva España!' 'Down with the traitors!' 'Spain yes, Russia no!'" Similar punishments were inflicted in other small towns nearby, like Alcanadre, Sartaguda, and Sesma. Each day these women had to present themselves at the Civil Guard barracks for registration. The political authorities' "visits" to "communist" men and women continued to persuade them to live "peacefully and honorably." The result had been an increase in attendance at Mass by "communists," more Catholic marriages, and more baptisms, some of them sponsored as *padrino* (godfather) by the Requeté chief himself.

In the Republican zone, it was certainly the case that the Church was a prime target of the revolution. Hundreds of ecclesiastical buildings and parish churches were burned, many of them destroyed, and priests were pursued by anticlerical revolutionaries throughout Republican territory, both urban and rural, once the rebellion took place. A dreadful and bloody purge ensued during the early months of the war, alongside the killing of thousands of other "enemies of the Republic," many known right-wingers, and also an unquantified number who had no political affiliation or public role. According to the most exhaustive study, 4,184 secular priests were killed in the Republican zone and 2,648 members of religious communities (2,365 monks and brothers and 283 nuns and sisters).[44] This was a purge in the very real sense of extirpation and affected most regions of the country. Some 65 percent of the total number of priests (270 from a total of 410) in the Catalan diocese of Lérida were killed, for example, and 48 percent in Málaga. In revolutionary Barcelona, there were more priests than average (1,251) and the percentage of those killed was lower (22.3 percent), though the number of deaths (279) was high. After barely two months of war, 3,400 religious had been murdered, almost 50 percent of the total number of clerical victims during the war.[45]

Historians have long debated the relationship of the anticlerical violence to categories of social class.[46] Until recently the orthodox view has been that priests and religion were targeted simply because the Church was perceived as a central part of the ruling order. The reality may not have been so simple. One man who admitted to killing a parish priest in Aragón declared that the victim had been "a very good man. But we had to kill all the priests." In another Aragonese pueblo, the revolutionaries spared the landowners but not the priest, as to do so would have been too conspicuous.[47] A number of recent studies have therefore shifted our focus on the wartime anticlerical violence. These analyses have built upon the highly suggestive study by the cultural anthropologist Bruce Lincoln, which examined the exhumation and display in the summer of 1936 of mummified corpses of nuns and priests.[48] In doing so, these investigations concentrate on the performative, iconoclastic, and ritualized aspects of revolutionary violence. The gestures of the revolution and of the violence, the seeming imperative of display (often of human bodies, dead and alive), the significance of desecration, the occupation of sacred space, and the carnivalesque inversion of Catholic values and rituals, have begun to be seen as highly significant. They symbolized and dramatized the corruption of the old order, the challenge to existing power represented by the revolution, and the arrival of a new, triumphant, proletarian order and a new time.[49] A Republican psychologist argued that the revolutionary acts he had observed represented "affective currents of collective aspirations towards justice." These could only be satisfactorily expressed through spectacular gestures. The determined revolutionary, because of his or her beliefs or reaction to charismatic leadership, is thrown into a state of "transcendence, above equanimity and judgment," where the law of all or nothing reigns.[50] It also seems clear that, in some regions at least, especially in Andalucía, these cultural markers of meaning behind the violence were intimately bound up with popular ideas about gender roles (primarily the *masculine* element in gender relations) and sexual fears.[51]

Some places that remained under the control of the Republican government were closer to the front and subject to a state of more or less constant siege; Madrid is the obvious example of the threat of shelling, bombardment, and occupation. This situation, and the fact that the conflict encapsulated a social revolution, meant that there was a fear of invisible enemies. There was an inevitable sense of insecurity and provisionality to daily life. Revolution also seemed to demand that all oppressive structures and organizations be thrown off and a new order and morality be given freedom to express itself. This freedom, and the cathartic sense of violence as an emotional release, was gradually, though ineffectively, controlled by the setting up, towards the end of August 1936, of formalized Tribunales Populares to hear the cases of denounced enemies of the Republic. These popular courts were a reaction to the storming of the Model Prison in Madrid and in the aftermath of the killing of right-wing prisoners there in revenge for both the bombing raids on the capital and the Nationalist massacre of Republican laborers following the capture of Badajoz in Extremadura.

There was also violence amongst Republican forces that fed from a generalized sense of fear. The exhausting exceptionality of the war—the hunger, the declining fortunes of the Republican war effort, the propaganda and rumors generated from behind the Nationalist lines, the use of political terror against "fifth columnists"—all of this played into hands of Stalinists associated with the PCE and accentuated the tension. By 1937 the communist security service was carrying out a purge of dissident leftists and Trotskyites in order to suppress the revolution.

Francoist violence arose from a somewhat different situation. While in the Loyalist zone repression and death had to do with the collapse of political power and state authority, in the insurgent zone repression and death were a part of the construction of a new power, although the daily experience of terror and fear must have been similar in both zones.[52] In Nationalist Spain, in particular areas, such as the latifundio south where landowners' black lists were drawn up to identify leftist laborers, there was a clear correlation between social class and violence. The desire of the landowners to return to the pre-1931 social order formed the context of violence and determined who was considered an enemy.[53] This was also the case in urban areas that fell quickly to the rebels, such as Zaragoza.[54] The influence of social class, though not the only factor, can be seen all over Spain, no matter what the nature of regional and local economic structures.[55] Nationalist repression during the occupation of territory followed a consistent motivating pattern and practice. The military coup of July 1936 had been backed up with a plan to "purify" Spain. In many places all over the country, the conflict consisted firstly of the elimination of a certain number of "enemies" and a transfer of political power without any real military conflict at all. Of the 12,000 or so executed by the Nationalists between 1936 and 1945 in the area of Badajoz, in Extremadura in southwestern Spain, some 4,700 were killed in 1936.[56] A purge of this scale cannot be explained solely through the mechanism of neighbor denouncing neighbor but, rather, by reference to the repressive structure of prewar social relations, a cathartic ideology of purification, and the class nature of the military rebellion.[57] Because occupation by the Nationalists occurred throughout the entirety of the war, the repression remained fierce throughout. Though the numbers killed slightly decreased in 1939 and although a formal process of military justice was put in place from the spring of 1937, large numbers of Republican civilians were tried and executed after April 1, 1939, often for spurious accusations of political crimes.

Localities that had seen a violent purge under Republican control were likely to suffer similarly once the Nationalists had gained control (the city of Málaga is one example). There were also places where the Republican revolution had been violent and destructive but where Nationalist violence was relatively light (Barcelona and Madrid are two key instances, which suggests that there were difficulties in locating and processing political enemies in the largest cities—which fell late in the conflict to Franco—and in the chaotic aftermath of the war with thousands of refugees on the move). There were many more cases where the occupiers' violence followed on after a quite peaceful period under Republican authority (urban Zaragoza, Segovia, Burgos, Valladolid, in particular). In the city of Zaragoza, there were 2,598 executions by Nationalists from July to December 1936, although there had been no clash between competing military forces. The victims were middle-class Republicans, liberals, political functionaries, trade unionists, manual workers, and peasants.[58] In Huelva, in the south, the word *guerra* only meant thorough political repression by Nationalists because there had been hardly any fighting.[59] During the first days of the rebellion in Logroño, there were 30 executions on average per day. Some 2,000 were executed in total although, again, there had been no war.[60] More research is required, but it seems very likely that denunciations were highly significant in this process in conservative towns where social conflict had been very slight but where radical politics and progressive ideas stood out and Nationalist authorities made public appeals to "deliver Spain's enemies to justice."[61] The denunciations came from ordinary neighbors, in order to demonstrate loyalty to the occupiers, as well as (possibly more frequently) from priests, Falangists, and employers, for broadly political reasons or because of personal disputes.

Much of the research suggests that it was those groups that became more visible as a result of the Republic's reforms that became the main targets of the violence.[62] Women, the younger generation, lay teachers, liberal professionals, the lower classes—groups we might call the social carriers of modernization—were disproportionately affected. Francisco Morente Valero has studied the question of the repression of teachers during and after the civil war in depth and found that on average between a quarter and a third throughout Spain were purged, receiving some sort of sanction for alleged political crimes.[63] Young adults figured very highly amongst the victims, particularly where large numbers were killed: Málaga, La Coruña, Valencia, Badajoz, and Huelva, where the violence was concentrated on those between 25 and 45 years of age.[64]

DEFEAT AND VICTORY: RESOURCES, MORALE, AND THE STRUGGLE FOR SURVIVAL

In contrast to the generally well-provisioned Franco zone, conditions in Republican Spain, centered on the principal urban areas, were precarious from the beginning of the war. General health deteriorated principally because of the shortage of food. Such was the poverty of many urban communities before the war that the pressures of the conflict quickly led to everyday hunger. On top of this, by October 1936 the first major problem of wheat supply arose. The scarcity of staple foods, such as potatoes, olive oil, maize, and fish, became the primary cause of a steep elevation in prices in the Republican zone. The municipal authorities in Madrid began to intervene to fix food prices and control profits within months of the start of the war. The public was advised to refuse to pay abusive prices, but without a reliable legal framework, and with the reality of daily hunger, this was clearly a vain hope. As the war progressed and the Nationalists swallowed more territory, it became ever more difficult to find effective remedies for the crisis of food production and distribution. While agriculture lacked vital inputs, such as animal feed, industry suffered shortages of cotton, paper, chemicals, gasoline, and coal. Substitution through importation became increasingly difficult for the Republic in the face of the blockade of the Spanish coast, with the result that industry had to rely on the demand of a depressed internal market while the rebels were able to continue exporting agricultural produce. The food crisis became part of class struggle and of politics within the Republican zone so that the turn towards "rationality" in the spring of 1937 was reflected in public by reference to short supplies. In early May, when the capital had suffered several days without bread, *El Socialista* made clear on its front page that "Madrid is lacking the most indispensable goods." The paper also asked who was to blame and took the opportunity to call for direct government intervention by suggesting that "spontaneous and disorganized generosity" was not enough to deal with the question.[65]

A regime of rationing had gradually been imposed throughout Loyalist Spain, instituted in Barcelona in October 1936 and justified rhetorically by the egalitarian principles of the revolution. In Madrid, full rationing was delayed until March 1937 in order to avoid any sense of defeatism, but a family card began to be issued in the city as early as September 1936 with the intention of "improving distribution of articles of primary necessity" and to "normalize consumption" for the working and middle classes.[66] If an objective of the revolution had been to equalize resources across society, then food shortages in Madrid made some inroads in this direction and an American doctor reported in 1939 that the incidence of gout, diabetes, and gall-bladder diseases, usually complaints of the wealthy, had been marked by a noticeable decline during the war. Food became extremely precious, almost regardless of social class. The journalist Martha Gelhorn remembered how one of the architects who was responsible for assessing the state of shelled buildings in Madrid brought with him each day, wrapped in newspaper, his ration of bread, and how he would climb gingerly among the debris, careful not to drop the bread: "he had to take it home—there were two small children there, and come death and destruction and anything else, the bread mattered."[67] In practice, official institutions were unable to ensure an efficient system of distribution and supply to such an extent that numerous collective protests were mounted, largely by women defending their generally accepted role as providers. The image of the food queue had become part of the urban landscape by the autumn of 1936 and women spent a large part of each working day in long lines that often snaked around several city blocks for hours. In December 1937, the Madrid Socialist newspaper *Claridad* paid tribute to the sacrifices of the women of the city in feeding families under fire from the enemy:

> For a year now food in Madrid has not only been extremely scarce but to obtain the little there is, nothing short of heroism has been needed. The queues suffer two dangers: first, the shelling and, then, the cold. At times, in spite of the freezing rain, they were there from three or four in the morning until mid-day or the afternoon, out in the open, in a temperature of 3 or 4 degrees below zero. And they have borne this suffering day after day.[68]

Some priorities needed to be met. A doctor's prescription was required to obtain rationed eggs, fish, meat, and milk. The supply of bread, the mainstay of the humble working-class diet when it could be located, was limited to 5.3 ounces per person. Clean water and coal were also hard to find. This general scarcity created the conditions for the vertiginous growth of a black market with which mainly women were forced to deal, and they did so with an impressive level of ingenuity. For many reasons, money was scarce, and women whose husbands were at the front had to fit in paid employment around time needed for queuing. The family benefit they received in lieu of the men's absence was not enough to compensate for the loss of income. Many women were forced habitually to leave their places of residence in the town and travel on foot, by bicycle, or by train to the countryside to obtain basic necessities, either through purchase or bartering. A woman from a small town in Catalonia explained how her wartime existence was largely shaped by the constant search for food:

> I'd go to Falset to look for olive oil, to Mora d'Ebre, to Monzón, to Cambrils . . . Sometimes they (the authorities) confiscated the items of food. In Barcelona and Tarragona we were caught by tremendous bombing raids. . . . Rationing just didn't provide for us, and we had no alternative but to go searching for food. There were many of us who did it.[69]

A nutritionist and contemporary observer of events calculated that the minimum daily intake required for a relatively sedentary individual was some 2,300 calories, 2,800 for a working person, and 3,000–3,200 for each individual working intensely in war industries or fighting at the front. From August 1937 to February 1939, real average consumption was much lower: some 1,060 calories. This malnutrition was not as extreme as that which would be suffered in many parts of Western Europe, let alone Eastern Europe, during the 1939–45 war (indeed, hunger was probably more extreme in Spain in the early 1940s), but it was serious enough to cause an epidemic of deficiency diseases in the spring of 1938. A food crisis was reached in December when average recorded consumption slumped to 770 calories per day. A study of the diet of the populace of Madrid suffering from deficiency diseases in 1938 and 1939 revealed that the average daily intake had been some 957 calories, slightly more than 40 per cent of the basic necessary adult minimum.[70]

Conditions hardly improved with the occupation of communities by Nationalist forces. As territory fell to the occupiers, a local section of the Falangist social aid organization, Auxilio Social, would normally be established to administer food, clothing, and shelter, much of it donated by foreign governments or international humanitarian organizations. This distribution was often chaotic and inefficient. The Director of Relief of the American Friends Service Committee in Spain reported how in the southeast of the country he would regularly see food rotting within half a mile of hungry people, "at a time when trucks were hauling soldiers and thousands of able-bodied men were marching in victory parades."[71]

Malnutrition caused rickets, scurvy, pellagra, and a great increase in active tuberculosis, all of which were compounded by overcrowding and the movement of refugees. Dramatic population shifts were produced by the war and endured into the postwar period. The decline in births and increase in mortality were not merely provoked through the fighting but because of health deterioration, poor sanitation, and the lack of food. In 1936, 1,103 Spaniards died from diphtheria but, by 1938, the official figure had leaped to 2,930, and in 1939 to 4,058. The Madrid infectious diseases hospital was overcrowded by 1939 with cases of smallpox, which had originated in Portugal and been brought to Spain as volunteers and refugees came and went across the frontier. More significantly, hundreds of thousands of people fled from the agrarian south, Andalucía, Extremadura, and New Castile, primarily, towards Republican areas, particularly the larger cities, Madrid, Barcelona, Valencia, in search of refuge, safety, and work.[72] Contrary to Francoist propaganda, in most areas many more people were fleeing the Nationalists than were migrating towards "liberated" territory. Fear of political violence was part of what motivated between 200,000 and 500,000 refugees to arrive in Madrid by October 1936. The populations of many smaller cities also doubled in size.

One clear effect was to increase the urban death rate substantially above mortality in the countryside, a development that reversed the modernizing trend set in train since the 1920s.[73] Ways needed to be found of providing hygienic refuge or of moving people on to other areas of Republican

A crowd gathers as a man and woman quarrel over a
ration of bread distributed by the Nationalists in Barcelona, January 29, 1939. Courtesy of AP Photo.

Spain further from the battle. By mid-December 1936, it was reported that
60,000 people (30,000 children and 30,000 elderly) had been evacuated
from the capital in a single week through an operation of the Republican
Committee for Children's Aid, although it was admitted that this action
was insufficient to deal with the problem. In an effort to make the city
truly impregnable, it was claimed, an intense campaign was undertaken
to persuade those of the civil population who could contribute little to the
defense of the city to leave, and combatants were encouraged to advise
their families to do so. In March 1937, in the interests of public health,
underground Metro stations were no longer to be deployed as permanent
homeless refuges but only as transitory shelters to be used for the duration
of air raids.[74] The socialist censorship officer in wartime Madrid, Arturo
Barea, reported on what he had seen of the living conditions of refugees
in a "pit of misery," a half-destroyed hall in the city in late September
1936: "The stench of excrement and urine hit me in the face . . . a horde of
women and children and old people, filthy, unkempt, evil-smelling, living in a litter of truckle-beds, crockery and pieces of furniture. . . . During
the days that followed, the caravans of donkeys and carts with tired men,

women, and children squatting on their bundles, never ceased." Within months of the beginning of the siege of the city in November 1936, no soap at all could be had. The sweat and lice of "the multitude" wrapped in damp and soiled blankets made the air dense and sour.[75] A policy was agreed in March 1937 to encourage the conservation of cats in the city because they were an important ally in the struggle against rats.[76]

The Republican government in Catalonia, in the northeast, calculated that by the end of 1936 some 300,000 refugees had arrived there. Many of the refugees who flooded towards the eastern coast were housed in rural colonies because of the aerial bombardment of densely populated urban areas such as the city's fishing quarter of Barceloneta. Feeding the neediest was a problem because of the lack of transportation. Infants were particularly in danger because of a grave shortage of milk from very early in the war.[77] The death rate among small children in Madrid in 1939 was estimated to be about 12 times the normal level.[78] By the second half of 1937, around 300,000 refugees in Republican Spain, including thousands from the south of Spain, mostly women and children, were being fed in emergency canteens established for destitute families. The population of the Republican zone, the latter by this stage constituting of only 40 percent of the total land mass of Spain, had increased by 25 percent above its average prewar level and was cut off from the principal food-producing areas in central and Southern Spain.

The capacity of the still-developing Spanish public health system was stretched to breaking point and the work of a relatively united group of political organizations, dominated on the home front by Spanish women, shouldered a huge burden.[79] The war had split the already patchy provision of health facilities in Spain into two disjointed organizations.[80] Given the conditions, the fact that there was no major epidemic during the war is testament to the health work that was carried out. The Republican Health Service of the Army of the Center carried out regular programs of delousing soldiers' bodies and uniforms while still at the front. These procedures prevented the onset and spread of typhus, which only struck after the war, especially in Madrid and Málaga in 1941. In the Republican zone, health provision was aided by such bodies as the Federación Universitaria Española (FUE), the Federación Española de Trabajadores de la Enseñanza (FETE, the teachers' association), International Red Aid, the International Brigades, and the Ajut Infantil de Reraguarda (Children's Aid for the Home Front) in Catalonia, which had 71 residences in 1938. The Department of Infant Hygiene of the Ministry of Public Health and Instruction took responsibility for the care of 40,000 children in 38 dispensaries throughout Republican Spain, and the National Council for Evacuated Children ran 74 refuge camps in Catalonia alone in 1938. The anarchist women's movement, Mujeres Libres, established a refugees' committee. The communist-backed Agrupación de Mujeres Antifascistas took responsibility for the care of orphans, as did the Catalan Women's Union in Barcelona; they also encouraged refugees to organize themselves. Neutral international organizations offered assistance to both zones, though the need was much greater on the Republican side: the Friends Service Council (in London and the United States), the Service Civil Internationale (Berne), International Save the Children Union (Geneva), and the Red Cross.[81] The Catholic International Commission for the Assistance of Child Refugees reported that at least 100,000 Spanish children in the summer of 1938 were starving or in a condition of "pre-starvation."[82] Given the dimensions of the refugee problem, in the end much of the assistance offered was given by ordinary women and families who were willing to offer some form of shelter.

CONCLUSIONS

Once political and social conflicts descend into open civil war, the contest between social groups and identities becomes simplified in public perception; the war becomes a struggle between *us* and *them*. The rhetorical and practical requirements of war—and of revolution—heighten this tendency to impose a framework of straightforward binary opposition. During the war, this simplification perpetuates hostilities and gives impetus to the violence. After the end of the war, the polarization of the war continues to affect deeply the writing of its history; civil wars are reduced, both in propaganda and often in more considered analyses, to struggles between democracy and dictatorship (in the Spanish case, fascist dictatorship), between revolution and counter-revolution, or between religion and atheism. According to the widely accepted international image of the civil war, and with good reason, Spain became the epicenter of world history in the late 1930s. The civil war and the social revolution encased within it exemplified the clash of extremes.[83]

These classic dualities have a place in explanations of the Spanish war, as does the notion of the war as a struggle to define the meaning of "the nation" and to impose one vision of the nation upon others. These grand narratives leave out the responses of the millions of anonymous protagonists, however; the orthodox historical explanations largely fail to address the internalization of the "big ideas" and the significance of the social conditions in which political messages were absorbed and assimilated. The military rebellion on July 18, 1936, only led to total war because of popular resistance to the coup and, in turn, because the generals' counter-revolutionary blow was quickly to be backed up by assistance from Hitler and Mussolini. Neither the revolution in the Republican zone nor the reaction in the rebel zone, and the inherent violence of both processes, represented merely the application of doctrinal positions. Both consisted of relatively confused actions that responded, in part, to ideological precepts but also to preexisting social relations, customs, and cultures, and to the enormous and specific pressures of civil (and *un*civil) warfare; and which were internal to each zone. The daily experience of the Civil War was thus shaped by the common effort of those who were caught up in the maelstrom of extreme political, economic, and psychological circumstances and who struggled to make sense of the public and personal tragedy unfolding before them.

NOTES

1. For instance, see Arthur Marwick and Clive Emsley, eds., *Total War and Historical Change* (Buckingham: Open University Press, 2001).

2. Nazi and Fascist involvement, and later that of the Soviet Union, indicates how the domestic Spanish war was also part of an ongoing and incipient international conflict. The peculiar context of Europe in the 1930s, characterized by a highly public politicization of many areas of collective and private life, shaped the Spanish war and its daily experience to a considerable extent. See Michael Richards, "The Popular Front," in *A Companion to Europe, 1900–1945*, ed. Gordon Martel (Oxford: Blackwell, 2006), pp. 375–90.

3. Julián Casanova, "Rebelión y revolución," in *Víctimas de la guerra*, ed. Santos Juliá (Madrid: Temas de Hoy, 1999), p. 63.

4. See Juan Martínez-Alier, *La estabilidad del latifundismo* (Madrid: Ruedo Ibérico, 1968).

5. See, for the impressions of participant-observer, the classic George Orwell, *Homage to Catalonia* (London: Penguin, 2003 [1938]).

6. This is the implication of the reductive understanding of the war as a struggle of individual egos in Michael Seidman, *Republic of Egos: A Social History of the Spanish Civil War* (Madison: University of Wisconsin Press, 2002), relying uncritically on accounts by official Nationalist historians. See especially pp. 11, 38, 47–52.

7. Helen Graham, *The Spanish Republic at War, 1936–1939* (Cambridge: Cambridge University Press, 2002).

8. See the front page of *El Socialista,* October 1, 1936.

9. Josep M. Bricall, "La economía española (1936–1939)," in *La guerra civil española 50 años después*, ed. Manuel Tuñón de Lara, Julio Aróstegui, A. Viñãs, G. Cardona, and Josep M. Bricall (Barcelona: Labor, 1985), p. 365.

10. For anarchist collectivization, see Julián Casanova, *El sueño igualitario: campesinado y colectivizaciones en la España republicana (1936–1939)* (Zaragoza: Institución Fernando el Católico, 1988). Also Casanova, *Anarchism, the Republic and Civil War in Spain: 1931–1939* (London: Routledge, 2005), especially pp. 130–45.

11. See Manuel González Portilla and José María Garmendia, *La guerra civil en el País Vasco* (Madrid: Siglo XXI, 1988).

12. Félix Carrasquer, cited in Ronald Fraser, *Blood of Spain: The Experience of Civil War 1936–1939* (Harmondsworth: Allen Lane, 1979 [1988 reprint]), p. 138.

13. Bricall, "Economía Española," p. 385.

14. Carme Molinero, M. Sala, and J. Sobrequés, eds., *Una inmensa prisión: Los campos de concentración y las prisiones durante la guerra civil y el franquismo* (Barcelona: Crítica, 2003).

15. María José González Castillejo, "Realidad social de la mujer: vida cotidiana y esfera pública en Málaga (1931–1936)," in *La mujer en Andalucía,* ed. Pilar Ballarín and Teresa Ortiz, vol. 1 (Granada: Universidad de Granada, 1990), p. 427.

16. *El Socialista,* April 10, 1937, p. 1; April 14, 1937, p. 1.

17. *El Socialista,* November 1, 1936, p. 2.

18. Mary Nash, *Rojas: Las mujeres republicanas en la guerra civil* (Madrid: Taurus, 1999), pp. 159–66.

19. See Martha Ackelsberg, *Free Women of Spain: Anarchism and the Struggle for the Emancipation of Women* (Bloomington: Indiana University Press, 1991).

20. Nash, *Rojas,* pp. 212–13, p. 252.

21. Teresa Gallego Méndez, *Mujer, falange y franquismo* (Madrid: Taurus, 1983).

22. Michael Richards, *A Time of Silence: Civil War and the Culture of Repression in Franco's Spain, 1936–45* (Cambridge: Cambridge University Press, 1998).

23. See, for example, José Madalena Calvo, "Los lugares de la memoria de la guerra civil en un centro de poder: Salamanca, 1936–39," in *Historia y memoria de la guerra civil,* ed. Julio Aróstegui (Valladolid: Junta de Castilla y Léon, 1988), 3 vols.

24. Manuel Tuñón de Lara et al., *Juan Negrín López: El hombre necesario* (Las Palmas: Gobierno de Canarias, 1996).

25. See Angelina Puig i Valls, "Mujeres de Pedro Martínez (Granada) durante la guerra civil," in *Las mujeres y la guerra civil española: III Jornadas de estudios monográficos* (Madrid: Ministerio de Cultura, 1991), p. 41.

26. Gallego Méndez, *Mujer, falange y franquismo,* p. 154.

27. *Diario de Navarra,* September 2–6, 1936, pp. 1, 3; *El Correo de Andalucía,* September 5, 1936; *Heraldo de Aragón,* September 3, 1936.

28. "Plegaria de los niños al Santo Crucifijo de sus escuelas," *Diario de Navarra,* August 30, 1936, p. 1; *El Ideal Gallego,* August 28, 1936, p. 1.

29. Francisco Morente Valero, *La escuela y el Estado Nuevo* (Barcelona: Ámbito, 1997).

30. *Heraldo de Aragón,* September 3, 1936, 1; *ABC* (Sevilla), September 2, 1936, p. 9.

31. The "public" had always to remain "merely as spectators" in all military, civil, or religious marches and processions. See *Heraldo de Aragón,* October 11, 1936, p. 4.

32. Karl Stahli, *Cristo en las trincheras,* Publicaciones del Consejo Superior de la Juventud de Acción Católica (Bilbao: La Editorial Vizcaíno, 1938), pp. 51–52. Also see *Diario de Navarra,* August 30, 1936.

33. For this debate and discussion of incipient Church-state conflicts see Michael Richards, "'Presenting arms to the Blessed Sacrament': Civil War and Semana Santa in the city of Málaga, 1936–1939," in *The Splintering of Spain: Cultural History and the Spanish Civil War, 1936–1939,* ed. Chris Ealham and Michael Richards (Cambridge: Cambridge University Press, 2005).

34. *Diario de Navarra,* September 1, 1936, p. 1. See also the path-breaking study by Martin Blinkhorn, *Carlism and Crisis in Spain, 1931–1939* (Cambridge: Cambridge University Press, 1975). Also Javier Ugarte Tellería, *La nueva Covadonga insurgente: Orígenes sociales y culturales de la sublevación de 1936 en Navarra y el País Vasco* (Madrid: Biblioteca Nueva, 1998).

35. *Heraldo de Aragón,* September 8, 9, 1936, p. 1.

36. *Diario de Navarra,* August 30, 1936, p. 4; September 6, 9, 1936; *El Correo de Andalucía,* September 4, 1936, p. 10.

37. Fraser, *Blood of Spain,* p. 119.

38. See Juan Díez Nicolás, "La mortalidad en la guerra civil española," *Boletín de Demografía Histórica,* vol III, no. 1, 1985, pp. 42–45.

39. Maria Jesus Souto Blanco, *La represión franquista en la provincia de Lugo* (Madrid: Ediciós do Castro, 1998), pp. 251, 272.

40. Juliá, *Víctimas,* pp. 410–12.

41. *El Correo de Andalucía,* September 4, 1936.

42. On Carlist identity, see the essay by Francisco Javier Caspístegui in Ealham and Richards, *The Splintering of Spain,* pp. 177–95.

43. *Diario de Navarra,* August 30, 1936, p. 4.

44. See Antonio Montero Moreno, *Historia de la persecución religiosa en España, 1936–1939* (Madrid: Biblioteca de Autores Cristianos, 1960).

45. Jesús Iribarren, *Documentos colectivos del episcopado español, 1870–1974* (Madrid: Biblioteca de Autores Cristianos, 1974), pp. 42–43, cited in Mary Vincent, "'The Keys of the Kingdom': Religious Violence in the Spanish Civil War, July–August 1936," in *The Splintering of Spain,* ed. Ealham and Richards, pp. 68–89.

46. See Casanova, "Rebelión y revolución," in Juliá et al., *Víctimas,* pp. 153–57.

47. See Vincent, "The Keys of the Kingdom," and Manuel Delgado, "Anticlericalismo, espacio y poder: la destrucción de los rituales católicos, 1931–39," in *El anticlericalismo,* ed. Rafael Cruz, special issue of *Ayer,* 27 (1997): 149–80; Julio de la Cueva, "Religious Persecution, Anticlerical Tradition and Revolution: On Atrocities against the Clergy during the Spanish Civil War," *Journal of Contemporary History* 33, no. 3 (1998): 361, 367.

48. Bruce W. Lincoln, "Revolutionary Exhumations in Spain, July 1936," *Comparative Studies in Society and History* 27 (1985): 241–60.

49. See Michael Richards, "Morality and Biology in the Spanish Civil War: Psychiatrists, Revolution and Women Prisoners in Málaga," *Contemporary European History* 14, no. 1 (November 2001): 418–21.

50. Resumé of a paper presented at the Institut Psicotècnic of the Generalitat of Catalunya, 1937–38 term, Emilio Mira, "Psicología de la conducta revolucionaria," *Universidad de La Habana,* September–December 1939, pp. 43–59. Richards, "Morality and Biology," pp. 418–21.

51. This is the important and persuasive argument of Vincent, "The Keys of the Kingdom."

52. Juliá, *Víctimas,* p. 25.

53. For a detailed update of historiography, see Michael Richards, "The Limits of Quantification: Francoist Repression and Historical Methodology," in *¿Política de exterminio? El debate acerca de la ideología, estrategías e instrumentos de la represión,* ed. S. Gálvez, Dossier monográfico, Universidad Complutense Madrid, *Hispania Nova: Revista de Historia Contemporánea* 7 (2007), http://hispanianova.rediris.es/7/dossier/07d015.pdf.

54. Julián Casanova et al., *El pasado oculto: Fascismo y violencia en Aragón (1936–1939),* 2nd ed. (Zaragoza, 1999).

55. See Manuel Ortiz Heras, *Violencia política en la II República y el primer franquismo: Albacete, 1936–1950* (Madrid: Siglo XXI, 1996).

56. Francisco Espinosa Maestre, *La justicia de Queipo: Violencia selectiva y terror fascista en la II División en 1936* (Seville: n.p., 2000), p. 23.

57. See Francisco Espinosa Maestre, *La columna de la muerte: El avance del ejército franquista de Sevilla a Badajoz* (Barcelona: Crítica, 2003); and Richards, *A Time of Silence.*

58. Casanova et al., *El pasado oculto.*

59. Francisco Espinosa Maestre, *La guerra civil en Huelva* (Huelva: Diputación, 1996), p. 16.

60. Hernández García, *La represión en La Rioja durante la guerra civil* (Logroño: n.p., 1984), vol. 1, pp. 25, 28–29.

61. For instance, on Málaga, see Richards, "Presenting Arms to the Blessed Sacrament," in *The Splintering of Spain,* ed. Ealham and Richards, pp. 196–222.

62. On the purge of teachers in Badajoz, see José María Lama, *La amargura de la memoria: República y guerra en Zafra (1931–1936)* (Badajoz: Diputación Provincial, 2004).

63. Morente Valero, *La escuela y el Estado Nuevo.*

64. See Antonio Nadal Sánchez, *Guerra civil en Málaga* (Málaga: Editorial Argúval, 1988), p. 192.

65. *El Socialista,* May 5, 1937, p. 1.

66. *El Socialista,* September 30, 1936, p. 3.

67. Martha Gelhorn, "The Besieged City," from Gelhorn, *The Face of War* (London: Granta, 1993 [1959]).

68. Cited in Nash, *Rojas,* pp. 205–6.

69. Nash, *Rojas,* p. 207.

70. Francisco Jiménez García and Francisco Grande Covián, "Algunas observaciones sobre las dietas consumidas por los enfermos carenciales de Madrid," *Revista Clínica Española* 1, no. 1 (July 1940): 43.

71. Howard Kershner, *Quaker Service in Modern War* (New York: Prentice-Hall, 1950), p. 92. See also pp. 40, 89–98.

72. Carles Santacana, *Victoriosos i derrotats: el franquisme a l'Hospitalet 1939–1951* (Barcelona: Publicacions de l'Abadia de Montserrat, 1994), pp. 73–91.

73. J. Villar Salinas, "Mortalidades 'urbanas' y 'rurales' de España," *Revista de Sanidad e Higiene Pública* 18 (1944): 274–86.

74. *El Socialista,* December 15, 1936, p. 2; January 9, 1937, p. 2; March 26, 1937, p. 3; March 29, 1937, p. 3.

75. Arturo Barea, *The Forging of a Rebel: The Clash* (London: Fontana, 1984 [1946]), pp. 187–88, 238, 318.

76. *El Socialista,* March 2, 1937, p. 3.

77. *Famine Faces a Million in Spain* (London: National Joint Committee for Spanish Relief, 1937), pp. 9–10.

78. Kershner, *Quaker Service,* p. 66.

79. On the attempted far-reaching reforms of public health during the Second Republic, see Rafael Huertas, "Política sanitaria: De la dictadura de Primo de Rivera a la II República," *Revista Española de Salud Pública* 74 (2000): 35–43.

80. League of Nations, *Quarterly Bulletin,* 1937, p. 56.

81. The Spanish Red Cross was also divided by the war. See J. C. Clemente, *Historia de la Cruz Roja Española* (Madrid: Cruz Roja Española, 1986).

82. D. J. Collier, F.R.C.S, "Children in Republican Spain," *The Catholic Medical Guardian* 16, no. 1 (January 1938): 146–52. Also Francisco Grande Covián, "Sobre los trastornos carenciales observados en Madrid durante la guerra," *Revista Clínica Española* 1 (1940).

83. Eric Hobsbawm, *Age of Extremes: The Short Twentieth Century, 1914–1991* (London: Michael Joseph, 1994).

FIVE

The Civilian Experience of World War Two: Displacement, Government, Adjustment, Comportment

Nicholas Atkin

To seize hold of the day-to-day life of civilians in World War Two is no easy matter. The extent of the Nazi and Soviet occupations, the extent of the fighting fronts, the extent of the killing, the extent of economic mobilization, the extent of material shortages, the extent of government interference into everyday lives, and the extent of the moral choices forced on ordinary men and women make any generalizations hazardous. Civilians inevitably experienced these intrusions, challenges, and upheavals in different ways. Nonetheless along the *unique* experiences of the war, there were also the *universal*.[1] These can be summarized as follows: displacement, government, adjustment, comportment. Before the fighting, with the fighting, after the fighting, came the displacement of populations on an unparalleled scale. Not only did civilians flee oncoming armies, they were also shuffled around by regimes. When the dust of battle settled, civilian lives were conditioned by the governments under which they lived, whether in the Soviet territories or Nazi-occupied Europe. Wherever one lived, civilians underwent a process of adjustment as they overhauled daily routines: much effort went into making do, finding enough to eat, keeping warm, and holding on to the familiar. Yet, in so doing, civilians had to ask questions about their political comportment. Few were happy to see the arrival of either the Nazi or Soviet occupier. Most endeavored to get on with their business regardless, a phenomenon known by the French term *attentisme*, a waiting on events; a small number chose to collaborate with the occupier; others chose to resist. These were not clear-cut choices, with the result that people's behavior was often ambivalent.

DISPLACEMENT

First came the fighting itself, and with it the massive upheaval of peoples. Europe had a foretaste of this reshuffling during World War One, especially the Russian empire, a territory "where a minimum of six million fled their homes."[2] It has been calculated that there were over nine million refugees still at large across Europe in the mid-1920s, the majority concentrated in central and eastern countries. The 1930s brought further disruption, when 200,000 German Jews fled their homeland to avoid Nazi persecution,[3] and 500,000 Spanish Republicans crossed the border into France to escape the Nationalist Franco regime. Housed in makeshift camps and made wholly unwelcome by their hosts, by late 1939 approximately 150,000 Spanish remained on French soil. They endured a truly uncomfortable existence under the authoritarian Vichy government of Marshal Pétain, created after the French defeat (see below). Prominent Republican leaders were returned to Spain, and to certain death, while Vichy colluded in the shipment of over 7,000 of their supporters to Mauthausen concentration camp in Austria.

This movement was dwarfed by what followed.[4] On September 1, 1939, Hitler moved into Poland, prompting the Union of Soviet Socialist Republics (USSR) to promote its own territorial ambitions, made possible by the Nazi-Soviet Pact concluded two weeks before. Acquiring a chunk of eastern Poland in mid-September, over the next nine months Stalin appropriated the Baltic states of Lithuania, Latvia, Estonia, and parts of Finland, together with the former Romanian territories of Bessarabia and northern Bukovina, producing 2.5 million refugees. By the terms of the Nazi-Soviet pact, it was intended that the estimated 750,000 Germans resident in those Baltic states and former Romanian territories conquered by the Russians would be relocated in the Greater Germany that Hitler was building. The majority of them were assembled in makeshift settlements for the duration of the war, their futures never to be resolved.

Meanwhile, on April 9, 1940, Germany attacked Norway and Denmark, an operation lasting two months, and followed this, on May 10, with the invasion of France, Belgium, Luxemburg, and the Low Countries, a campaign won within six weeks. In the blazing hot summer of 1940, between 6 million and 8 million French, Belgian, Dutch, and Luxemburger civilians took flight to escape the German advance in what is known as the *exode* ("exodus"); in view of the temperatures and unsanitary conditions on the roads, it was astonishing this event was not accompanied by epidemic.[5] Over the Channel Britain had not been expecting the battle for western Europe to end so quickly, but had braced itself for the arrival of 250,000 Continental refugees.[6] Thanks to the speed of German victory, fewer than

25,000 came over, mainly Belgians, yet the United Kingdom would not entirely escape the dislocation experienced across the Channel. It is known that there were 60 million changes of address in Britain between 1939 and 1945, a remarkable statistic given an overall population of 48 million. Part of this ebb and flow was due to the evacuation of children to the countryside where they were relatively free from air raids; it was officially acknowledged there was "no place of absolute safety."[7] Whereas Germany protected its young in relief camps, a scheme known as the *Kinderlandesverschickung*, in the United Kingdom rural householders were obliged to take in families from the cities. Given that town and countryside knew little about each other's lives it was, as Richard Titmuss records, a strange encounter, not without difficulties, often reinforcing middle-class notions about the habits of the working class.[8] Perhaps 4 million were resettled in this way; a further 2 million made their own arrangements. There had been plans to evacuate children to North America, but the threat of U-Boats in the Atlantic ensured less than 2,000, known as "bundles from Britain," were relocated to the United States.[9] These were the lucky ones. One of the most pitiful sights in World War Two was of those children accidentally separated from their parents and left to forage for themselves, a common phenomenon in central Europe in 1945.

Further displacement had come with the German invasion of the Soviet Union on June 22, 1941 (Operation Barbarossa). Already used to being pushed around by their government during the collectivization programs of the 1930s, maybe as many as 16.5 million Poles, Russians, and Jews now traveled east to avoid the Nazis.[10] In the Baltic states, recently acquired by Stalin, the population was again on the move, an exodus made more painful by the explosion of ethnic tensions.

We will never know for sure just how many civilians were dislodged by the Nazi-Soviet war, even with the gradual opening of Russian archives: so much remains conjecture. We are aware, however, that in 1944–45 Soviet successes on the eastern front led to the evacuation of approximately 7 million German citizens and the forceful resettlement of 500,000 more (Poles, Romanians, Bulgars, and Germans), many of whom were in danger of ending up in the gulags, Soviet labor camps, where harsh working conditions, paltry rations, subzero temperatures and general neglect cost the lives of 4 million people over the period 1941–45.[11] For their part, the Germans rounded up and killed some 6 million, the majority of whom were Jewish, in the prosecution of the Holocaust. As we will see, roughly the same number of people, from all across Nazi-occupied Europe, were dragooned into German factories to keep Hitler's war machine functioning.[12] The Soviets did something similar. Following Barbarossa, approximately 16 million workers, along with their factories, were relocated by to the east, to Kazakhstan, the Volga, the Urals, and Siberia.

It has been calculated that possibly some 40.5 million Europeans were displaced during World War Two; some historians put the figure even higher.[13] Those left homeless at the end of the conflict—at least outside of the Soviet Union where, as mentioned, refugees were at risk of being packed off to the gulags[14]—came under the protection of the United Nations Relief and Rehabilitation Administration (UNRAA), created on November 9, 1943, by the fledging United Nations (UN). Labeled DPs, these displaced persons were assembled in camps, usually situated on the outskirts of the large towns of Italy, Austria, and Germany, where they were given food, schooling, medical assistance, employment, and entertainment. Though UNRRA was successful in repatriating large numbers, especially those rescued from concentration camps, and did much to prevent the outbreak of disease that had accompanied the end of World War One, the mood among DPs themselves was often described as "apathetic," perhaps not surprising given the awful experiences they had endured. UNRAA itself was also running out of energy and in 1947 bequeathed its work, together with 643,000 DPs still to be rehomed, to the newly founded International Refugee Organization (IRO).

During the war itself, the appearance of refugees was an ominous portent of what might follow. On June 1, 1940, the British writer George Orwell recorded the scenes at Victoria railway station in London where soldiers and civilians, rescued from the beaches of Dunkirk, were arriving. While the waiting crowds applauded the troops, the sight of refugees evoked silence, as though onlookers knew that this might soon be their own fate.[15] Within France itself, the exodus of civilians was growing apace and, through the contemporary descriptions of the *exode* and the many novels written about the episode,[16] we may piece together something of the experience. This was dominated by a series of questions: in the first instance, whether to take flight or not. Often the instinct was to follow the herd. Most civilians did exactly that, largely because they were swept away by panic and were desperately in want of advice—from the wireless, from local authorities, from newspapers and from the military, all of which were in chaos; only the Catholic Church appeared to stand firm. This confusion ensured that the *exode* was a class leveler. While the wealthy and well connected had earlier made good their escape, most social groups found themselves on the march, something borne out by statistical surveys carried out in 1940 among London refugee centres.[17] The English journalist Neville Lytton, a veteran of the 1940 exodus, recorded how in later newsreels of refugees, the homeless seemed "to be drawn from the poorer classes only, whereas in fact all classes were on the road."[18]

Having decided to flee, refugees questioned what belongings to take with them. The instinct was to carry as much as possible, yet it was those who traveled light, often by bicycle, who proved most mobile. Those who traveled with heavy items often had to discard these by the roadside. The next issue was where geographically to make for. The Soviet Union, which already had a practice of shuffling people around, had made extensive provisions for evacuation. This proved a formidable achievement but was

A displaced Belgian family is seen walking in front of a destroyed house during the German invasion of Belgium in 1940. The location is unknown. Courtesy of AP Photo.

not without its share of problems. In October 1941, with their city seemingly vulnerable, thousands of Muscovites panicked and made their journeys without official guidance, often without food and water, hampering military transport journeying in the opposite direction towards the front. Organization was conspicuously lacking in western Europe: some people headed for the homes of friends and relatives; others for resort towns where they had earlier enjoyed holidays; a majority had little notion where to go, other than away from the fighting.[19] Interviewing small groups of refugees in 1940, officials in London discovered some two-thirds had made no plans for their evacuation—it happened too quickly.[20] Such men and women also described life on the move. This experience was again peppered with questions, evoked in Jean-Paul Sartre's novel, *The Iron in the Soul.* On the road from Paris, the hapless Sarah and her child Pablo overhear conversations about the future. How would the war turn? What would the Germans be like? How would they behave towards civilians?[21]

However much they tried, it was difficult for refugees to escape violence. This was especially true of eastern Europe. In Poland, few people harbored any illusions about the German invader, or the Russian one for that matter. The same was not necessarily true of those Ukrainian villagers caught up in the opening stages of Barbarossa. Having endured Stalinist persecution and desirous of autonomy, some (though not a majority) mistakenly welcomed the Nazis as liberators, offering German soldiers flowers, bread, and salt. None had truly reckoned on Hitlerian ideology, which regarded Slavs as racially inferior. They were further ignorant that their homeland had been targeted by Hitler as *Lebensraum* or "living space" to be populated by Germans. Nor had they anticipated the Einsatzgruppen, or SS killing squads, which followed the regular army, the Wehrmacht, as they had done in Poland. Memories instead were of the German army of World War One. As one of the partisans in Primo Levi's novel *If Not Now, When?* reflects, the Germans he had known in 1914–18 were "civilized people" who "would give the land back to the peasants."[22] The Einsatzgruppen were a different breed. Protected by the Barbarossa Jurisdiction Decree, which excused German soldiers from the Hague Convention governing crimes against civilians, their task was to eliminate Communist Party members and Jews—in sum, anyone who got in the way. Along with the scorched earth policy that Hitler pursued in the USSR, possibly 10 million Soviet civilians were killed between 1941 and 1945. Small wonder that the Red Army later responded with equal barbarity. As has been observed, though Stalin did not practice or preach systematic extermination, the Soviet authorities "only acted to stop their troops from misbehaving when their behavior threatened military discipline." Thus the Russian invasion of Germany, notably the siege of Berlin (1945), was accompanied by "an orgy of looting, raping and murder."[23]

Depressingly, German armies retreating in western Europe behaved in a similarly brutal fashion, abandoning the discipline they had maintained in 1940, though let it not be thought that their conduct then was temperate. Rapes, arbitrary violence, and savage punishments frequently accompanied the 1940 invasion of France and Belgium, as they had in 1914. German behavior steadily deteriorated over the course of the war and reached a nadir in 1944–45. One of the most infamous incidents was at Oradour-sur-Glane, a small village just west of Limoges in southern France.[24] Here, on June 10, 1944, men from the SS Das Reich Panzer Division stopped unexpectedly, rounded up all the men, women, and children they could find, and butchered them—642 lives in total. After the war, the charred ruins of the town were preserved as a memorial. There were several other notorious episodes of arbitrary reprisals and violence, among them: De Woeste Hoeve, Holland (March 6, 1945); the Fosse Adreatine, Italy (March 24, 1944); Tulle, France (June 9, 1944); Distomo, Greece (June 10, 1944); and Bande, Belgium (December 24, 1944).

Wherever refugees and civilians congregated, it was hard to escape violence, especially that perpetrated from the skies. World War One had offered a glimpse of what could be achieved through air power, giving rise to a doctrine of strategic bombing, that is the targeting of economic and military bases. Military planners quickly appreciated how these bombardments undermined general morale, as civilians were inevitably killed in such raids. Although the Hague Convention, League of Nations, and U.S. President Roosevelt warned against targeting civilian centers, the economic and terror possibilities of strategic bombing—greatly enhanced by rapidly developing technology in aircraft design, explosives, and radio—ultimately proved too great for belligerents to resist, at least in the western theater. As Richard Overy writes, on the eastern front air power was less crucial, partly because of the long distances involved, and partly because both sides "remained committed to the Clausewitzian view" that success lay in knocking out forces in the field,[25] though it should not be forgotten that the aerial assault on Moscow lasted as long as the *Blitz* and that, at the end of the war, the Russians exploited their superiority in the air to clear the way for the Red Army's invasion of Germany.

The *Blitz* was the name given to the Luftwaffe's campaign of prolonged night attacks on British cities (August 1940–May 1941). The "silence,"

German school teachers and children wear gas masks as they are drilled in how to conduct themselves in the event of a war in Berlin, Germany, August 31, 1939. Courtesy of AP Photo.

"purity," and "transience" of the London summer, as described by one French exile, gave way to an autumn and winter of unrelenting noise and violence.[26] Remarkably among Londoners, a spirit of defiance evolved, this despite the fact that, nationally, the *Blitz* left 45,000 dead and 139,000 injured. As the commentator Vera Brittain observed, fear of the raids was real, yet the newspapers did not need to make up the tales of courage and gaiety as a resolve had taken root that the bombs could not dislodge.[27] Whether London could have remained defiant is another matter. The capital was fortunate in its geographical size, which meant different parts of the city were hit at different times, though this was not always how it appeared to those living close to industrial centers, especially in the East End. For provincial towns, such as Coventry and Portsmouth, devastation was ubiquitous. Amid the rubble, fantastic tales about social disintegration quickly spread. It was fortunate for all British cities that the German invasion of the USSR siphoned off the Luftwaffe's energies.

Britain was also fortunate in that this bombing was not as severe as that which the Royal Air Force (RAF) meted out on Germany. The United Kingdom had been nurturing a policy of strategic bombing since the creation of Bomber Command in 1936, and let this loose in mid-May 1940 with raids on industrial plants along the Ruhr. By 1942, the RAF, assisted increasingly by the USAAF, intensified the campaign, choosing targets throughout Europe. The destruction of military and economic bases remained the aim, yet it again proved impossible to avoid heavy civilian casualties, many more than in the *Blitz,* creating anxieties among allied planners that they might alienate the support of the very people whose loyalty they were trying to win over. As the newspaper *Le Courrier de Saint-Nazaire* remarked in February 1942, after a particularly heavy raid on the local area, "How can a people as civilized as our former British allies be seized by such a fury of destruction, devastation and death without in the least advancing their military cause?"[28] Ultimately, military needs prevailed. As D-Day drew closer, an increasing number of attacks were launched against the French coastal towns of Royan, Saint-Nazaire, Le Havre, and Caen.[29] The propaganda value of these strikes was not lost on the Germans. Following an especially intense strike on Rouen, the Germans produced an arresting poster of Joan of Arc, who had been tried and burned in the city by the English during the fifteenth century. "The assassins always return twice," it announced. The Germans further retaliated, in 1944–45, with V1 and V2 rockets launched in the general direction of London—the missiles' trajectories were so unreliable they could not help but fall on civilians, which was the whole point.

The morality of strategic bombing was brought into relief by the allied raid on Dresden. On February 13 and 14, 1945, this picturesque German town, capital of Saxony, was showered with incendiary devices and high explosive bombs, first by British, then by American bombers, resulting in a ferocious firestorm depicted in Kurt Vonnegut's 1969 absurdist novel

Slaughterhouse-Five. Critics argue that the attack was unnecessary, a terrible revenge for the earlier bombing of British cities, notably that on Coventry of November 14 and 15, 1940, which left 380 dead, 865 injured, and the fourteenth-century cathedral in ruins. In 1945, it is argued, the war was won; Dresden was of no economic importance; and a beautiful cultural center was destroyed. Recent scholarship has alluded to the attack as a war crime, and parallels have been drawn with the Holocaust.[30] Other historians have argued otherwise: the town was an important war-manufacturing base; it was a Nazi stronghold; and it was a departure point for Jews in the area to be shipped off to concentration camps. The bombing actually saved the lives of those remaining Jews earmarked for the camps, notably the diarist Victor Klemperer. Nor was the bombing as fateful as sometimes thought. Those killed numbered between 25,000 to 40,0000, not the 100,000 sometimes claimed, though this is not to belittle the magnitude and appalling nature of the slaughter.[31]

Whatever the morality of strategic bombing, we will never know for sure the number of civilians who lost their lives as a result of aerial campaigns. It was often difficult to recognize body parts, never mind identify and count the cadavers, discovered amid the rubble. The process of killing might have become more mechanized in World War Two, distancing the artilleryman or bomber from the carnage he had caused, but the messiness of death could not be hidden from civilians, a process already evidenced in 1914–18. For their part, historians are uncertain of overall civilian losses in World War Two, whether as a result of strategic bombing, deportations, concentration camps, the gulags, and other war-related factors, for instance, population movement, disease, malnutrition, reprisals, and arbitrary violence. What may be safely said is that the human cost was greater than any conflict before or since.

NUMBERS OF EUROPEANS KILLED IN WORLD WAR TWO

For the belligerent nations as a whole (including non-European), one authoritative account (always remembering these figures are still imprecise and are constantly being revisited), has calculated that 22 million military personnel lost their lives, alongside 28 million civilians—this latter figures includes the 7.5 million Chinese killed in the multitudinous conflicts that raged in the Far East.[32] On the part of the Axis powers, Germany suffered most: 4.5 million military deaths, the eastern front being the chief killing ground, and 2 million civilian. Italy experienced 400,000 military, 100,000 civilian; Romania 300,000 military, 200,000 civilian; Austria 230,000 military, 144,000 civilian; Hungary 160,000 military, 270,000 civilian; and Finland 84,000 military, 16,000 civilian. Among the Allies, the United Kingdom lost 300,000 military, 50,000 civilian.

It was countries knocked out in the early stages of the war where civilian deaths were higher than military ones: France 250,000 military, 350,000 civilian; Belgium 10,000 military, 78,000 civilian; Holland 6,000 military, 204,000 civilian; and Norway 2,000 military, 8,000 civilian. Because of the Nazi persecution of Jews and

Slavs, and the willingness of resisters to partake in military actions, Poland suffered still higher civilian losses: 123,000 military, 4 million civilian. Figures for the USSR are disputed. Various Russian leaders exaggerated these so as to enhance the legend of the "Great Patriotic War," though they were also eager to hide the deaths in the gulags. Some recent calculations have suggested that, overall, 30 million Russian civilians died—more sober estimates hazard 10 million military losses, and the same number of civilian ones. Controversy and uncertainty also surround the numbers who perished in the Holocaust. Though the overwhelming majority were Jewish, anywhere between 150,000 and 500,000 gypsies were slaughtered, alongside 150,000 to 200,000 handicapped, 10,000 homosexuals, and 2,500–5,000 Jehovah's Witnesses.

Historians are on stronger ground when they point to how the war destabilized the gender balance of populations—adult males suffered far more than women and children—and how it contributed to a decline in birth and marriage rates, though this was not the same everywhere. As in the aftermath of 1914–18, Europe quickly made good its shortfalls, a phenomenon partially to be explained by longer-term demographic trends and the atmosphere of peacetime. "The horrors of war, with its separations and instabilities," reflects one historian, "brought longings for domesticity, marriage and parenthood."[33]

GOVERNMENT

Death, the fear of death, the death of a loved one, friend or colleague, or that of a faraway relative or casual acquaintance—this was a constant in the civilian experience in World War Two. Yet remarkably people strove to get on with their lives as best they could. Their ability to do so was largely determined by where in Europe they lived, bringing us back to the second variable identified earlier, that of government. This varied throughout Europe largely because Hitler had no blueprint for his empire, other than a wish to create a Greater Germany—"power without plan or purpose" is one description.[34] Historians such as Michael Burleigh have, however, determined a series of factors that shaped the ways in which Germany treated its subjugated territories: race, the strategic value of an area, and economic importance, to which could be added another factor, that of time.[35] When the war turned badly, Berlin squeezed its possessions ever more tightly, ruthlessly seeking out raw materials, foodstuffs, manpower, and Jews.

Greater Germany

The complexities of Hitler's Europe have been neatly unraveled by Henri Michel.[36] At its hub, he writes, lay the Germany, as established by the 1919 settlement, to which were eventually bolted on Austria, the Sudetenland, Memelland, Alsace-Lorraine, Luxemburg, Eupen and Malmédy, Poznan, Silesia, the Polish corridor, and Danzig so as to form the so-called *Grossraum* (Greater Germanic Estate), though there was no precise understanding as what this should comprise. All these territories were to be Germanified, though no unitary administration was ever accomplished. As historians stress, Hitler's priority was to win the war, seize yet more land, and rid Europe of its Jews. The time-consuming task of designing a uniform administrative template, suitable for everywhere, and craved by the Ministry of the Interior, would have to wait until final victory, though whether the ramshackle bureaucracy of the Nazi state, already well out of hand by 1939, would have permitted such codification is another matter.[37]

Whatever the case, in several parts of the Greater Germany—Austria, the Sudetenland, Memelland, and Eupen and Malmédy—the population largely regarded itself as German, and did not consider itself as under foreign rule. This was not true of those minorities, caught in the Greater Reich, that were damned as racially inferior, notably Poles and Lorrainers. The disputed provinces of Alsace-Lorraine had been seized by the Prussians in 1870–71, only to be handed back to France in 1918. In Hitlerian ideology, they were marked to rediscover their "true German identity." To this end, shortly after their conquest, 105,000 Alsace-Lorrainers, deemed unsuitable for Germanification, were herded onto trains for Lyon and other towns in France. Within Alsace-Lorraine, French street signs, notices, and newspapers were "Germanized," and the organs of the Nazi state supplanted existing administrative units. More brutal was the treatment of the Poles. The campaign of 1939 saw the Einsatzgruppen at their deadly work. In 1940, with the campaign won, the population was ruthlessly shuffled around. Those deemed unsuitable for Germanification were expelled into what was known as the General Government (to be considered later), forced to leave their houses without belongings, and ferried in cattle trucks without provisions. Their homes were taken over by those Germans from the Baltic states. Although these settlers never arrived in numbers, in preparation for their migration the Germans removed traces of indigenous culture, especially from those areas of Poland once occupied by Prussia, notably the Wartheland.

Holland, Denmark, and Norway

In the case of northern European countries—Holland, Denmark, and Norway—it has been said that their experience of occupation was initially that of a "Nazism lite" variety. This was because of their supposed Nordic descent which, in Hitlerian racial terms, meant that they were essentially Aryans, and could ultimately be assimilated.[38] In Holland, Queen Wilhelmina and her cabinet fled to London to establish a government-in-exile. Their place was taken by a German Reich commissioner, Arthur Seyss-Inquart, who ran the country in collaboration with the Dutch civil service, hopeful that the autonomy permitted the Dutch would convince them of their Aryan destiny. In Norway, King Haakon VII and his ministers emulated their Dutch counterparts by taking up exile in London.

Once again, a German Reich commissioner was appointed in their stead, Josef Terboven, who governed with the assistance of Nazi officials and members of Vidkun Quisling's fascist Nasjonal Samling party, though Quisling was so unpopular he had to be kept in the background.[39] In Denmark, Christian X stayed, as did parliament, which functioned under the watchful eye of the Germans, and the Nazi-sponsored government dominated by the veteran politicians Thorvald Stauning and Eric Scavenius.[40]

The promise was to interfere as little as possible in the affairs of these northern states, yet everywhere the Nazis failed to keep their promises and took whatever they wanted, provoking a series of strikes and general noncompliance. Such behavior was commonplace in Holland and Norway by 1942, and belatedly overtook Denmark where, in August 1943, a state of emergency was declared thanks to widespread sabotage and industrial action. Earlier that year, free elections had been permitted, but produced an overwhelming majority for the Social Democrats, hostile to the Germans, though ready to work with Scavenius. For the final months of the war, the occupier effectively administered most of the country's institutions.

France and Italy

Less indulgent were the arrangements within France, a nation that Hitler regarded with suspicion, partly because of its traditional rivalry with Germany, partly because of its racial complexion, and partly because of its revolutionary heritage.[41] As Julian Jackson writes, the country was effectively "Balkanized," divided up into a series of zones, in preparation for its eventual disappearance.[42] Alsace-Lorraine constituted the annexed zone and, as mentioned, was to be absorbed in the Greater Germany. There further existed a prohibited zone containing the industrial departments of the Nord-Pas-de-Calais, run by the German High Command in Brussels, which also oversaw the government of Belgium. An industrial area, with latent Anglophile sentiments, this prohibited zone was unwelcoming toward the Germans, as was the neighboring forbidden zone, a small strip of northern France, which served as a *cordon sanitaire*. The main occupied zone comprised the majority of northern France and the Atlantic littoral, effectively the wealthiest and most densely populated parts of the country, and was ruled by the Germans in Paris. Here, the occupying authorities went out of their way, at least in the early stages of the war, to assuage the anxieties of the population, though the curtailment of civil liberties, the plundering of economic resources, and the growing roundups of Jews, communists, and others sent out a sobering message. As one German report of September 1940 summarized, "the population is on the whole calm, on occasion welcoming, but for the majority of the time reserved, often unfriendly and to a certain degree hostile."[43]

The remainder of France, essentially the southern third, known as the unoccupied zone and separated from the rest of the country by a heavily patrolled Demarcation Line, was governed by Marshal Pétain, a hero of World War One, who was invested with dictatorial powers, and whose government took up residence at the little spa town of Vichy. Though Vichy had considerable autonomy, and though Pétain was hugely admired, thanks to his compassionate image cultivated during the 1914–18 conflict, a reputation strengthened during the *exode* when he seemed genuinely concerned for the fate of the compatriots, his regime was hugely unpopular. It attempted a back-handed overhaul of the country's institutions through a National Revolution, whose deficiencies propaganda could not hide; there grew considerable resentment at the way in which the marshal's government collaborated with the Germans; there was a residual sympathy for the British and General de Gaulle, leader of the French resistance overseas; there was growing dissatisfaction at material shortages, deliberately exacerbated by the Germans; and there developed a dislike of the discriminatory measures Vichy took, under its own initiative, against Jews, foreigners, and communists. It was telling that many French Jews increasingly sought refuge in the Italian occupied zone, a tiny part of southeastern France that Mussolini had seized in 1940, and where Italian discriminatory legislation proved less severe than that practiced by the French. Numbers swelled after November 1942 when wider developments in the war prompted Germany to occupy all of France, and the Italians widened their zone of occupation, though let it not be thought that Italian fascism was in any sense soft-hearted. Richard Bosworth has shown that the popular image of Italian fascists as awkward amateurs, interested primarily in children, good food, wine, and women—an image, noted *The Economist* magazine, perpetuated in Louis de Bernières' 2001 popular novel *Captain Corelli's Mandolin*—is grossly misleading. Mussolini's Italy might not have been preoccupied by Jews, but was wholly intolerant of Blacks, Arabs, and Slavs, and in its search for empire may well have murdered 1 million people from these groups.[44]

Czechoslovakia

Severest were the arrangements in Eastern Europe. Czechoslovakia was divided up, partially along racial grounds. While the German-dominated Sudetenland was incorporated into the Greater Reich, and while Slovakia became one of Berlin's puppet states, the rump of Czechoslovakia was translated into the Protectorate of Bohemia and Moravia, under the Reichsprotektor, Baron von Neurath, succeeded in 1941 by the SS man Reinhard Heydrich. Jews in the area were eliminated (possibly 118,000); the Czech aristocracy and middle classes, viewed as decadent by the Nazis and potential leaders of any resistance, were endlessly bullied; all nonwar industries were closed down; and Czech labor was drafted into the service of the German economy.

Poland

Similar geopolitical and ethnic considerations informed the division of Poland. Whereas the Wartheland region was Germanized, what remained of Poland, together with pieces of Ukraine (Galicia and Volhynia), became known as the General Government run by Hans Frank, one of Hitler's keenest disciples, and became "the racial laboratory of Nazidom."[45] With a population of 12 million the General Government was intended as a slave-labor colony and dumping ground for Europe's Jews, and was subject to unspeakable horrors from the start. As Frank himself remarked, "If we had one notice posted for every seven Poles we have shot, the forests of Poland would be inadequate to produce the paper for them."[46] Those Jews who escaped the firing squads were herded into ghettos, which were walled off from the main parts of cities and governed by Judenräte, councils of Jewish elders. With a veritable army of conscripted bureaucrats at their disposal, these councils have been described as "collaborative shadow states," though it must be stressed that those who served on these bodies were given absolutely no choice in the matter; death was the alternative.[47] Survival in the Ghetto proved a matter of enormous ingenuity and good fortune, as revealed in Roman Polanski's 2002 film *The Pianist,* based on the autobiography of the memoirs of the eminent musician, Wladyslaw Szpilman.[48] It was from the ghettos that Germany fed the extermination camps, many of which were on Polish soil: Auschwitz, Lublin-Majdanek, Chelmo, Treblinka, Sobibor.

Ukraine

It is invidious to establish a hierarchy of suffering, yet the horrors perpetrated in Poland were perhaps still less than those committed in the USSR, especially in Ukraine, which the Soviets themselves had systematically abused in an attempt to crush national identity. The Germans were equally hostile to the emergence of an independent nation, hence the quick dismemberment of the territory in 1941. Land closest to Germany was placed under army rule; the fate of Galicia and Volhynia has been mentioned; the remainder fell under the control of the Nazi Gauleiter, Erich Koch, whose regime "was probably the most exploitative in the whole of Europe."[49] The indigenous peoples, some of whom had mistakenly believed the Germans might be liberators, were wholly confused, as the Nazis pursued an uncompromising policy of terror. Kiev was left to starve in the campaign of 1941; the Ukrainian intelligentsia was systematically eliminated; indigenous culture was expunged (though paradoxically it was encouraged in Galicia where the Nazis were keen to destroy Polish identity); arbitrary arrests and executions were commonplace; the labor force was mobilized in the service of the Reich; and Ukraine's Jews (possibly 600,000) were extinguished.

ADJUSTMENT

It is not possible to detail all the complicated arrangements the Nazis made elsewhere to support their empire, for instance the puppet states created in Greece, Serbia, and Croatia. Nor is there space to examine the ways in which Berlin interfered in the running of its so-called ally states: Finland, Romania, Bulgaria, Hungary, and, increasingly, Italy. The overriding point is that the experience of civilians was determined by where they lived and when they lived; as the war progressed, material conditions worsened. That said, people everywhere attempted to get on with their lives as best they could and, in so doing, confronted the third variable mentioned at the start of this essay, that of adjustment. What is astonishing is that, in modifying their lives, Europeans underwent similar experiences, especially within the workplace, where governments demanded more; at the shops, whose empty shelves begged questions about strategies for survival; and in the home, where many hardships fell on women.

The Workplace during War

The workplace was paramount. Hitler was especially alive to the fact that this was a war to the last. He was haunted by the experience of 1914–18 when he believed that defeat had been precipitated by a nonindustrious home front—corrupted by Jews and left-wingers who had sought domestic comfort ahead of national sacrifice. This obsession with the myth of the "stab in the back" has led some historians to argue that Hitler deliberately shielded the German people from the full demands of wartime at least until 1942, and that a wholly mobilized economy was not achieved until 1944.[50] There is now growing consensus that the high-level management of Germany economy, directed by a multitude of agencies (among them, the 1936 Four Year Plan, Göring's Council of Ministers for Reich Defense, the Organisation Todt, the Speer Plan) was never sufficiently supple to allow sudden movements from civilian to military expenditure. The latter had been growing at the expense of the former since 1936. The upshot was that two-thirds of national income was spent on defense by 1941, in comparison to one-fifth three years earlier; civilian spending within that time had fallen sharply, hardly surprising given that most factories were supplying the military.

For the German people, this meant full employment, yet at a price. Work was central to Nazi ideology and those deemed work-shy were shipped off to camps for reeducation; workers' representation, in the shape of trade unions, had been eliminated in the 1930s to be replaced with welfarism and the "Strength through Joy" movement that hoped to eliminate boredom on the factory floor; whether standards of living for urban workers actually rose under Hitler is still a disputed issue, yet there is evidence to suggest that it was becoming easier for manual workers to enter white-collar professions.[51] The paradox was that amid the propaganda and erection of a police state, German workers, mindful of the Depression years of 1929–33, were grateful for new opportunities. Whether they welcomed the aerial attacks on their factories is another matter. Life was safer in the countryside. As one historian has observed, bombing "was principally an urban phenomenon," yet it will be recalled that nowhere was secure.[52] What is remarkable is that despite the daily worry of air raids, the constant injunctions to toil harder, the setting of unrealistic production targets, the introduction of longer hours, the conscription of women, the initiation of severe punishments for supposed slackers, and the disruption brought about to routines by the relocation of industries, the workforce labored until the end, not merely because of coercion, or fear of the Russians. "Deference to the Nazi regime," writes one historian, ended only when it was blindingly obvious that it "could no longer protect its subjects."[53]

However much they worked, and they certainly worked hard, German workers could not provide enough. To compensate, the Nazis conscripted foreigners, a process overseen by Fritz Saukel, onetime Gauleiter of Thuringia, appointed Plenipotentiary for Labor in March 1942. By August 1944, a series of decrees had drafted 4,375,882 civilians into the service of the German war economy, among them: 177,451 Belgians; 465,729 French; 114,898 Italians; 174,358 Dutch; 1,890,299 Soviet; 1,415,276 Poles; and 117,679 civilians from the Protectorate of Bohemia-Moravia.[54] Nor should it be overlooked that Germany deployed 1,424,047 prisoners of war in its workforce, the majority of whom were Soviets and Poles. By 1944, one-fifth of Germany's labor force was of foreign origin. Inevitably, among these conscripts, it was the eastern workers (*Ostarbeiter*) who suffered most, often put to work in camps, deprived of rations, and overseen by ruthless officials. Those of Nordic stock and from western Europe were treated more indulgently, and it is sometimes conveniently overlooked that a minority of French workers were reluctant to return to their homeland in 1945 because they found working conditions in wartime Germany more favorable than in peacetime France. This is not to believe that labor conscription, introduced in France in early 1943, was popular. A sizeable proportion (30–40,000) avoided enlistment by escaping into the scrubland (*maquis*) where they became resistance fighters, *maquisards*. More understandable was the reluctance, at the end of the war, for Poles, Yugoslavs, and especially Soviet civilians to leave Germany and return to their homelands where they feared possible reprisals and material hardships.

Without doubt, of all the home fronts, it was Russian workers who underwent the greatest adjustments.[55] Thanks to the Bolshevik defensive mentality, the centralized nature of the Soviet economy, and the growing expectation of war with Germany, much hoarding of goods had been accomplished by the late 1930s, though it was understood that the Five-Year

Plans had not met targets, and that collectivization had led to a slump in agricultural production. Yet further state controls were required should the USSR withstand invasion, a recognition hardened by early military reverses in 1941–42 that left 40 percent of the Soviet population and nearly two-thirds of Russian armaments factories in German hands. "From being the world's third largest industrial economy, behind the United States and Germany," writes Overy, the USSR had been reduced "to the rank of smaller economies, such as France, Italy and Japan."[56]

The challenge was partly met by the *dirigiste* State Defense Committee (GKO), a small war cabinet, appointed in June 1941 and charged with "the rapid mobilization of all the country's resources."[57] Under the GKO, the Soviet war economy rose to the challenge. Factories producing consumer goods were turned over to war manufacture; evacuation of plant machinery was stepped up, with factories being disassembled and transferred away from the front by railway, possibly one million wagonloads of plant machinery in total, along with their workers; new railways were laid to overcome the logjams; and there ensued an exploitation of neglected oil and coal reserves in Siberia. The Russian aircraft engineer Alexander Yakovlev recalled how at Moscow, "with the enemy only 150 miles away," factories producing Yak-1 fighters kept their conveyor belts rolling, with aircrew waiting at the gates to take delivery of their machines; only at the very last moment was the plant equipment disassembled and transported eastwards to Siberia.[58] Frequently things did not go to plan, shortages were commonplace, and the GKO never struck the right rhythm when directing targets; indeed, as is frequently stressed, there is no simple explanation to account for the Soviet economic achievement. Yet, crucially, Soviet war production outmatched that of Germany's, even if exploitation of raw materials lagged behind, something compensated for through Allied assistance in the form of Lend-Lease.

For workers themselves, already used to being exhorted to toil more, there were severe hardships, both on the factory floor and in the fields. Hours were long and frequently extended, a 55-hour week by 1942; holidays were suspended; accommodation for workers was basic, often comprising primitive wooden huts with few amenities; rations were meager; and many categories of civilians were enlisted, young boys, women, and the elderly. Yet, as the British writer Alexander Werth observed, it was understood that without work, death was the most likely outcome as there were no official ration entitlements for the unemployed, or even for those who lost their ration cards.[59] As with Nazi Germany, the irony was that the Soviet regime did not solely rely on its commissars to intimidate the people. During the war, civilians rediscovered their love for "eternal Russia," and a Stalin personality cult evolved. That this love for the Russian leader was genuine was testified by Werth, who was struck by the way in which people applauded Stalin in newsreels: "people don't cheer in the dark unless they really feel like it."[60]

It is widely acknowledged that the home front that adapted most effectively belonged to a liberal democracy, the United Kingdom. Here, in the buildup to 1939, a peacetime economy prevailed. Although some industries had been overhauled, for instance those producing fighter aircraft, unemployment was disturbingly high, and the "phoney war" only seemed to engender what one diarist described as "a strange somnambulistic quality" in which neither government nor people seemed alive to the urgency of the situation, though the blackouts were observed stringently.[61] That urgency was spelled out by events in 1940, notably the fall of France. Thereafter Britain, and its empire, was on its own, notwithstanding the enormous material aid provided by the United States in the shape of Lend-Lease. Civilians met the challenge and beyond. Unemployment evaporated; several people held down more than one job; absenteeism in the workplace was slight; and women became prominent in many occupations.

Credit for this mobilization must partly go to government. In April 1940, the Lord President's Committee, a cabinet subcommittee, asserted its right to set production targets. It was assisted by the appointment, the following year, of Sir John Anderson, celebrated as a man who got things done. March 1941 saw the initiation of the Essential Work Order, authored by Ernest Bevin, brought in from the Transport and General Workers Union (TGWU) to become minister of labor. Though some historians have since argued that, in the longer term, such initiatives hindered the economy by enshrining outdated management and work practices,[62] this legislation allowed government to register the entire work force so as to direct its workers to those industries most in need. The corollary to government intervention was the inspired leadership of Winston Churchill, prime minister from May 1940. It is widely acknowledged that his speeches, particularly in the bleak years of 1940 and 1941, convinced the public that self-sacrifice and tough measures were needed if the United Kingdom was to stay in the war. Historians have further pointed to the values of unity and tolerance among the British people, values that withstood pressures of wartime. Many intellectuals and left-wing politicians thus characterized World War Two as the "people's war." Just how harmonious British wartime society truly was is a source of contention.[63] Foreigners, especially in the invasion scare of 1940, were greatly feared; anti-Semitism was never far from the surface; internment of enemy aliens was more draconian than in 1914; crime rates rose, and looting accompanied the "Battle of Britain" (the vital air campaign conducted in June–September 1940 over the south of England as the Germans prepared for invasion); the press was tightly controlled; and class differences were never truly reconciled. As one historian has remarked, while the war resulted in the "temporary throwing together of social groups," there was "no equalising effect upon income" or significant redistribution in the ownership of property.[64]

Shortages in Food and Other Products

Where governments were not slow to bark orders, and where civilians had to make significant adjustments, was in the rationing of basic commodities and foodstuffs. Contrary to what is occasionally believed, Germany started rationing for essential goods as early as 1939. Although Berlin could requisition resources from its conquests, luxury items quickly disappeared from the shelves and people, at least in the towns, became acclimatized to a dreary diet largely comprising bread, potatoes, and occasional meat. In the countryside, people ate more plentifully, partially because farmers could squirrel away their produce without the state always noticing. Bread, potatoes, and fats also figured prominently on the menus of the Soviet workforce, which experienced rationing on a calorie basis immediately after the invasion and which was entitled to a quarter of the food distributed daily to its German equivalent. Digging antitank ditches outside Moscow, women workers received a daily ration comprising a small roll of bread and a sausage. Best nourished were those engaged in heavy industry, and blood donors, though this is saying little. In the winter of 1941, "more Leningraders starved to death every month than the total of British civilians killed by German bombs in the entire war."[65] In the United Kingdom, rationing was resisted in 1939, lest it undermine morale. In early 1940, however, ration books were issued with instructions to households to register with local retailers. It proved a cumbersome system, not helped by a steady drip of merchandise made subject to controls: initially butter, sugar, bacon, and ham, followed by various meats, cheese, preserves, tea, butter, cooking fats, though not tobacco. Individual allowances for several products fell sharply in 1941 as the U-Boats attacked Atlantic convoys, and the home economy struggled to meet demand. Though rationing produced much grumbling, the irony was that the emphasis on vital foodstuffs, together with their equitable distribution and plentiful government propaganda as to their best use, may have improved the vitamin and calorie intake of the working classes, who had suffered badly during the Depression years.[66] In some of the poorer rural areas of France, a similar process might have occurred, though this might also be put down to the wily ways of a peasantry that withheld produce for its own tables. A tension soon evolved between town and countryside, reminiscent of that which existed in the nineteenth century when French towns suspected peasants of deliberately hoarding supplies. A similar process also appears to have overtaken Italy and Greece, though not all farmers could exploit their position, especially those in "monocultural areas that did not produce food."[67]

Let it not be thought that occupied Europe was well fed. The Germans took whatever they wanted, leaving the indigenous people the scraps. Paul Simon, a French resister, observed, "The food problem is such that one must give up work in order to queue and eat, or work and not eat.

Food is the main topic of conversation."[68] By 1944, with Germany ever more rapacious, famine stalked Europe, notably in Greece and in Holland, which underwent the "hunger winter" of 1944. As one Dutch survivor recalled, "Nothing was so important as food—with fuel on its heels. I remember getting up in the morning thinking of food; the whole day we talked about food; the whole day long we talked about food; and I went to bed hungry and dreaming about food."[69] Children and adolescents were especially badly affected; puberty and general growth were delayed as a result of shortages. Always last in the food line were Jews and Slavs. Szpilman records how widespread hunger kicked in within two days of the creation of the Warsaw Ghetto, and how, when escorted on work detail out of the walls, he marveled at the "fruit and vegetables" and the sparkling scales of the fish he spied on market stalls.[70]

Among the many effects of these shortages, four are worth highlighting. First, the black market flourished, and in occupied Europe was often supplied and encouraged by the Germans themselves so as to undermine morale, though Nazi propaganda always depicted illegal trafficking as the work of Jews. Second, queuing became commonplace. Foreign exiles in the United Kingdom were astonished by the orderliness of the British, who seemed to accept the drudgery of long waits with extraordinary patience. In occupied Paris, queues occasionally became riotous as people jockeyed for position. Frequently they formed early in the morning and had to be dispersed by the police. Whenever they assembled, queues were a source of gossip, and the Germans were known to place spies among them to pick up local news, spread anti-British sentiments, promote defeatist talk, and recruit informers. Third, civilians became good at improvisation. In Paris and Brussels, window boxes were turned over to cultivating vegetables; in the Soviet Union, vegetables were grown in the smallest of flower pots; in the United Kingdom, the number of allotments numbered 1.5 million by 1942, producing around a tenth of the nation's food. Municipal parks, playing fields, railway embankments, bomb sites—any suitable land was put aside for cultivation. Fourth, imitation products proliferated. Civilians proved especially adept at improvising clothes, though it is questionable how many Venetian women responded to government propaganda urging them to maintain their elegance by donning coats made out of tabby cat fur.[71] It was ersatz food products where ingenuity prevailed—and no doubt indigestion. In Germany, coffee was made out of barley, in France out of chicory; in the United Kingdom, a popular BBC radio program entitled *The Kitchen Front* suggested how to make traditional dishes using ingenious recipes containing whatever products were plentiful at the time. More people ate out in Britain than ever before, as prices were fixed and coupons were not used as currency, yet sitting down to a meal in a restaurant was often a puzzling experience as customers tried to work out exactly what they were eating.

Women line up outside a butcher shop to buy meat in North Cheam, Surrey, England, on April 17, 1942 during World War Two. Courtesy of AP Photo.

Women's Roles

It was women who were at the sharp end of these scarcities. Women were the ones who dominated the food lines, who adapted the family budget to cope with the demands of the black market and rationing, and who did their utmost to hold families together. In part, this was to be expected. European society traditionally viewed women as homemakers, on whom the chores of daily life naturally fell, even if those chores were greater than usual, a viewpoint reinforced by the chauvinistic ideology of Nazi Germany and Fascist Italy. The short supply of men (killed in action, conscripted into the armies, deported for labor, or held as POWs) further underscored the prominence of women. At the close of the war, in Soviet Russia, "the number of women exceeded men by 20 million."[72] Some writers have thus characterized World War Two as "a woman's war."[73] Yet, as others have countered, this was still very much "a soldier's war," and it should not be overlooked that women had always played a part in conflict by keeping the home fires burning, contributing to the welfare of armies, operating as nurses, and very occasionally serving as fighting troops.[74]

It is generally agreed that what made the 1939–45 conflict different was the extent of mobilization, which forced the "second sex" into unaccustomed roles. On the fighting fronts, women were used as auxiliaries, the United Kingdom being the first country to introduce female conscription. Only the Soviet Union actually used women in battle, enlisting thousands in readiness for the siege of Moscow. On the home fronts, women discovered, as in 1914–18, that they had to take on men's jobs but on a scale greater than before. In the United Kingdom, women were steadily conscripted, and by 1943 comprised 43 percent of the entire labor force. It is said that it was virtually unavoidable for a woman under 40 not to be in a job unless she was pregnant, had a large number of children to look after, or was providing lodgings for war workers. As to the USSR, in 1940 two-fifths of those in industry were women; by 1943, the proportion was

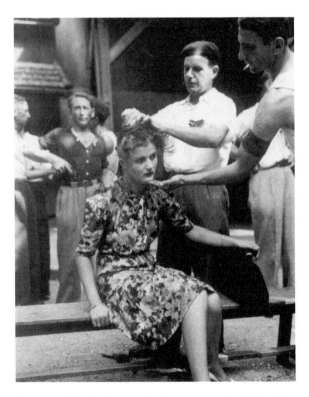

As a penalty for having had a personal relationship with a German during the time of occupation, this young woman gets her head shaved in public by a French civilian, while another man is holding up her chin, in the Montelimar area in southeastern France, in 1944. Courtesy of AP Photo.

over a half. As to Germany, there persists a notion that the Nazis resisted women's employment, partially on ideological grounds and partially to cushion the home front from wartime realities. Though exemptions from war work were more generous than those in the United Kingdom, statistics reveal that women predominated on farms and, by 1944, made up half the industrial workforce.

The ability of women to work as well as men did not bring about a leveling of the sexes. Women still earned less than men; they still lacked equal opportunities; and they were still likely to face redundancy come peacetime, though this was less true of those who had managed to break into white-collar professions, a phenomenon especially apparent in Germany, whose male adult population had been devastated. Whether war created freedoms for the "second sex" in other regards is also open to question. It is frequently said that women in France and Italy were granted the vote in 1944 because of their involvement in resistance, yet there were redoubtable institutional and cultural barriers to surmount. Historians have subsequently spoken of women in these two countries being given "citizenship without liberation." Nor did it help that, in the 1950s, there were social pressures "to recreate the mother" and modern housewife.[75] This trend was reinforced by the appearance of glossy magazines, a response to the austerity of the war years, in which women were given a glimpse of a new world of *haute couture* and labor-saving gadgets, yet such images only buttressed existing gender stereotypes, and were, in any case, too expensive for many. Within sexual relations, there may have been some easing of codes of behavior, though this was not acknowledged during the "prudish" 1950s, and was forgotten during the "permissive" 1960s. It took the wartime-based novels of Mary Wesley, published in the 1980s, to remind a UK public that people in World War Two had sex, and quite a lot of it.[76] Leaving to one side the psychological theory that war acts as a sexual stimulant, the ever-present fear of death was an imperative for people to seek pleasure whenever they could and, in the blackouts and curfews, there were plenty of opportunities, something also true of same-sex liaisons. As the flamboyant actor, writer, and model Quentin Crisp recalled of wartime London, "As soon as the bombs started to fall, the city became like a paved double bed. Voices whispered suggestively to you as you walked along; hands reached out if you stood still and in dimly lit trains people carried on as they had once behaved only in taxis."[77]

Governments everywhere were concerned at the ways in which war chipped away at traditional moral values. In the French department of the Nord, the prefect reported in 1941 that there existed 65,000 young, unemployed people who were "demoralized."[78] While boys partook in homosexual behavior, the girls worked as prostitutes, with the result that a venereal disease clinic, dedicated to adolescents, had been established in Lille. VD was indeed the great anxiety of all belligerent nations, and was the subject of enemy propaganda that played on fears of servicemen about the fidelity of their spouses at home. British troops especially fretted over the arrival of American forces into the United Kingdom. Viewed as overpaid and oversexed, the presence of GIs led to a hike in extramarital affairs and a surge in illegitimate births. Recent records released in the United Kingdom have indicated that the London police was alarmed at the number of "feckless" teenage girls, playing truant from reform schools (schools for difficult adolescents), sleeping with American soldiers and spreading sexual diseases.[79] Yet, in calling for restraint, governments everywhere were guilty of double standards, notably when it came to prostitution. This was frequently condemned, yet frequently organized by governments and fraternized by troops, for instance the trains of women who accompanied the Soviet westward advance in 1944–45. In Paris, the Nazi authorities issued prostitutes with cards, written in both the German and French languages, outlining their prices and the types of sexual services they offered.[80] Forgotten always was the fact that women, especially the increasing number of young adolescent girls, had little choice in the matter. The alternative was poverty, unemployment, and hunger.

Double standards were particularly evident at the Liberation when no acknowledgement was made of rapes.[81] As has been observed, rape in war is omnipresent: "[S]oldiers for the most part are young, sexually segregated males, who carry knives and firearms."[82] All armies offended, yet it was the Red Army that offended the worst: in Hungary, Romania, Slovakia, Yugoslavia, and most brutally in Germany itself. Rape was viewed as part of the collective punishment to be meted out on the Germans, and one of the spoils of war. Statistics suggest that 95,000 to 130,000 female Berliners were raped in the siege of their city, and possibly 2 million German women overall during 1945. In addition, it has been calculated that anywhere between 150,000 and 200,000 babies fathered by Russian soldiers were born in Soviet-occupied Germany in 1945–46, a figure that excludes the many abortions that took place.[83]

Brutal treatment was visited on those women who were alleged to have slept with the enemy, what is sometimes called "horizontal collaboration." In the Soviet Union, their fate was the gulag; in France, Denmark, Italy, and throughout much of the rest of Europe they were in danger of public humiliation, of having their heads shaved, and possibly being paraded semi-naked with swastikas daubed on their breasts. During the war itself, the SS had tried to prevent fraternization with troops, especially in eastern Europe where the Nazis looked down on Slav women as racially impure, a concern the Italian occupying forces shared in the Balkans. In practice, such prohibitions were regularly flouted, for understandable reasons. Often separated from their own menfolk, women were confronted by occupying troops in large numbers who, in the words of the historian Anette Warring, presented both "a threat and an opportunity."[84] The threat of rape was always a consideration, forcing women into difficult situations when responding to sexual advances. It is small wonder that many chose to submit "voluntarily." Nor is it any surprise that, amid the uncertainties and drudgeries of war, the imperative to live for the moment, and the loosening of sexual mores, women were drawn to German soldiers, who were often better off, much younger, and more numerous than the indigenous male adult population. In France it is calculated that 200,000 children were born to German fathers.[85] The mothers of these infants, Warring suggests, were not necessarily "victims" or "collaborators" but ordinary people trying to navigate exceedingly difficult circumstances.

COMPORTMENT

The issue of fraternizing with the invader raises the final variable highlighted at the start of this essay, that of comportment.[86] What attitude should the population adopt towards the occupier? Few people welcomed either the Germans or the Soviets into their lives—the instinct was to adopt a wait-and-see attitude. This was understandable. It was a bold choice to enter into the Resistance, or join a collaborationist movement. It also appeared to many, in 1940–41, that protest was futile as the Germans seemed all-powerful, an image strengthened by the use of propaganda. Posters and newspapers were traditional forms of communication; new was the cinema and, crucially, the radio. In Nazi Germany, Goebbels mercilessly exploited the fact that most civilians possessed the *Volksempfänger*, the so-called people's radio, a cheap and relatively portable device. His broadcasts played up German victories, minimized Axis losses, and put out what is termed black propaganda, that is misleading and fabricated material designed to embarrass the enemy. However, control was never complete. More and more Europeans tuned in to the British Broadcasting Corporation (BBC), which Churchill himself utilized in the dark days of 1940. Overseen by the Ministry of Information, the BBC transmitted to the whole of the Continent, sending bulletins in numerous languages, renowned for their truthfulness, though Broadcasting House was not above putting out its own black propaganda, plus coded messages to resisters. Despite attempts to jam the airwaves, the Gestapo was aware that by 1944 most Germans were tuning in to the BBC rather than home stations.

Given the way in which the war was turning and the unpopularity of the occupier, it might seem strange that anyone chose to throw in their lot with the Nazis, yet there existed several collaborationist groups. Most emanated out of prewar far-right organizations: Quisling's Nasjonal Samling (Norway), Fritz Clausen's Storm-Afdelingr (Denmark), Doriot's Parti Populaire Français (France), and Léon Degrelle's Rexists (Belgium), to name but a few. There were also various separatist movements who welcomed the Germans, most infamously the Ustaša, which set out to destroy the two million Serbs caught within borders of the Nazi puppet-state of Croatia. Among Serbs themselves, national identity also influenced behavior patterns. Whereas Tito's communist-dominated Partisans sought to expel the Germans, there also emerged another partisan group, comprising elements of the army known as the Četniks, who wanted the restoration of Yugoslavia under a Serbian monarchy, but who were not always averse to working with the Germans. Separatism, ideological affinity with Nazism, anti-Semitism, hatred of communism, opportunism—these were some of the motivations behind collaborationism. It could also be added that many young collaborators may have been psychologically disturbed, misfits in society, looking for excitement, violence, and an authority otherwise denied them, for instance those *miliciens* portrayed in Jean Genet's 1947 novel, *Pompes funèbres (Funeral rights)*.[87]

Collaborationist movements were heterogeneous in their leadership, less so among the rank and file. Crudely speaking, in western Europe, the peasantry and working classes were under-represented; those predominating were urban based, young, male, and largely from the middle classes, broadly defined. Nowhere did collaborationist groups muster much support. In France, membership numbered around 150,000, though caution is needed when handling these figures. Support was deliberately exaggerated and was occasionally based on the distribution of newspapers, which were often dumped for want of sales. It was said Parisians bought collaborationist newspapers because German subsidies ensured they were printed on better quality paper good for starting fires and lining drawers.

The lack of a popular base is not hard to comprehend. Collaborationists were deeply factionalized, ideological differences from the 1930s spilling out into the open; they were associated, in the public mind, with the hardships of the war, notably hunger, though the collaborationists themselves seemed to prosper, frequently through the black market; their leaders were often opportunistic second-raters, lacking the charisma of a Mussolini or Hitler; and they were tainted by their close relationship with the Germans. Paradoxically it was this relationship that held them back the most. As the historian Dick Martin has remarked about the Netherlands, the Germans had no trust in collaborationist parties that were recognized to be unpopular, yet the Nazis made no effort to change this state of affairs. Hitler worried that these movements might become too powerful, thus challenging the Reich's hegemony.[88] Romania's ethno-fascist Iron Guard was especially feared, and Berlin drew a sigh of relief when it was suppressed by the Romanian government itself in 1941. Elsewhere a close watch was kept on collaborationists. In Hitler's eyes, their true worth lay in their military contribution: for instance, those Alsatians conscripted into the SS who took part in the last-ditch defense of Berlin; the Légion des Volontaires Français contre le Bolchevisme (LVF), which enlisted young Frenchmen to fight on the eastern front; the SS Galicia Division, composed of Ukrainian nationalists, which guarded the concentration camps; and the ad hoc armies composed of Ukrainian, Lithuanian, and Latvian POWs that cleared the Jewish ghettos in 1943–44.

It is frequently said that it was not essential to belong to a collaborationist group in order to collaborate in the widest sense of the term. The very presence of the occupier forced an element of association on local populations. Administrators, civil officials, and police officers (especially in Holland, Denmark, and Norway) quickly found that they were working alongside Germans, and later in the war, many were drawn into the maw of the Holocaust. Industrialists discovered that production had to be geared to the Nazi war economy, though some concerns, notably Renault, Gnome and Rhône, and Schneider-Creusot in France, adapted their markets without little demur. Shopkeepers and café owners were called upon to serve their German customers, and were not always above partaking in the black market. Playwrights, authors, actors, and singers had to decide whether to continue their activities, even though their audiences had changed. And, on a day-to-day basis, civilians had to determine their behavior towards occupying troops; for instance, whether to give up a seat in the train for a German. It is no surprise that relations with the occupier were ambiguous, and open to criticism at the Liberation. It was even possible to be both a resister and a collaborator. A frequent example given is that of railwaymen in France who were vaunted as resisters par excellence, for their role in disrupting the German war machine; yet these were the same railwaymen who had driven cattle trucks laden with Jews destined for the death camps. Perhaps the only way to escape suspicion was to avoid any open acknowledgement of the occupier, something nigh on impossible. Rare must have been the situation described in Vercors' 1951 novel, *Le Silence de la mer,* where an old man and his niece refuse to have anything to do with the German soldier billeted in their home, though even their resolve wavers in the end.

Generally speaking, resistance was slow to develop across Europe, its evolution determined by a series of factors, beginning with the behavior of the occupying forces themselves. Where the Nazis were reasonably well behaved, for instance Denmark, Holland, and Norway, people were slow to protest; it was when the Germans' conduct deteriorated that opposition mounted. Where the actions of the Nazi were wholly repugnant, for example in Poland, resistance was immediate, though the intensity of the German presence was another factor influencing the relative strength of resistance. This has been demonstrated in the case of France.[89] It might have been expected that it would have been in the northern areas, where the Germans were most evident, that resistance would have been strongest, yet historians have shown that clandestine groups were more influential in the Vichy zone, precisely because the Germans were absent. France, too, offers another insight into how resistance evolved. Historians have shown how protest frequently erupted in areas that had a long history of defiance, such as the Cévennes, where in the seventeenth century Huguenot protesters had challenged Louis XIV. Habits of protest were manifold in Poland, subject to occupation ever since the partitions of the late eighteenth century. Contrary to what is sometimes thought, Germany also possessed long traditions of protest—dating back to the 1848 revolutions and beyond—yet with the rise to power of Nazidom a conformist legacy had come to prevail, enforced by an extensive police apparatus. Dissent was further stifled by the propaganda of Nazi military triumphs. It was as the victories dried up that Germans became more questioning, though resistance was still a fragmented affair, perpetrated most energetically by individuals, church leaders, former trade unionists, and university students such as the White Rose group, which distributed anti-Hitler propaganda in the main entrance to Munich University. Resistance found its firmest expression among senior soldiers who had once worked with Hitler and who labored under the least suspicion—for instance, those involved in the abortive July 1944 bomb plot, orchestrated by Colonel von Stauffenburg, to assassinate the Führer.

Resistance behavior was extremely varied. Frequently this is associated with violent opposition. Within western Europe, military actions were in fact slow to emerge as the risks were too great: German reprisals were swift and indiscriminate in their choice of victims. In the East, the brutality of the conflict meant that violence was unceasing, especially in the USSR where partisans roamed behind enemy lines and were extensively supplied by the Red Army. As Konstantin Simonev's poem proclaimed, "Kill a German, kill him soon / And every time you see one—kill him!"[90] Other forms of resistance action were less spectacular, but no less significant: the publication and distribution of clandestine newspapers, some 3,500 titles alone in Holland, France, Belgium, Norway, and Denmark, which were vital in order to put across a different viewpoint to that peddled by the Nazi media; the setting up of networks so as to pass on military intelligence and facilitate the escape of allied airmen shot down over Europe; and industrial sabotage, go-slows, and strikes, commonplace in Italy, Holland, and Belgium by 1943–44. Alongside these varieties of active protest, which by their very nature drew on particular groups of civilians, there existed other forms of passive resistance, less spectacular types of protest, in which everyone could partake. The Germans gradually woke up to the ingenuity of this behavior, as evidenced in the following selective list of actions deemed punishable in occupied France: "chalking the V sign on military vehicles"; "adopting an anti-German attitude"; "ringing the doorbell of the German military police without reason"; "jostling German officers"; "listening to foreign radio stations"; "adopting an incorrect attitude to a German sentry."[91] Insulting the Germans had, in effect, become a national task. Police in fascist Italy proved equally sensitive, cracking down severely on those who spread jokes and made "pointed gossip" about the regime.[92]

In the eyes of some commentators, the manner in which Jews and others responded to genocide constituted another form of resistance—a refusal to give up one's cherished beliefs before the barbarity of Nazism.[93] It has even been claimed that a form of spiritual resistance was demonstrated by those Christians who observed regular patterns of religious observance, for instance attending weekly communion. Though such actions were certainly brave in Poland, where many clergy were persecuted and murdered, this ignores the fact that much of Europe underwent a religious revival during the war as people clung to their faith as a sign of continuity and turned to religion in search of personal solace. Pews were full again; the authority of priests was enhanced; pilgrimage sites, such as that at Le Puy in France, enjoyed a renewed popularity; a cult of the Virgin Mary flourished; crucifixes were placed in prominent places; and many Catholics took to carrying scapulas and amulets to ward off misfortune. This use of religion as a type of personal comfort had been witnessed before in World War One and, as has been observed, harked back even earlier to the tradition of "dearth, disease, devotion," noticeable in the eighteenth and nineteenth centuries.[94] The Cardinal of Mechelen in Belgium was so agitated by the reappearance of certain practices that he warned his flock to include others in their prayers and not just themselves. This spiritual revival would not last much beyond 1945, yet as a result of their shared sufferings Christians of all denominations frequently discovered that they had more in common with nonbelievers and their purported enemies than they had once assumed, notably communists. This was not, of course, the situation in the Nazi puppet states of Slovakia and Croatia, where the Catholic regimes of Jozef Tiso and Ante Pavelić attempted to eliminate their many ethno-religious enemies. It was fortunate for the longer-term reputation of the Roman Catholic Church that, elsewhere in Europe, Catholics were prominent in resistance, protecting Jews and others, this despite unambiguous teaching from Pius XII, who was hesitant to denounce the Holocaust for fear of intensifying persecution, a reluctance that some historians have since called wise and others (both Catholic and non-Catholic) have been highly critical of.[95] Within Holland and Belgium notably, Catholic prelates openly protested against the Nazification of their countries and came to encourage civil disobedience without necessarily intensifying the misery of Jews and other minorities.

Resistance drew on civilians from all walks of life, and was not just the work of eminent individuals. Entering a *maquis* camp in 1943, the writer Jean Guéhenno discovered several occupations represented: postmen, doctors, students, and schoolteachers like himself.[96] Because of the secrecy involved, and because of the ambiguity of resistance behavior, historians have been unable to quantify how many people were involved, but they are beginning to appreciate the involvement of groups hitherto ignored, in particular women, who partook in both active and passive resistance, yet who were overlooked in the distribution of honors at the end of the fighting. Thanks to the Nazi belief that women were biologically unassuming and unlikely to behave in a political manner, they were often able to carry out resistance acts unobserved, for instance the ferrying of information and the smuggling of armaments, though this chauvinistic mindset did not apply to Eastern Europe where everyone, men, women, and children, were perceived as putative partisans. Within western Europe, too, the Nazis grew increasingly suspicious of seemingly innocent activities, yet the absence of men within society meant that women could still perform resistance acts unnoticed.

The relationship between partisans and civilians was a complicated one. The need for secrecy meant that resisters were careful not to mention their activities to those among whom they lived and worked. This was despite the fact that many underground movements began among friends and professional networks. After the war, there was amazement when people learned that, unbeknown to one another, they had belonged to the same organization. When resistance groups became operational, they posed a series of dilemmas to civilians in the vicinity, something especially true in the countryside, where partisans were often dependent on supplies from villagers. These provisions were sometimes willingly given, sometimes not. The French novelist Georges Perec recalls how as a schoolboy, evacuated to southern France, he and other children were sent into the neighboring countryside with supplies in their rucksacks to be handed over to the *maquis*.[97] It was a considerable risk. Peasants and townspeople understood that, however much they disliked the Nazis, the presence of partisans could well attract unwelcome German attention, and visit reprisals on an area. Nor were resisters themselves always well behaved. Some established spheres of influence, and were not above organizing contraband, for instance in American cigarettes, which were highly prized throughout Europe. Everywhere there was a fear of the communists who came to dominate movements in Italy, France, and Greece. It was understood that the communists were not just fighting a war against the Nazis but often against their former adversaries. At the Liberation, summary justice was more often than not the work of the far left.

CONCLUSIONS

It would be reassuring to write the history of everyday life as a rejection of totalitarianism, but this was not so. The overriding instinct among civilians was to survive. Their ability to do so was largely determined by a series of factors over which people had little control: the proximity of battle; air raids; the behavior of the occupier; deportation and genocide; and the availability of food, warmth, and shelter. Small wonder war was experienced in a variety of ways. It is because of this diversity that many writers have preferred not to write the social history of World War Two on a European-wide scale, but have concentrated on a single country, or even a specific region. Yet, as this essay has shown, it is still possible to highlight certain generalities in the European experience. In the belligerent nations, this was a war impossible to avoid, one that equated to *displacement*. This was a war in which *government* intruded into all walks of life. This, too, was a war in which *adjustment* was a must as civilians held on to the familiar. The accompanying instinct was to do little to attract the attention of the authorities. That was not always possible, begging questions about *comportment.* Choices could not be put off forever, and left an agonizing legacy. The decisions made in wartime could not easily be sloughed off in peacetime, however much governments attempted to rewrite the past, burying uncomfortable truths about collaboration, resistance, and the Holocaust. Much remains to be said about the civilian experience of the World War Two; still more needs to be said about how that conflict has been remembered.

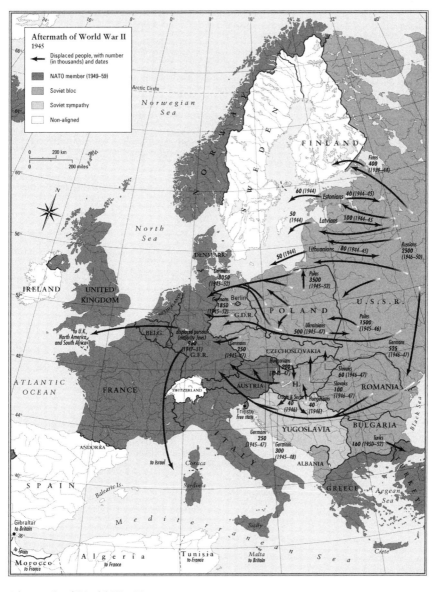

Aftermath of World War Two.

NOTES

1. These terms are borrowed from David S. Heidler and Jeanne T. Heidler, eds., *Daily Lives of Civilians in Wartime Early America* (Westport, Conn.: Greenwood, 2007).

2. Peter Gatrell, "World Wars and Population Displacement in Europe in the Twentieth Century," *Contemporary European History* 16, no. 4 (2007): 418.

3. See especially Daniel Snowman, *The Hitler Emigrés: The Cultural Impact on Britain of Refugees from Nazism* (London: Chatto and Windus, 2002).

4. Much of the subsequent discussion on movement is drawn from the author's article, "The Home Fronts: Europe at War, 1939–1945," in *A Companion to Europe, 1900–1945,* ed. Gordon Martel (Oxford: Blackwell, 2005), pp. 456–71, which also addresses several of the other themes in this chapter. The figures come from Peter Calvocoressi and Guy Wint, *Total War: Causes and Courses of the Second World War* (Harmondsworth: Allen Lane, 1972), pp. 218–19. For the movement of peoples, see the maps in G. Frumkin, *Population Changes in Europe since 1919* (London: George Allen and Unwin, 1951).

5. Richard Vinen, *The Unfree French: Life under the Occupation* (London: Allen Lane, 2006), p. 30.

6. TNA, HO 213 464 203/2/8, report of January 18, 1940.

7. Quotes from Juliet Gardiner, *Wartime: Britain, 1939–1945* (London: Headline, 2004), p. xvi, p. 17.

8. Richard Titmuss, *History of the Second World War: Problems of Social Policy* (London: HMSO, 1950), p. 111.

9. See especially the memoir by the English historian Alistair Horne, *A Bundle from Britain* (London: Macmillan, 1994); and Michael Henderson, *See You after the Duration: The Story of British Evacuees to North America in World War II* (London/Baltimore: PublishBritannica, 2004).

10. See Rebecca Manley, "The Perils of Displacement: The Soviet Evacuee between Refugee and Deportee," *Contemporary European History,* 16, no. 4 (2007): 495–509.

11. See especially Anne Applebaum, *Gulag: A History of the Soviet Camps* (London: Penguin, 2004).

12. See Ulrich Herbert, *Hitler's Foreign Workers: Enforced Foreign Labour in Germany under the Third Reich* (Cambridge: Cambridge University Press, 1997).

13. Eugene M. Kulischer, *Europe on the Move: War and Population Changes, 1917–47* (New York: Columbia University Press, 1948), p. 253.

14. Primo Levi, *The Truce* (London: Abacus, 1987).

15. George Orwell, *The Collected Essays: Journalism and Letters of George Orwell,* vol. 2, *My Country, Right or Left: 1940–1943* (London: Secker & Warburg, 1968), pp. 342–43, also quoted in Nicholas Atkin, *The Forgotten French: Exiles in the British Isles, 1940–1944* (Manchester: Manchester University Press, 2003), p. 30, which makes the same point as here.

16. Among the most recent of these is the extraordinary novel by the Russian *émigré* to France, Irène Némirovsky, published posthumously in 2004 after her death in Auschwitz: *Suite Française* (London: Chatto and Windus, 2006).

17. Atkin, *The Forgotten French,* pp. 51–52.

18. Neville Lytton, *Life in Unoccupied France* (London: Macmillan, 1942), p. 13.

19. See H. R. Kedward, "Patriots and Patriotism in Vichy France," *Transactions of the Royal Historical Society*, 5th series, 32 (1982): 175–92.

20. See Atkin, *The Forgotten French*, p. 38.

21. Jean-Paul Sartre, *Iron in the Soul* (London: Penguin, 2004).

22. Primo Levi, *If Not Now, When?* (Harmondsworth: Penguin, 2000), p. 56.

23. David French, "The Real War," in Martel, *A Companion to Europe*, p. 452.

24. On Oradour see Sarah Farmer, *Martyred Village: Commemorating the 1944 Massacre at Oradour sur Glane* (Berkeley: University of California Press, 2000).

25. Richard Overy, "The Second World War," in *The Oxford Illustrated History of Modern War*, ed. C. Townshend (Oxford: Oxford University Press, 1997), chapter 17.

26. Robert Mengin, *No Laurels for de Gaulle* (London: Constable, 1967), p. 69.

27. Vera Brittain, *England's Hour* (London: Continuum, 2005), pp. 142–43.

28. Quoted in Robert Gildea, *Marianne in Chains: In Search of the German Occupation, 1940–45* (London: Macmillan, 2002), p. 305.

29. See Andrew Knapp, "The Destruction and Liberation of Le Havre in Modern Memory," *War in History*, 14, no. 4 (2007): 476–98.

30. See Jorg Friedrich, *The Fire: The Bombing of Germany, 1940–1945* (New York: Columbia University Press, 2006); and A. C. Grayling, *Among the Dead Cities: Is the Targeting of Civilians in War Ever Justified?* (London: Bloomsbury, 2007).

31. See Frederick Taylor, *Dresden, Tuesday 13 February 1945* (London: HarperCollins, 2004), as well as Paul Addison and Jeremy Crang, eds., *Firestorm: The Bombing of Dresden 1945* (London: Pimlico, 2006).

32. Figures, and much of the information for this paragraph, come from I.C.B. Dear, ed., *The Oxford Companion to World War Two* (Oxford: Oxford University Press, 2001), pp. 224–27. See too Tony Judt, *Postwar: A History of Europe since 1945* (London: William Heinemann, 2005), pp. 18–19; and Norman Davies, *Europe at War, 1939–1945: No Simple Victory* (London: Allen Lane, 2006), pp. 364–68.

33. R.A.C. Parker, *Struggle for Survival: The History of the Second World War* (Oxford: Oxford University Press, 1989), p. 285.

34. The words belong to Werner Rings, *Life With the Enemy: Collaboration and Resistance in Hitler's Europe, 1939–1945* (London: Weidenfeld and Nicolson, 1982), p. 21.

35. Michael Burleigh, *The Third Reich: A New History* (London: Pan, 2000), p. 410.

36. Henri Michel, *Shadow War: Resistance in Europe, 1939–1945* (London: Deutsch, 1972), pp. 21–22. See, too, Atkin, "The Home Fronts," p. 457.

37. On German administration, see Bernard Kroener, R.-D. Muller, and Hans Umbreit, eds., *Germany and the Second World War* (Oxford: Oxford University Press, 2000), vol. 5, part 1. For the experience of East Europeans, see D. Mayer, *Non Germans under the Third Reich* (Baltimore, Md.: John Hopkins, 2003).

38. Much of the information here comes from Jill Stephenson, "Occupation and Resistance," in *The Experience of World War II*, ed. John Campbell (London: Grange, 1989), pp. 182–83.

39. See Hans Fredrik Dahl, *Quisling: A Study in Treachery* (Cambridge: Cambridge University Press, 1989).

40. See Nathaniel Hong, *Sparks of Resistance: The Illegal Press in German Occupied Denmark* (Odense: University of Southern Denmark Press, 1996).

41. The classic work on occupied France remains Robert O. Paxton, *Vichy France: Old Guard and New Order, 1940–1944* (New York: Knopf, 1972). On civilian

life, see Richard Vinen, *The Unfree French: Life Under the Occupation* (London: Penguin, 2006).

42. Julian Jackson, *The Dark Years: France 1940–1944* (Oxford: Oxford University Press, 2001).

43. Quoted in Philippe Burin, *La France à l'heure allemande* (Paris: Seuil, 1995), p. 188.

44. Richard J. B. Bosworth, *Mussolini's Italy* (London: Allen Lane, 2006). See too Louis de Bernières, *Captain Corelli's Mandolin* (London: Vintage, 1995). See the review of this book in *The Economist*, October 6, 2005, which draws the comparisons with *Captain Corelli's Mandolin*.

45. Davies, *Europe at War*, p. 306.

46. Quoted in Rings, *Life with the Enemy*, n.p.

47. Rings, *Life with the Enemy*, p. 138, stresses how Jewish elders were given no choice in the matter. See Yirael Gutman and Cynthia J. Haft, eds., *Patterns of Jewish Leadership in Nazi Europe, 1933–1945* (Jerusalem: Yad Vashem, 1979).

48. Walter Szpilman, *The Pianist* (London: Orion, 2005).

49. Davies, *Europe at War*, p. 306. See too K. C. Berkhoff, *Harvest of Despair: Life and Death in Ukraine under Nazi Rule* (Cambridge, Mass.: Harvard University Press, 2001).

50. Richard Overy, *The Dictators: Hitler's Germany and Stalin's Russia* (London: Allen Lane, 2004), p. 504, for a discussion and firm rebuttal of this argument. See, too, Atkin, "The Home Fronts," for a similar discussion.

51. M. Roseman, "World War II and Social Change in Germany," in *Total War and Historical Change. Europe 1914–1955*, ed. Arthur Marwick, Clive Emsley, and W. Simpson (Buckingham: Open University Press, 2001), p. 247.

52. Davies, *Europe at War*, p. 298.

53. Anthony Beevor, introduction to *A Woman in Berlin: Diary 20 April 1945 to 22 June 1945* (London: Virago, 2005), p. 7.

54. Figures are from Dear, *The Oxford Companion*, p. 302.

55. For an introduction to the Russian home front, see J. Barber and Mark Harrison, *The Soviet Home Front: A Social and Economic History of the USSR in World War II* (London: Longman, 1991) and S. J. Linz, *The Impact of World War II on the Soviet Union* (Totowata, N.J.: Rowman and Allanheld, 1985).

56. Richard Overy, *Why the Allies Won*, 2nd ed. (London: Pilmlico, 2006), p. 223.

57. Alexander Werth, *Russia at War* (New York: Dutton, 1964), p. 168.

58. This episode is recalled in Overy, *Why the Allies Won*, p. 220.

59. Werth, *Russia at War*, p. 218.

60. Quoted in Rodric Braithwaite, *Moscow 1941: A City and Its People at War* (London: Profile Books, 2006), p. 170.

61. Mollie Panter-Downes, *London War Notes, 1939–1945* (London: Longman, 1971), p. 21.

62. See Corelli Barnett, *The Audit of War: The Illusion and Reality of Britain as a Great Nation* (London: Macmillan, 1986).

63. On Britain, see Sonya Rose, *Which People's War? National Identity and Citizenship in Wartime Britain, 1939–1945* (Cambridge: Cambridge University Press, 2003) and Jose Harris, "Britain and the Home Front during the Second World War," in *The World War Two Reader*, ed. Gordon Martel (London: Routledge, 2004).

64. Ian F. W. Beckett, "Total War," in Marwick, Emsley, and Simpson, *Total War*, p. 38.

65. Mark Harrison, " 'Barbarossa': The Soviet Response," in Marwick, Emsley, and Simpson, *Total War*, p. 222.

66. See, for example, the collections of government recipes reproduced in *Eating for Victory: Healthy Home Front Cooking on War Rations*, Reproductions of Official Second World War Instruction Leaflets (London: Michael O'Mara Books, 2007).

67. Polymeris Voglis, "Surviving Hunger: Life in the Cities and Countryside during the Occupation," in *Surviving Hitler and Mussolini: Daily Life in Occupied Europe*, ed. Robert Gildea, Olivier Wieviorka, and Anette Warring (Oxford: Berg, 2006), p. 29, pp. 16–41.

68. Paul Simon, *One Enemy Only—The Invader* (London: Hodder and Stoughton, 1942), p. 117.

69. Henry A. Van der Zee, *The Hunger Winter: Occupied Holland* (Lincoln: University of Nebraska Press, 1998), p. 147. See too Ralf Futselaar, *Lard, Lice and Longevity: A Comparative Study of the Standards of Living in Occupied Denmark and the Netherlands, 1940–1945* (Amsterdam: Aksant Academic Publishers, 2007).

70. Szpilman, *The Pianist*, p. 110.

71. Bosworth, *Mussolini's Italy*, p. 483.

72. Judt, *Postwar*, p. 19.

73. For an introduction, see K. Anderson, *Wartime Women: Sex Roles, Family Relations and the Status of Women during World War II* (Westport, Conn.: Greenwood, 1981); and Penny Summerfield, *Women Workers in the Second World War: Production and Patriarchy* (London: Croom Helm, 1984).

74. See the discussion by Janet Howarth in Dear, *Oxford Companion*, pp. 997–1002.

75. Susan K. Foley, *Women in France since 1789* (Basingstoke: Palgrave, 2004), p. 235.

76. Of Mary Wesley's work, see especially her *The Camomile Lawn* (London: Black Swan, 1984).

77. Quentin Crisp, *The Naked Civil Servant* (London: Harper Perennial, 2007), pp. 157–58.

78. William D. Halls, *The Youth of Vichy France* (Oxford: Clarendon, 1981), pp. 175–76.

79. *The Guardian*, March 31, 2006.

80. Vinen, *The Unfree French*, p. 171.

81. See Joanna Bourke, *Rape: A History from the 1860s to the Present* (London: Virago, 2007).

82. Davies, *Europe at War*, p. 338.

83. Judt, *Postwar*, pp. 20–21.

84. Anette Warring, "Intimate and Sexual Relations," in Gildea et al., *Surviving Hitler and Mussolini*, p. 90, pp. 88–128. See too Fabrice Virgili, *Shorn Women: Gender and Punishment in Liberation France* (Oxford: Berg, 2002) and M. R. Higonnet, Jane Jenson, Sonya Michel, and M. C. Weitz, eds., *Behind the Lines: Gender and the Two World Wars* (New Haven, Conn., and London: Yale University Press, 1987).

85. Jean-Paul Picaper and Ludwig Norz, *Enfants Maudits* (Paris: Editions des Syrtes, 2004).

86. See Rab Bennett, *Under the Shadow of the Swastika: The Moral Dilemmas of Resistance and Collaboration in Hitler's Europe* (Basingstoke: Macmillan, 1999).

87. Jean Genet's 1947 novel, *Pompes funèbres*, was originally published anonymously by Gallimard because of its homosexual subject matter.

88. Dick Martin, "The Benelux Countries During the Second World War: Between Collaboration and Resistance," in *Conditions and Politics in Occupied Western Europe, 1940–1945* (London: Thomson, 2006), p. 3.

89. H. R. Kedward, *Resistance in Vichy France* (Oxford: Oxford University Press, 1978).

90. Quoted in Joanna Bourke, *The Second World War: A People's History* (Oxford: Oxford University Press, 2001), p. 135.

91. Halls, *Youth*, p. 53.

92. Bosworth, *Mussolini's Italy*, p. 477, p. 480.

93. Atkin, "The Home Fronts," p. 466.

94. Much of the information and argument here comes from Nicholas Atkin and Frank Tallett, *Priests, Prelates and People: A History of European Catholicism since 1750* (London: Tauris, 2003), p. 262.

95. The controversial role of Pius XII can be followed in John Cornwell's hostile work, *Hitler's Pope: The Secret History of Pius XII* (New York: Viking, 1999); Susan Zuccotti's scathing book, *Under His Very Windows: The Vatican and the Holocaust in Italy* (New Haven, Conn.: Yale University Press, 2001); and J. M. Sánchez's defense, *Pius XII and the Holocaust* (Washington, D.C.: Catholic University Press, 2001).

96. Jean Guéhenno, *Journal des Années Noires, 1940–1944* (Paris: Gallimard, 1973).

97. Georges Perec, *W, or the Memory of Childhood* (Boston: Godine, 1988), p. 114.

SIX

Writing the History of Daily Life in the Cold War

Frank Tallett

NEW APPROACHES TO MILITARY HISTORY

The writing of military history has come a long way in recent decades. For a long time it remained the preserve of ex-military men concerned almost obsessively with operational details, and it was chiefly written and read in order to teach officers how to do their jobs better. This was quite proper, because past conflicts provide an essential guide to members of the military profession. However, in the hands of its worst practitioners, this form of military history became little more than the listing of "one damn battle after another." This approach is still to be found today. But it began to be challenged a generation ago by the rise of what is still termed the "new military history," even though this type of history is now anything but new. As Nicholas Atkin writes at the start of this volume, the "new military history" insisted that war had to be placed in its social, economic, and institutional contexts, by focusing upon the interface between war and society, and that to achieve this blend new methodological approaches would be required.[1] Accordingly, historians started to look at topics such as the social composition of armed forces,[2] the role of women in them,[3] the relationship between bureaucratic change and military conflict, and war's impact on the development of the state.[4] So pervasive did this approach to military history become that, for a time, it was all but impossible to produce a respectable monograph without the word "society" featuring at some point in its title. The defect of this approach was that it concentrated so much on the "peripheries" of warfare that it ceased to grapple, or in some instances to be concerned at all with, the central business of armies and navies: *fighting.*

Although the "war and society" approach to military history has not been dethroned, it has nevertheless tended to interlard with a third discourse, which takes the best of both preceding schools and finds new value in the study of operational details, provided these are set within a broader context. This third approach, which for brevity's sake might be referred to as the "newest military history," recognizes that, in the final analysis, armies and navies were there to fight, that in order to understand how they fought it is necessary to know about the complexity of war, especially in the industrial age, and that this knowledge needs to inform any assessment about the outcome of battles and campaigns, and their wider significance for the armed forces, states, and individuals involved in them.[5]

The reasons for this paradigm shift in the approach to military history are various. On the one hand, the "new military history" was born out of a recognition, particularly after World War Two, that the conduct of war was too serious a business to be left to the generals, and that the study of war was too important to be left in the hands of military men. It sprang, too, out of a wider vibrancy in the historical profession, which, in the 1960s and 1970s, began to discover novel areas of exploration, such as gender, race, and anthropology, and more recently themes of memory and culture, which were subsequently incorporated into the history of war. There was also some hint of self-preservation in the adoption of a wider agenda, an awareness that military history, which had never had much academic respectability, would simply cease to exist as a scholarly specialty if it did not broaden its vision. To be sure, the success of this new approach in rescuing military history from academic annihilation is questionable. In both Britain and the United States it remains popular with the public (albeit in its "drum and trumpet" form), but it still retains a rather shaky presence on university curricula, although it is now accepted that some knowledge of war is integral to an understanding of political and societal developments more generally.

A final spur to the development of the writing of military history has been the changing nature of warfare itself. Although the two World Wars fitted relatively easily into the state-versus-state paradigm of conflict that had held good since at least the nineteenth century, subsequent conflicts have been more obviously asymmetrical, often consisting of low-intensity, guerrilla, and counter-insurgency operations. There has been an increased diversity of force structures, fighting methods, and objectives since 1945; force of arms can no longer be used to impose political goals but instead must be used to create conditions in which those goals can be achieved; conflicts have been embedded in confrontations, and it is recognized that a victory may be achieved in one of these areas but not the other; the *theater* of operations has become increasingly exactly that, a public arena that participants in the conflict have to use to influence onlookers.[6] As warfare has altered, it has accordingly become necessary for military historians to review the sort of meta-narrative that privileged technological superiority as the key to victory in interstate conflicts and that assumed that there was some kind of ranking to military capabilities that could be used to predict the outcome of conflict.

The results of these new approaches to military history have been enormously impressive. Medieval and early modern specialists were among the first to recognize their value. Indeed, it might have come as a surprise to some medievalists to be told that they were writing "new military history," because they had long appreciated that they were dealing with a society dominated by, and imbued with, the ideals of a military caste.[7] In Britain, it was the seminal work of Michael Roberts, published in 1956, on the notion of a "military revolution" in early modern Europe that did much to bring about change in the writing of military history by positing a clear link between military change and wider developments.[8] Though his ideas remained untested and unchallenged for some while, his thesis has been the vehicle used by many scholars to revaluate the relationship between military and political/administrative developments in the early modern period. Gone are the days when a final, separate chapter entitled "Armies and Navies" was the obligatory ending to a textbook; military matters are now perceived as integral to an understanding of social, political, and intellectual movements, rather than being divorced from them.[9]

Modern historians, by contrast, were relatively slow to recognize the value of the new approaches to military history. But here too, enormous progress has been made. For example, François Cochet's *Soldats Sans Armes* probes the effects of imprisonment and repatriation on prisoners of war in a series of conflicts ranging from the Franco-Prussian war of 1870–1871 to the wars in the former Yugolsavia.[10] Gary Sheffield has explored the impact and use of memory in relation to World War One.[11] Denis Showalter has signaled the significance of military affairs at both the operational and strategic level for German unification.[12] Vejas Liulevicius has analyzed the implications for the populations of German-occupied Latvia, Kurland, and Lithuania of the interplay between operational details, strategy, and ideology after 1914.[13] Even the study of battle has been renewed, beginning with John Keegan's brilliantly evocative *The Face of Battle* and continuing with Joanna Bourke's *An Intimate History of Killing* and John Lynn's *Battle*.[14]

Civilians have been at the heart of new approaches to the writing of military history. This is scarcely surprising given military developments in the twentieth century. Not only did the two World Wars witness first a blurring then an eradication of the distinction between the home and fighting fronts but, as war *among* the people has replaced war *between* the peoples, and as troops are increasingly forced to operate in contact with civilians, so the study of war has increasingly come to encompass some greater consideration of how civilians affect and are affected by conflict.

Accordingly, civilians have figured in a variety of roles in scholarly studies: for example, as camp followers, as victims of the armed forces, as resisters to oppression, as black-marketers, as refugees and evacuees, and as workers in the war economies that were essential to military success, especially in the two World Wars.[15] The essays in this volume enshrine the very best of the "Newest Military History," because they encapsulate the view that the civilian experience should be studied both in its own right but also as part of a total explanation of how, why, and with what effects wars have been fought.

Approaches to the History of the Cold War

If much has been achieved, much remains to be done. A case in point is the Cold War. It has long been understood that relations between states "lay along a continuum ranging from all-out enmity to all-out friendship,"[16] with varying gradations of neutrality and cold war in between. However, the expression "Cold War" has come to be reserved for that period of history between, roughly, the end of World War Two on the one hand and the fall of the Berlin Wall in 1989 and the formal dissolution of the Soviet Union on December 25, 1991, on the other. The Cold War is appropriately named because it reflects the fact that, in the bipolar world inaugurated by World War Two, conflict between the two superpowers, the Soviet Union and the United States, never became an all-out conflagration, though on two occasions—the 1948–1949 blockade of Berlin and the Cuban missile crisis of 1963—it came very close.[17]

The historiography of the Cold War is now extensive, but it tends to center upon a number of core questions: when did it begin, who was responsible, was the Cold War inevitable or avoidable, what did the Cold War comprise, why did it endure for over 40 years?[18] Orthodox history, which placed the responsibility for the freezing over of the Cold War squarely on the shoulders of an expansionist Soviet Union, keen to secure a hegemony of Eastern Europe in defense of its security interests and to advance the cause of communism throughout the world,[19] began to be challenged in the 1960s and 1970s by revisionist scholars, influenced by U.S. involvement in Vietnam. Such writers were dissatisfied with notions of American "containment" of Soviet expansion and proffered a rethinking of the U.S. role in international affairs, for which Washington itself had to take responsibility.[20]

While shifting responsibility for the Cold War away from the Soviet Union, such scholars also challenged the assumption that the origins of the conflict dated no further back than the immediate postwar period, arguing for its emergence either with the use of atomic weapons against Japan; or with the failure of the Western Allies to open a second front early on in World War Two; or with the Bolshevik revolution of 1917, which created two antagonistic ideological camps; or with the trade rivalry between the United States and Russia in the nineteenth century; or even in the early modern period when Russia retained a distinct distance from European affairs.[21] These writers pointed out that decades of mutual suspicion preceded May 1945 and the traditional start of the Cold War, and that the USSR's war against Germany between 1941 and 1945 had merely masked long-standing distrust between the liberal democracies of the West and Russian/Soviet totalitarianism.

A post-revisionist phase in Cold War studies, prompted by the opening of U.S. archives, suggested an even more nuanced view of U.S.-Soviet relations and sought not so much to ascribe blame but to understand the actions of both sides as part of a process of interaction.[22] Thus the Soviet Union's explosion of its first atomic bomb, the formation of defensive alliances including NATO, SEATO (Southeast Asia Treaty Organization), and the Warsaw Pact in 1955 came to be seen as understandable responses of states looking after their national interests. After 1989, a new history of the Cold War began to take shape, helped by the ending of the conflict and the increasing availability of Warsaw Pact archive material, and drawing upon a methodology of multiarchival research and a multipolar analysis.[23] Much of this recent rethinking occurred within an emerging set of theories about the nature of international relations, which may broadly be characterized as neorealist and constructivist.[24]

There has been less ambiguity about the ways in which the Cold War manifested itself: in economic competition, in an arms race, in "little wars" fought by proxy in the developing world, and in "culture wars" in which both the Soviets and Americans vaunted the merits of their respective politico-economic systems.[25] Inevitably these struggles affected different states in different ways, most obviously the two Germanys; and the internal politics of the Eastern Bloc states have accordingly attracted considerable attention.[26] Remarkably few contemporaries foresaw the abrupt ending of the Cold War, which again has raised a series of questions: was it Western pressure or the inability of the Soviet Union to maintain its vast industrial-military complex that brought about collapse; and what have been the consequences of the breakup of the old Soviet empire?[27]

CIVILIANS IN THE COLD WAR

This historiography has enormously enriched our understanding of the origins of the Cold War and of the ideologies and economic/military standoffs that underpinned it. However, the Cold War has generally been approached from the standpoint of high politics, and its impact on civilians remains relatively neglected. Admittedly, there have been some recent attempts to shift the focus away from the negotiating table to everyday experiences and cultural meaning, and to examine in particular the politicization of daily life.[28] Additionally, there exists a formidable literature on how the United States experienced the "Red Scare,"[29] but the coverage of Europe is far less even.

This neglect of civilian experience may appear surprising, given that the Cold War was fought, at least in part, over "rival ways of life."[30] Yet the reasons for this overall lack of attention, and the patchy nature of Cold War studies, are not hard to discern. It is difficult to put together an overview of an experience that varied enormously between individual states as well as between the United States and the Western and Eastern Blocs more generally. In the case of the liberal democracies, the very openness and permeability of their societal structures makes generalizations hazardous. In the case of Eastern Europe, there was for a long time an absence of primary materials; and the inherent difficulties in researching archives that have only recently been opened up to historians have been compounded by government sensitivities about the conduct of their predecessors and alarm by Cold War contemporaries about revelations from the past. A book such as Anna Funder's 2003 *Stasiland*, which uses the recently released archives of the East German secret police to relive the bleak and oppressive world of the GDR would have been impossible to contemplate before 1990.[31] Troublingly, such a book might not again be possible as these archives are simply misplaced and destroyed.

Moreover, the civilian experience of the Cold War was mediated by a whole range of factors that again render generalization difficult. One was class, broadly defined. In Eastern Europe, for example, those groups on the *nomenklatura* had privileged access to goods and services that obviated the tedium and deprivations of everyday life. Religion was another important variable that operated in a number of ways. The end of World War Two and the extension of Russian hegemony brought several million believers, including over five million Catholics as well as Protestants and members of the Orthodox Church, into the orbit of an avowedly atheist Soviet regime.[32] Pius XII's decree of 1949, which prohibited Catholics from membership in the communist party, forbade them from reading communist literature, and removed the sacraments from any Catholic who was a party member or publicist, not only affirmed the tensions between communist regimes and Christianity, but confronted many priests and lay believers with difficult choices of conscience. Throughout the Eastern Bloc, ministries were established to oversee the conduct of religious life. The Orthodox Church complied fairly readily with this new bureaucratic intrusion, as did the Lutheran sects in East Germany (though they would later play a key role in creating a non-communist civil space). There was much more defiance in Protestant areas of Czechoslovakia, however, and from the hierarchical Catholic Church. Practicing believers found themselves discriminated against in a variety of ways, and prominent Church leaders, the best known of whom include Father Józef Tiso in Slovakia, Archbishop Stepinac in Yugoslavia, and Cardinal Mindszenty in Hungary, were imprisoned or put on trial. In practice, however, persecution of believers of all religious groupings varied both geographically and chronologically. It was probably worst in Albania, which did not of course fall directly into the Soviet orbit, though it was led by the hard-line communist Enver Hoxha. After the downfall of Khrushchev in 1964, there was some relaxation of pressure on religious believers as it came to be realized that outright violence could prove counterproductive.

In analyzing the civilian experience of the Cold War there is above all the difficulty of determining what elements of that experience to ascribe to the Cold War and what resulted from contingent circumstances. This is a judgment made more difficult because the experience was not consistent but altered over time. Accordingly, what follows is less a series of definitive conclusions than a set of preliminary analyses and suggestions for future research.

WHEN THE COLD WAR GOT "HOT"

It should be recognized at the outset that any understanding of the experience of civilians during the Cold War needs to be conducted at a number of levels. For some civilians, the Cold War was actually a very hot one. Although the two principals in the struggle, the United States and the Soviet Union, never came directly to blows, there were a number of proxy conflicts, of varying intensity, in which the two superpowers tested each other's weaponry, ideological commitment, and resolve. The best known of these proxy conflicts were the Korean, Indo-Chinese, and Arab-Israeli wars. But Africa would also become drawn into the rhetoric and divisions of the Cold War, especially after the Suez crisis in 1956. In the 1970s, 50,000 Cubans would be sent to Angola backed by Soviet money, arms, and advisers; and Soviet, Cuban, and South Yemeni troops operated in the Somali-populated Ogaden region. In the same decade, the Soviet Union, the United States, France, and Belgium sent aid to their respective client groups in Guinea, Mali, Mauritania, Nigeria, and Uganda. Moreover, despite U.S. determination to keep Cold War struggles as close to the Soviet Union and as far away from its own backyard as possible, superpower antagonisms spilled over into Latin America. U.S. covert operations in Cuba and Nicaragua were both located in the context of the Cold War, as was intervention in the Dominican Republic in 1965. U.S. advisers helped to train Colombian and Bolivian forces in counterinsurgency; and the United States supported coups against Marxist governments in Guatemala (1954) and Chile, where the Allende regime was toppled by general Pinochet (1973).

Not surprisingly, in many of these proxy conflicts the conditions for civilians resembled those in any conventional conflict. Civilians were forced out of their homes; they had to endure deprivation, rape and ill-treatment; and they became the victims of deliberate or accidental killing. However, these proxy conflicts often brought with them a heightened level of suffering and deaths, for a number of reasons.[33] They tended to be protracted affairs, sustained as they were by the resources and intervention of the superpowers. Moreover, they were embittered by ideological pressures. Some of these tensions derived from the fact that the wars were frequently struggles for self-determination and decolonization, but grafted onto them were the ideological tensions which lay at the heart of the Cold War. Ideological commitment commonly produced indifference toward civilian suffering and neglect of human rights. The war in Vietnam would be a case in point.[34]

The "limited war" theory that informed U.S. thinking in Vietnam, that unacceptable losses could be inflicted by each side on the other, was not shared by the North Vietnamese. The Viet Cong were prepared to accept heavy losses and were prepared to see the civilian population subjected to sufferings much greater than those considered acceptable by the United States government, which had to bear in mind the opinion of the public, which watched the war daily on its television screens.[35] The result was a conflict in which the civilians suffered terribly. Merely to take one instance among many: the city of Hué during the 1968 Tet offensive. Most of Hué had fallen into the hands of the Viet Cong by January 31 and was not regained by U.S. and South Vietnamese troops until February 25. In this short interval, around five thousand inhabitants had been killed by the Viet Cong or had otherwise "disappeared" on the grounds that they belonged to unacceptable social categories. Additionally, about half the city had been destroyed by artillery and air fire, resulting in some 100,000 refugees or homeless persons. During the war, civilian suffering extended beyond the borders of Vietnam. Cambodia came under attack in 1970 and there was an invasion of Laos by the North Vietnamese the following year. Over half of the $200 billion spent by the United States on the war went to air power, and over eight million tons of bombs were dropped on Vietnam, Laos, and Cambodia during the course of the struggle. South Vietnam suffered more than the North. It became the most bombed country in the history of warfare,[36] though if the proponents of air power had been allowed their way and operations such as Rolling Thunder (the unrestricted bombing of the North) had been allowed to continue after 1968, the South's unenviable record in this regard would have been challenged.

GETTING AND SPENDING: MATERIAL
CONDITIONS AND THE COLD WAR

If we turn from those areas where the Cold War became a hot one and look at the civilian experience in the United States and in Western Europe on the one hand, and at the Soviet Union and the rest of Eastern Europe on the other, there is an obvious contrast in the material conditions to be discerned. Much of Europe lay in ruins in 1945, and even those areas that had not been overrun or suffered directly from the fighting were exhausted. George C. Marshall, brought out of retirement to be secretary of state in 1947, recognized that there was a moral as well as an economic crisis to be addressed in Europe, though the two were intertwined. He and others in the United States feared that liberal democracy, being restored to France, Italy, West Germany, and elsewhere, might come to be equated with turmoil and hardship. For their part, the Soviets offered an alternative model to prewar capitalism, which had apparently brought little benefit, and in many states, including France and Italy, there existed communist parties with a strong electoral appeal. If Europe was to be saved for democracy, then American intervention was needed. This determination was confirmed by the Greek crisis of 1947, when Britain had to admit that it could no longer sustain the conflict there, opening up the possibility not just of the fall of that country to communism but of the whole of the eastern Mediterranean. Accordingly, Marshall brought forward to June 1947 the announcement of a project, carrying his name, designed to permit the emergence of social and political conditions in which democratic institutions could exist. The Marshall Plan, which involved the injection of around $17 billion in cash and the establishment of free trade conditions, would strengthen the hand of those in Europe who wanted free-market economics and open, pluralistic politics. Marshall was reasonably certain that the Plan would be well received in Europe, though inside the United States there was more opposition. An earlier project, the so-called Morgenthau Plan of 1941, had envisaged stripping Germany of its industrial base and reducing the country to a pastoral economy, and many Americans still considered in 1945 that something along these lines remained the best option. The Cold War helped Marshall to overcome his critics; in his view Germany, as well as the rest of Europe, had to be restored to prosperity if it was to be saved from communism.

Seventeen countries agreed to participate in the Marshall Plan, though this did not include Franco's Spain, nor the Soviet Union or its satellites, many of which came together in the Moscow-centered Comecon (the Council for Mutual Economic Assistance), established in 1948, and designed to facilitate cooperation among communist and Eastern Bloc nations. Comecon, however, could not hope to match Marshall aid, whose assistance began to be felt as early as 1948. To be sure, some slow economic recovery in Western Europe had already begun to get under way by that time. But it was greatly stimulated by American aid, and the Marshall Plan was enormously significant in helping to bring about the material well-being and high levels of employment that underpinned so many other social and political developments in the postwar era. In the last resort, the Plan was crucial as much for the psychological boost that it gave to Europe, as for its economic input. By raising optimism and proffering a different way forward, it helped a new generation of politicians to come to the fore with policies based on collaboration, open frontiers, and long-term investment, ideals that would be embraced within the project for European integration, and it thus helped to ensure that Western Europe would be rescued from a new totalitarianism.

In effect, the Marshall Plan and the Soviet domination of Eastern Europe established two models for economic, social, and political development: an American and a Soviet one. The new regimes in Eastern Europe, watched over by Comecon, followed the Soviet model of change, but accomplished in 5 years what had taken 30 years in Russia under Lenin and Stalin. Large landed estates were sequestrated and handed over to ordinary peasants and farmers. Such a redistribution not only accorded with a Soviet model, it was seen as a way of securing the loyalty of the peasantry who, the Left believed, had proved particularly susceptible to fascist and nationalist blandishments and who might again form the basis for a revival of right-wing regimes. Whole classes of landed gentry and large farmers thus disappeared in Poland, Hungary, Romania, Yugoslavia, and East Prussia. Collectivization of agriculture quickly followed within a few years. Although it proceeded without quite the same ruthlessness that had characterized the process in the Soviet Union under Stalin, those who resisted faced arrest, deportation, or financial coercion. Apart from Poland and Yugoslavia, by the 1960s most farmland was collectivized. At the same time as land was sequestrated, industry too was put under state control, and there was a push to develop heavy industries. Central planning institutions controlled the direction of the economy by establishing targets for output, prices for consumer products, and wage rates, while state banks orchestrated financial investment.[37]

The social impact of the managed economy was significant, involving as it did rapid industrialization and urbanization, though both of these probably would have happened in any event, albeit not so swiftly nor so extensively. There was a sharp decline in the proportion of the population living and working in the countryside, with the exception of Albania. This shift proved traumatic for many people, yet socialist polices promoting subsidized health care, housing, education, and guaranteed employment were better received. Moreover, as in the West, the immediate postwar period was one of dramatic economic growth, with the average increase in Gross National Product (GNP) standing at or above 3 percent.[38] This translated into higher living standards for a good number of people, though the statistics that would permit a precise quantification of this are not always available or reliable.

However, by the mid-1950s strains in the economies of the Soviet bloc were already beginning to become apparent. These stemmed partly from the ideologically induced inefficiency of economies directed to collectivization and the primary industrial output of heavy industries at the expense of high value, light industry, and consumer goods. The tensions were also due to the heavy expenditure on men and weaponry, including atomic bombs, as part of the ongoing Cold War. The policy of seeking military equivalence with the United States was perhaps understandable, but it was harmful to the economy, because it distorted investment and research strategies. Housing, transport, and communications in particular were neglected. By the 1950s, and throughout the 1960s, the effects on ordinary people of the high military spending and mismanagement of the economy were to be seen in the crowded cities whose inhabitants lived in soulless and poorly constructed housing blocks, in the shortage of consumer goods and their generally shoddy quality, and in the crumbling infrastructure and decay of the environment.

The economic strains on both the Western and Eastern Blocs intensified in the 1970s. In the West, and in the United States itself, there were inflationary pressures resulting both from the oil price hike of 1973 and the American decision to fund the war in Vietnam largely through borrowing rather than from higher taxes. Moreover, defense spending increased following the start of the so-called Second Cold War, as relations between East and West cooled, particularly following the clamp-down in Poland. The MX missile system, the Strategic Defense Initiative ("Star Wars"), together with official and clandestine aid to Afghanistan and Central America, caused U.S. defense spending in 1985 to rise by six percent, an increase that was unprecedented in peacetime, putting pressure on the American economy.[39] Yet much more severe were the strains on the economies of the Eastern Bloc. Around 30–40 percent of Soviet resources were devoted to defense spending, four or five times the American share, constituting a burden that could not be carried indefinitely. The debacle in Afghanistan—Russia sent in troops in 1979—also put severe social as well as economic strains upon the Soviet Union.[40] It has been estimated the by the early 1990s one in five veterans were alcoholic, while many others found it hard to gain employment and lived a fitful and rootless existence. By 1985, the Soviet Union's foreign debt stood at $30.7 billion; just four years later it topped $54 billion. Hence, under Gorbachev, it looked to the liberalizing policies of *perestroika* and *glasnost* to rejuvenate society and the economy. In the satellite states, too, the economic strains of military expenditure were being felt. Poland's national debt had reached a staggering $40 billion by 1986. The cost of servicing this mountain of debt required 27 percent of export income in 1974, 43 percent in 1975, and a staggering 70 percent in 1980.[41] Faced with deep-seated economic problems of its own, the Soviet Union was increasingly reluctant to take the pressure off its satellite territories by providing subsidized energy or by offering a market for shoddy East European goods, as had happened in the past. World economic conditions made matters worse. The flow of generous Western credit, which had financed economic growth in the 1970s, began to dry up, partly as a result of the oil shock and also as it became clear that Eastern governments were likely to default on their loans.

Living conditions consequently worsened for the populations of the Eastern Bloc. To be sure, in the 1970s most of the leaders of these countries accepted that the disillusionment of their peoples with the communist ideal meant that it was necessary to keep them happy through the provision of material goods. Measured by retail consumption, the standard of living rose accordingly. There was a fourfold increase in the number of privately owned cars in Poland between 1975 and 1989. In Hungary and

152 _Daily Lives of Civilians in Wartime Twentieth-Century Europe_

Czechoslovakia, roughly 4 out of every 10 people owned a TV. But such consumer goods were harder to come by in the Soviet Union, and everywhere the quality was poor, there was little choice, styling was drab, and spare parts were generally unavailable. There were also problems with the supply of basic commodities. In order to purchase a basic basket of foods, a shopper in Washington would have had to work 12.5 hours in 1979, in London 21.4 hours, but a staggering 42.3 hours in Moscow, despite high levels of subsidy. Things got worse. In Poland, for instance, consumer prices were raised by around 25 percent in 1987; the following year they were increased by a further 60 percent, and the inflation rate was reaching 1,000 percent per annum. Moreover, many hours had to be spent finding and then queuing for goods. Life was "expensive as well as exhausting."[42] It was also lived out in declining environmental conditions. By the early 1980s, northern Bohemia in Czechoslovakia had the worst air pollution in Europe as a result of the use of brown coal, 35 percent of all Czech forests were dead or dying, one third of the country's watercourses were severely polluted, and special children's hospitals had to be opened in Prague to deal with respiratory ailments.

To be sure, in making an assessment of the material conditions in the Eastern Bloc it is well-nigh impossible to determine precisely the extent to which economic difficulties derived from distortions to the economy caused by the high levels of Cold War military spending on the one hand, and how far they sprang from the inefficiencies inherent in a command economy, or from broader shifts in the world economy, on the other. Moreover, a full evaluation of material conditions also needs to take into account the so-called "second economy," the black market in goods and services that operated extensively in a number of Eastern Bloc countries. For instance, in Hungary by the early 1980s, less than 90,000 artisans met 60 percent of the local demand for services using equipment filched from state industries in their private enterprise. But the Cold War, as well as diverting resources, certainly helped to entrench the Soviet economic model across the Eastern Bloc, thus making reform more difficult and encouraging the existence of the parallel economy, which itself fostered a culture of sleight-of-hand and deception.

Repression

Popular unrest over economic issues developed in the Eastern Bloc, with varying degrees of intensity and expression, and might be linked to demands for wider changes, including greater national autonomy and political participation. Yet governments were reluctant to accede to such demands. Communism, after all, depended upon control: of the economy, of knowledge, of movement, and of opinions. To accept change in any one area was to challenge the whole system. For the Soviet Union, the maintenance of conformity and the suppression of diversity was especially important, because control of the Eastern Bloc was crucial to its security and influence. Consequently, extensive mechanisms of repression were established involving secret police forces (notably the Stasi in East Germany), restrictions on independent organizations and the media, censorship, restraints on travel, cessation of contacts with the West, and, of course, the direct use of force. To be sure, the existence of police states in Eastern Europe was not just a result of the Cold War. The Bolshevik regime had from the very start sought to protect itself and maintain its control through the creation of a widespread and highly ruthless secret police in the shape of the Cheka, which later became the KGB. Nevertheless, the Cold War provided the grounds for the continuation of mechanisms of repression, their extension to the satellite states, and their intensification in order to protect the state and its people against ideologically driven opponents. The Cominform (1947–1956), the successor to the Comintern, an umbrella organization that grouped together different European Communist parties under the watchful eye of Moscow, also fulfilled similar aims, though it could not prevent Tito's Yugoslavia from following an independent path.

The forces of repression were used, especially in the first half of the Cold War, with frightening ruthlessness. In Hungary, in 1956, about 2,000 people were killed and some 200,000 went into exile as a result of the military crackdown against disaffection, which, the Soviets maintained, had been inspired and driven by Western intelligence agencies. Earlier that year, the Polish army had crushed riots, and 56 strikers in Poznan were killed. In Czechoslovakia, in 1968, around 200 Czechs and Slovaks lost their lives as a result of a security operation, involving over one quarter of a million troops, designed to prevent the formation of a liberal Communist regime. In East Germany, around 130 people were killed trying to get over the Berlin Wall, built in 1961 in order to keep the citizens of the Soviet sector under a form of house arrest, though the precise figure still remains unclear and may be much higher. Though the loss of life in the Eastern Bloc was less than in areas where the Cold War became "hot," we should not underestimate the level of mortality in those regions where the Cold War remained "cold." Moreover, the mechanisms of repression involved an astonishing proportion of the population. The opening up of the archives in East Germany has revealed that nearly one in three ordinary citizens were complicit in the operation of the police state, spying on their neighbors, relatives, girlfriends, and business acquaintances, and providing both banal and shocking information about their daily lives. The psychological impact upon individuals of cooperating with the secret services and engaging in deceit has yet to be fully explored but was certainly significant.[43]

The Cold War did not give rise to comparable police states in the West, but here too, it drove the extension and elaboration of secret services. Thus in the United States, the Central Intelligence Agency (CIA) was created in 1947 under the National Security Act. Designed both to spy on foreign opponents and to locate and deal with domestic spying, communist infiltration, and sedition, these Western security services drew into their purview a wide range of "suspects" who had their movements logged and their telephones tapped, including politicians, trade union leaders, student militants, and others. The United States was unique in the extent to which the fear of Cold War communism led to an attempt, orchestrated at the highest levels, to ferret out "reds under the bed." The Federal Bureau of Investigation, the House Un-American Activities Committee, and the Permanent Investigations Subcommittee, whose most prominent member was Senator Joseph McCarthy and which arraigned 500 witnesses, were all indefatigable in this regard.[44] No one was immune, and people from all walks of life were challenged. Even George C. Marshall was accused of being a communist sympathizer, something from which his one-time *protégé*, Dwight D. Eisenhower, did nothing to defend him. A black waitress in the Pentagon was challenged because her husband received the *Daily Worker*. However, artists and writers were especially vulnerable. So, too, were homosexuals. They were not only regarded as a security threat; they also suffered from a backlash against their perceived takeover of the civil service during the New Deal era.[45]

RHETORIC AND THE CULTURE WARS

Outside of the areas of "proxy" conflict, the two principals in the Cold War did not confront each other with guns and bullets. Instead, the struggle was waged through words, symbols, and more covert means as both sides sought to manage public opinion, expectations, and morale. For example, the United States funneled millions of dollars to the Vatican and the trade unions to fund anti-Marxist propaganda in advance in the crucial elections in Italy in April 1948, helping to ensure that the Christian Democrats emerged with 48.5 percent of the vote as against 31 percent for the socialist/communist Popular Front alliance. Promising Italian intellectuals in particular were provided with scholarships and educated in America. In the early 1950s, and especially in response to the crisis in Korea, which was seen by many as the prelude to World War Three, the United States and NATO stepped up their use of propaganda, using radio broadcasts in particular. In Eastern Europe, there was a more concerted attempt at an ideological mobilization of the people. Communist ideology and the triumphs of the socialist system were rehearsed, and the defects and inevitable collapse of Western capitalism were highlighted in the state-controlled newspapers, TV, and radio, on posters in the workplace, through public architecture, and in the educational system. The launch of the satellite Sputnik I in 1957 was used by the Soviet Union as part of a wider drive to assert the ascendancy of its technology and its economic and social system, a claim backed up with the release of statistics about standards of living. Defense studies were even introduced as a compulsory element into East German schools in 1977 to raise awareness of the threat from the West.

In addition to the more obvious forms of propaganda orchestrated through the public media, artists, writers, and intellectuals were drafted in to give legitimacy to the respective systems of East and West as part of what have been termed the "culture wars." These affected theater, film, music (both classical and popular), painting and sculpture, and sports, and involved some of the most prominent artistic figures of their generation, such as Wadja, Eisenstein, Brecht, Miller, and Ionesco. In a move designed to get out the anti-communist vote for the 1948 elections in Italy, the U.S. State Department secured the cooperation of Paramount Pictures in the reissue of *Ninotchka,* while crooners such as Frank Sinatra and Bing Crosby sang on Italian radio, with the political cadenza that voting communist meant the end of freedom. More concerted attempts to use culture as part of the Cold War struggles came with Stalin's launch of the Movement for Peace in 1949. Designed to stress U.S. bellicosity and the peaceful intentions of the Soviet Union and its allies, it was backed by prominent communist authors who were sponsored to give talks, sign books, and speak on behalf of the Soviet Union. A response from Western intellectuals came with the formation of the Congress for Cultural Freedom, founded in 1950, whose goal was to rally support against communism. A further response came with the establishment of American-supported radio networks and "America houses" across Europe, which contained libraries of carefully selected books and newspaper reading rooms, and which hosted guest lectures.

Quite how far and in what ways the ordinary population was affected by the propaganda and culture wars is unclear and remains the subject of ongoing investigation.[46] For instance, modernism, whether in art or in music, was condemned in the Soviet Union and championed by the Congress for Cultural Freedom in the West. The abstract expressionist, Jackson Pollock, may even have received some financial support from the CIA. Yet if modernism was the dominant idiom in Western art, it remained an elite movement with little popular appeal. Socialist-realist art was promoted in Russia and the Eastern Bloc, where art forms had a much greater public presence than in the West. But here, too, it is unclear how much genuine popular appeal this had, though both modernism and socialist-realism received more prominence because of official backing than they would otherwise have enjoyed. Soviet attempts to portray American culture as crass and banal undoubtedly enjoyed some success. They were shrewdly targeted at a European population that both needed American help and feared "Coca-colonisation." Hostility toward Americanization was especially prevalent in Italy and in France: in the latter country, the sale of Coca-Cola was prohibited until 1950, other than in tourist areas. On the other hand, the popularity of American popular music and cinema is widely attested. American films dominated European cinemas and over half of the income of the U.S. film industry was derived from overseas in the late 1950s. If the erosion of the communist vote in Western elections through the 1950s and 1960s is any guide, America made better use of its "soft power" and emerged the victor in the culture wars.

The Psychological Impact of the Cold War

If it is not always easy to assess the impact of the culture wars on civilians, it is equally difficult to gauge the psychological effects of the Cold War. It undoubtedly served to create a climate of mistrust and fear. In the West, a commonly used phrase was "living under the shadow of the bomb"; and the 1960s witnessed the emergence of a powerful peace movement, notably in West Germany, though it was less influential in Britain and hardly figured at all in France, where General de Gaulle and his successors as presidents of the Fifth Republic pursued a defense policy nominally independent of NATO and the United States, thus avoiding the stationing of American missiles and bases on French soil. In the East, the propaganda onslaught against Washington and Western bellicosity was relentless, though there are indications that with the passage of time people became inured to the effects of such sloganeering because of its very ubiquity.

Despite the anxieties over nuclear conflagration, the postwar years were a time of optimism for many. In the West, this was underpinned by rising standards of living (though stubborn thickets of poverty remained numerous) and, for those on the broad Left, by a belief in the eventual triumph of socialism, which proffered the roadmap to the future. In the Eastern Bloc, living standards also rose, and there was a state guarantee of housing, education, and employment. Lip service was also paid to the equality of the sexes, and women were given ready access to contraception, family planning, and abortion, though many women saw through communist propaganda. Indeed, optimism would eventually turn to cynicism. This occurred after the 1960s in the West but came earlier in the East. True, the death of Stalin in 1953 eased some of the ferocity of state repression. Life was no longer dominated by terror, but it was still gray and drab. There was growing disillusion with the communist ideology and with an apparently inclusive political system (98 percent participation rates in elections) that seemed to offer so much but failed to give people any meaningful voice. Speaking in 1967, one Czech hardliner acknowledged the increasing alienation, noting that "[In 1948] we had posters in the shop windows about how socialism is going to look, and people were receptive to it. That was a different kind of excitement and a different historical time."[47] The dismal performance of the economy and declining living standards removed the system's last claims to legitimacy.

As a response, some took refuge in drink. The per capita consumption of alcohol in the Soviet Union more than quadrupled from the 1960s to the

1980s. More significantly, dissent, which in the 1950s had been largely confined to the intellectuals, began increasingly to assume a popular form. The dissident movements had already begun to articulate a new view of civil society in which the individual would be able to live outside the structures and patterns associated with the communist authorities, for example by buying goods outside the controlled economy, reading *samizdat* literature, or belonging to independent organizations.[48] This had a wider resonance with those feeling frustrated and resentful. In Poland, for instance, it eventuated in the establishment of local unions and factory councils, a rejuvenation of the Catholic Church, and pressure for real workplace rights. The articulation of a new view of civil society was linked to a rediscovery of national and ethnic culture, typically associated with the concept of Central Europe. The term was widely used by the Czech Vaclav Havel, and the Hungarian Gyorgy Konrad, but it was first developed by Milan Kundera in his 1983 essay *The Tragedy of Central Europe*. In this he argued that the traditional ordering of Europe into two distinct spheres had been upset by the 1945 settlement. Several nations that had always been tied to the West suddenly found themselves in an alien, Soviet-dominated theater. Kundera's arguments, like those for a civil society, suggested that politics and the communist ideology were irrelevant to the formation of individual and national identity. Instead, this was to be affirmed above all by culture.

CONCLUSIONS

The historian who seeks to make an assessment about the impact of the Cold War on civilians is faced with an uphill struggle. As we have seen, there are problems in establishing an overview, when there was so much regional diversity. Local studies of high quality are beginning to emerge, but they are as yet too few to permit anything but a chequered account. There are ongoing difficulties with primary sources, which are all too often unreliable or nonexistent: economic statistics and measures of public opinion in the Eastern Bloc in particular would fall into this category and have to be treated with the utmost caution. The military historian also needs to have an appreciation of unfamiliar methodologies and historical approaches, including economics, politics, film, and literary criticism, if a full appreciation of the evolving experience of civilians is to be gained. Nevertheless, the track record of military historians in broadening their approach to a study of the civilian experience in hot wars is a good one and augurs well for future studies on civilians in the Cold War.

NOTES

1. See for example Donald R. Shaffer, *After the Glory: The Struggles of Black Civil War Veterans* (Lawrence: University of Kansas Press, 2004), which is based on

a study of pension records; and A. Corvisier, "Le Moral des Combattants, Panique et Enthousiasme: Malplaquet," *Revue Historique des Armées* 12 (1977): 7–32, which rests upon a study of wounds sustained in battle.

2. See for instance Brian Bond, *War and Society in Europe, 1870–1970* (London: Fontana, 1984) and Geoffrey Best, *War and Society in Revolutionary Europe, 1770–1870* (London: Fontana, 1982).

3. On women see Elizabeth D. Leonard, *Yankee Women: Gender Battles in the Civil War* (New York: Norton, 1994); and John A. Lynn, *Women, Armies, and Warfare in Early Modern Europe* (Cambridge: Cambridge University Press, forthcoming).

4. See for example John Brewer, *The Sinews of Power: War, Money and the English State, 1688–1783* (London: Unwin Hyman, 1989); Jan Glete, *War and the State in Early Modern Europe: Spain, the Dutch Republic and Sweden as Fiscal-Military States, 1500–1660* (London: Routledge, 2002); I.A.A. Thompson, *War and Government in Habsburg Spain, 1560–1620* (London: Athlone Press, 1976); Richard Bonney, ed., *The Rise of the Fiscal State in Europe, c. 1200–1815* (Oxford: Oxford University Press, 1999); Martin Daunton, *Trusting Leviathan: The Politics of Taxation in Britain, 1799–1914* (Cambridge: Cambridge University Press, 2001); and Christopher Storrs, ed., *The Fiscal-Military State in Eighteenth Century Europe* (Aldershot: Ashgate Press, forthcoming).

5. See for example Robert Foley, *German Strategy and the Path to Verdun* (Cambridge: Cambridge University Press, 2005).

6. Rupert Smith, *The Utility of Force* (London: Allen Lane, 2005). W. Chin, "The Transformation of War in Europe, 1945–2000," in *European Warfare, 1815–2000,* ed. Jeremy Black (Basingstoke: Palgrave, 2002), pp. 192–217; Mary Kaldor, *New and Old Wars: Organised Violence in the Global Era* (Cambridge: Cambridge University Press, 1999); and Colin Gray, *Postmodern War: The New Politics of Conflict* (London: Routledge, 1997). For an attempt to predict future developments on the basis of current trends, see Michael Evans, Russell Parkin, and Alan Ryan, eds., *Future Armies, Future Challenges: Land Warfare in the Information Age* (Crows Nest, Australia: Allen and Unwin, 2004) and Makhmut A. Gareev, *If War Comes Tomorrow: The Contours of Future Armed Conflict* (London: Frank Cass, 1998).

7. K. de Vries, *Guns and Men in Medieval Europe, 1200–1500: Studies in Military History and Technology* (Aldershot: Ashgate, 2002) is good on the relationship between technology and wider changes and is a healthy antidote to the technologically determinist ideas about the evolution of the Middle Ages to be seen in Lynn White, *Medieval Technology and Social Change* (Oxford: Oxford University Press, 1962).

8. Michael Roberts, *The Military Revolution, 1560–1660* (Belfast: Queen's University Press, 1956), reprinted in an amended form in his *Essays in Swedish History* (London: Weidenfeld and Nicolson, 1967), pp. 195–225. The best survey of the debate is in C. J. Rogers, ed., *The Military Revolution Debate: Readings on the Military Transformation of Early Modern Europe* (Boulder, Colo.: Westview Press, 1995).

9. See for example Euan Cameron, ed., *Early Modern Europe: An Oxford History* (Oxford: Oxford University Press, 2001) and R. Mackenney, *Sixteenth Century Europe: Expansion and Conflict* (Basingstoke: MacMillan, 1993).

10. *Soldats Sans Armes: La Captivité de Guerre: Une Approche Culturelle* (Brussels: Bruylant, 1998). See, too, his *Les Exclus de la Victoire: Histoire des Prisonniers de Guerre, Déportés et S.T.O. (1945–1985)* (Paris: Éditions S.P.M. et Kronos, 1992).

11. *Forgotten Victory. The First World War: Myths and Realities* (London: Review, 2001). On this theme, see also Paul Fussell, *The Great War and Modern Memory* (New

York: Oxford University Press, 1975); Jay Winter, *Remembering War: The Great War and Historical Memory in the Twentieth Century* (New Haven, Conn.: Yale University Press, 2006); and Susan Rubin Suleiman *Crises of Memory and the Second World War* (Cambridge, Mass.: Harvard University Press, 2006).

12. Dennis E. Showalter, *Railroads and Rifles: Soldiers, Technology and the Unification of Germany* (Hamden, Conn.: Archon Books, 1975).

13. V. G. Liulevicius, *War Land on the Eastern Front: Culture, National Identity and German Occupation in World War I* (Cambridge: Cambridge University Press, 2000).

14. John Keegan, *The Face of Battle: A Study of Agincourt, Waterloo and the Somme* (London: Cape, 1976); Joanna Bourke, *An Intimate History of Killing: Face-to Face Killing in Twentieth-Century Warfare* (London: Granta, 1998); and John Lynn, *Battle: A History of Combat and Culture* (Boulder, Colo.: Westview Press, 2003).

15. As a personal selection, among many, see Clifford J. Rogers, *Civilians in the Path of War* (Lincoln: University of Nebraska Press, 2002); Susan R. Grayzel, *Women's Identities at War: Gender, Motherhood and Politics in Britain and France during the First World War* (Chapel Hill: University of North Carolina Press, 1999); Jay Winter and J.-L. Robert, eds., *Capital Cities at War: London, Paris, Berlin, 1914–1919* (Cambridge: Cambridge University Press, 1997); Donald Thomas, *The Enemy Within: Hucksters, Racketeers, Deserters and Civilians during the Second World War* (New York: New York University Press, 2003); Roger Chickering and Stig Förster, eds., *Great War, Total War: Combat and Mobilisation on the Western Front, 1914–1918* (Cambridge: Cambridge University Press, 2000); and Martin Parsons, *War Child: A History of Children in Conflict* (London: The History Press, 2008).

16. W. Roosen, "The Origins of the War of the Spanish Succession," in *The Origins of War in Early Modern Europe*, ed. Jeremy Black (Edinburgh: John Donald Publishers, 1987), p. 155.

17. It is worth noting that between 1950 and 1953, U.S. and Russian fighter pilots fought in the skies over North Korea, and from 1965 to 1973 their military personnel manned air defense missile systems in Vietnam, but neither of these instances of direct conflict was acknowledged.

18. An excellent introduction to the themes of the Cold War and its aftermath is to be found in David S. Mason, *Revolution in East-Central Europe: The Rise and Fall of Communism and the Cold War* (Boulder, Colo.: Westview Press, 1992), while the historiography and approaches are well reviewed in Odd Arne Westad, ed., *Reviewing the Cold War: Approaches, Interpretations, Theory* (London: Frank Cass, 2000).

19. Typified by T. A. Bailey, *America Faces Russia: Russian-American Relations from Early Times to our Day* (New York: Oxford University Press, 1950), and A. M. Schlesinger Jr., "Origins of the Cold War," *Foreign Affairs* 46 (1967): 22–52. A good entry into the debate on the origins of the Cold War is Martin McCauley, *The Origins of the Cold War, 1941–1949*, 2nd ed. (London: Longman, 1995), pp. 1–30.

20. William Appleman Williams, *The Tragedy of American Diplomacy* (Cleveland, Ohio and New York: World Publishing Co., 1959) is the key text.

21. On dating the start of the Cold War, see T. G. Paterson, *The Origins of the Cold War* (Boston: Houghton Mifflin, 1999); G. Alperovitz, *Atomic Diplomacy: Hiroshima and Potsdam: The Use of the Atomic Bomb and the Confrontation with Soviet Power* (New York: Simon and Shuster, 1965); W. LaFeber, *America, Russia and the Cold War, 1945–1971*, 2nd ed. (New York: John Wiley and Sons, 1972); and his *New Empire: An Interpretation of American Expansion, 1860–1898* (Ithaca, N.Y.: Cornell

University Press, 1963). The famous long telegram of February 22, 1946 from the Sovietologist and diplomat George Kennan, which traced Russian paranoia about the Western world back to the early modern period, when the Tzars feared the destabilizing impact of any outside influences despite talk of "Westernization," can be found in George F. Kennan, *Memoirs, 1925–50* (New York: Bantam, 1969), pp. 549–51.

22. J. L. Gaddis, *The United States and the Origins of the Cold War, 1941–1947* (New York: Columbia University Press, 1972); Geir Lundestad, *The American Non-Policy Towards Eastern Europe, 1943–1947* (Tromsö, Norway: Universitetsforlaget, 1975); and T. G. Paterson, *Soviet-American Confrontation: Postwar Reconstruction and the Origins of the Cold War* (Baltimore, Md.: John Hopkins University Press,1973).

23. Steven Morewood, "Divided Europe. The Long Postwar, 1945–89," in *Themes in Modern European History Since 1945,* ed. Rosemary Wakeman (London: Routledge, 2003), p. 14; M. Leffler, "Inside Enemy Archives: The Cold War Reopened," *Foreign Affairs* 75 (1996): 120–35 and his "The Cold War: What do 'We Now Know'?," *American Historical Review* 104, no. 2 (1999): 501–24. J. L. Gaddis changed some of his postrevisionist views and published *We Now Know: Rethinking the Cold War* (Oxford: Clarendon Press, 1997).

24. See Kenneth Waltz, *Theory of International Politics* (Reading, Mass.: Addison-Wesley, 1979), who embodies the approach of neorealism, while A. Wendt, "Anarchy Is What States Make of It: The Social Construction of Power Politics," *International Organization* 46 (1992): 391–425 and his *Social Theory of International Politics* (Cambridge: Cambridge University Press, 1999) opened the way for a constructivist approach. For an overview of the historiographical and conceptual approaches to the Cold War, see Westad, *Reviewing the Cold War.*

25. A gargantuan literature exists on these questions, too vast to summarize here. For a historical conspectus, see Tony Judt, *Postwar: A History of Europe Since 1945* (London: William Heinemann, 2005).

26. See Patrick Major, *Behind the Berlin Wall: East Germany and the Frontiers of Power* (Oxford: Oxford University Press, forthcoming).

27. A starting point is Jacques Lévesque, *The Enigma of 1989: The USSR and the Liberation of Eastern Europe* (Berkeley: University of California Press, 1997).

28. See for example Patrick Major and Rana Mitter, eds., *Across the Blocs: Cold War Cultural and Social History* (London: Frank Cass, 2004); Arnd Bauerkämper, ed., *Britain and the GDR: Relations and Perceptions in a Divided World* (Berlin: Philo, 2002); Patrick Major and Jonathan Osmond, eds., *The Workers' and Peasants' State: Communism and Society in East Germany under Ulbricht, 1945–1971* (Manchester: Manchester University Press, 2002); and Saki and Geraint Hughes, eds., *Palgrave Advances in Cold War History* (London: Palgrave, 2006).

29. See H. W. Brands, *The Devil We Knew: Americans and the Cold War* (New York: Oxford University Press, 1997); Robert J. Corber, *Homosexuality in Cold War America: Resistance and the Crisis of Masculinity* (Durham, N.C.: Duke University Press, 1997): Hermann and Kate Field, *Trapped in the Cold War: The Ordeal of an American Family* (Stanford, Calif.: Stanford University Press, 1994); Richard M. Fried, *The Russians are Coming, The Russians are Coming: Pageantry and Patriotism in Cold War America* (New York: Oxford University Press, 1998); Margot A. Henrikson, *Dr Strangelove's America: Society and Culture in the Atomic Age* (Berkeley: University of California Press, 1997); E. Tyler May, *Homeward Bound: American Families in the Cold War Era* (New York: Basic Books, 1988); Edward Pessen, *Losing*

Our Souls: The American Experience in the Cold War (Chicago: I. R. Dee, 1993); and Stephen J. Whitfield, *The Culture of the Cold War* (Baltimore, Md.: John Hopkins Press, 1991).

30. Jeremy Isaacs and Taylor Downing, *Cold War* (London: Bantam Press, 1998), p. 247.

31. Anna Funder, *Stasiland: Stories from Behind the Berlin Wall* (London: Granta, 2003).

32. Owen Chadwick, *The Christian Church in the Cold War* (London: Allen Lane, 1992), p. 5 for the statistics; and Nicholas Atkin and Frank Tallett, *Priests, Prelates and People: A History of European Catholicism Since 1750* (London: I. B. Tauris, 2003), especially chapter 6. There is useful material in Michael Burleigh, *Sacred Causes: Religion and Politics from the European Dictators to Al Qaeda* (London: Harper Press, 2006).

33. Martin van Creveld, *The Transformation of War* (New York: Free Press, 1991), pp. 20–21, notes that, in post-1945 conflicts, more civilians than military personnel have generally been killed.

34. The conflict in Southeast Asia is set firmly in the context of the Cold War in M. A. Lawrence and Fredrik Logevall, eds., *The First Vietnam War: Colonial Conflict and Cold War Crisis* (Cambridge, Mass.: Harvard University Press, 2007).

35. Ronnie E. Ford, *Tet 1968: Understanding the Surprise* (London: Frank Cass, 1995); William J. Duiker, *Sacred War: Nationalism and Revolution in a Divided Vietnam* (New York: McGraw-Hill, 1995). Limited war is dealt with in R. Brown, "Limited War," in *Warfare in the Twentieth Century: Theory and Practice*, ed. Colin McInnes and Gary Sheffield (London: Unwin Hyman, 1988).

36. Jeremy Black, *War Since 1945* (London: Reaktion Books, 2004), p. 64.

37. J. M. Montias, *Central Planning in Poland* (New Haven, Conn.: Yale University Press, 1962).

38. True, living standards did not always match those in Western Europe, but the economies of Eastern Europe were coming from a lower baseline.

39. For much of what follows, see Judt, *Postwar,* especially pp. 570–77, 581, 593–95, 605–7.

40. J. J. Collins, *The Soviet Invasion of Afghanistan: A Study in the Use of Force in Soviet Foreign Policy* (Lexington, Mass.: Lexington Books, 1986).

41. There is much statistical and other information on Poland in John Clark and Aaron Wildavsky, *The Moral Collapse of Communism: Poland as a Cautionary Tale* (San Francisco: Institute for Contemporary Studies, 1990).

42. Judt, *Postwar,* p. 581.

43. See Funder, *Stasiland* for an excellent exploratory narrative.

44. On McCarthy himself and his wider significance, see David M. Oshinsky, *A Conspiracy So Immense: The World of Joe McCarthy* (Oxford: Oxford University Press, 2005). On Senator Pat McCarran from Nevada, another key figure in the anti-Communist campaign, see Michael J. Ybarra, *Washington Gone Crazy: Senator Pat McCarran and the Great American Communist Hunt* (Hanover, N.H.: Steerforth Press, 2004).

45. David K. Johnson, *The Lavender Scare: The Cold War Persecution of Gays and Lesbians in the Federal Government* (Chicago: University of Chicago Press, 2004). On investigations into the film industry, see Lary Ceplair and Steven Englund, *The Inquisition in Hollywood: Politics in the Film Community* (Berkeley: University of California Press, 1979).

46. David Caute, *The Dancer Defects: The Struggle for Cultural Supremacy during the Cold War* (Oxford: Oxford University Press, 2003) is an outstanding study. See also Whitfield, *The Culture of the Cold War.*

47. Cited in Judt, *Postwar,* p. 580.

48. For much of what follows see T. G. Ash, *The Uses of Adversity: Essays on the Fate of Central Europe* (New York: Vintage, 1990), especially his essay "Does Central Europe Exist?" pp. 161–91.

SEVEN

Staying Behind: Civilians in the Post-Yugoslav Wars, 1991–95

Maja Povrzanović Frykman

The key in politics is to make certain identities more relevant than others, and others irrelevant to politics; and to impute very particular meanings to the relevant ones, meanings that seem to lead "naturally" to particular policies or outcomes. This doesn't necessarily require changing people's self-perceived identifications. Rather, it means forcing them in particular contexts to act—or not act—within the narrow range of one "identity" defined in a very specific and particular way. (V. P. Gagnon Jr., *The Myth of Ethnic War,* pp. 26–27)

YUGOSLAVIA: THE POLITICAL BACKDROP

Thousands of pages have been written on Yugoslavia. Its twentieth-century history may be summarized thus. The first, royal Yugoslavia came about as the Kingdom of Serbs, Croats, and Slovenes (1918–29), and was later called the Kingdom of Yugoslavia (1929–41). In April 1941, it ceased to exist thanks to the Nazi invasion. The Germans kept a portion for themselves (northern Slovenia, Banat, and Serbia); an "Independent State of Croatia," including Bosnia and Herzegovina, was established under Ante Pavelić and his fascist supporters, the Ustaša; and the remainder was given over to Berlin's Axis partners, Italy, Bulgaria, and Albania.

---

*Note: Parts of this chapter appear in an article in another publication, *Ethnologie Française.* (Maja Povrzanović Frykman, "The Forgotten Majority: On Civilians' War Experiences," *Ethnologie Française* 38, No. 2, 2008, pp. 315–324.) Used by permission.

The Former Yugoslavia. Map by David S. Heidler.

In the course of World War Two, Yugoslavia was at war with both the occupiers and its own peoples. The Germans and their supporters, in the Ustaša, were locked in a bitter conflict with the Četniks (essentially the rump of the former army and police force, under the leadership of Draža Milhailović who sought a Serbian-dominated Yugoslavia under a restored monarchy), who were also fighting the Partisans, essentially the Communists, under Josip Broz Tito.

At the end of World War Two, the state of Yugoslavia was reestablished, and comprised six republics (Slovenia, Croatia, Bosnia-Herzegovina, Serbia, Montenegro, and Macedonia), along with two autonomous provinces (Vojvodina and Kosovo, both within the Republic of Serbia). At the head of this new state was the victorious Tito, though unlike other East European communist regimes, Yugoslavia retained an independence of the USSR, much to Stalin's displeasure. Tito would retain a strong grip of Yugoslavia until his death in 1980, and for many analysts his death was the beginning of the country's disintegration.

The 1980s proved a destabilizing decade for Yugoslavia: growing international debt, international opprobrium, and mounting unemployment gave the impression of permanent economic, political, and social crisis. It was one that the socialist system seemed incapable of resolving. The long-term results were social disintegration, intense political infighting, ethno-nationalist movements, and eventually armed conflicts.

Long before the legal dissolution of Yugoslavia, political power was shifting from central federal institutions to those of the republics and provinces. The 1974 (and final) constitution ensured that each republic had its own central bank, its own communist party, its own independent educational and juridical system, as well as its own police force. The only remaining exclusively federal institution was the Yugoslav People's Army (JNA) along with the eight-member presidential body which, after Tito's death, served as its commander-in-chief.

The 1974 constitutional amendments had been intended as a progressive response to demands for local autonomy.[1] Yet they inadvertently turned the republics into rivals of the central state, as well as into rivals of one another. In this situation, leading politicians appealed to ethno-national loyalties, and played on lingering grievances dating back to World War Two. Irreconcilable national historical narratives helped sustain separate identities that undermined a shared Yugoslav identity.

Without doubt, memories of the terror unleashed in World War Two played a central role in the nationalist discourses that prefigured the wars in the 1990s, and in the prolongation of the conflicts. However, scholars are divided as to the importance of these recollections. The anthropologist Stef Jansen points out that the past was primarily a propaganda tool in the hands of nationalist politicians,[2] a point reinforced by the political scientist V. P. Gagnon, Jr. In his view, history and the (ab)use of historical memories is misleading in any understanding as to why the wars broke out, as all sides had a selective view of the past, conveniently overlooking the absence of tensions before 1941.[3] Gagnon thus observes that Yugoslavia never saw the kind of religious wars seen in Western and Central Europe, and that Serbs and Croats never fought one another before the beginning of the 1990s. Ustaša forces did perpetrate massive atrocities against Serbs and others during World War Two, but it should be remembered that they were a marginal party imposed by the Germans and Italians after the highly popular Croatian Peasant Party refused to collaborate. And while the Četniks perpetrated atrocities against Muslims in Bosnia, most Serbs in Croatia and Bosnia joined the multiethnic Partisan forces, rather than purely nationalistic Četnik groups.[4] Gagnon rightfully claims that the image of ethnic groups in conflict, even during World War Two, must be seen as "part of a selective, ideological construct in which 'ethnic groups' are portrayed as actors by nationalist politicians and historians."[5]

There is thus a substantial body of thought that believes the dissolution of Yugoslavia did not spring from ethnic tensions.[6] The real importance of these tensions was that they contributed to the maintenance of intergroup boundaries and fostered a distrust that enabled politicians to mobilize "their" group against others, with terrible consequences.[7] The real reasons behind the country's dissolution are consequently to be found elsewhere in the political and economic spheres: the imposition of communism, which was seen by much of the population as an illegitimate act; a decline in living standards common to command economies; systemic structural flaws (most notably of the federal system); the failure of Yugoslav peoples to develop a common historical narrative; and the role played by Slobo-dan Milošević and other ambitious political leaders and intellectuals in several of the republics.[8] The lack of perceived legitimacy was probably crucial, since "illegitimate" systems are much more vulnerable to collapse than long-established systems and are harder hit by economic crises.

Slovenia, the nationally homogenous westernmost republic, and the one economically best suited for independence, expressed its intention to secede in 1989. The first democratic elections were held there in April 1990, sweeping the communists from power. Elections were subsequently conducted in the remaining republics, Serbia being the last to organize them. The results of these elections signaled an end of the supra-national Yugoslav project: nationalist politicians and parties were the clear win-ners. Milošević, in particular, emerged as the champion of the Serb people. In his political discourse, he warned Serbs across Yugoslavia that their rights were under assault—from the province of Kosovo (whose ethno-mix was 90 percent Albanian Muslim, 10 percent Serb), to the republic of Croatia, whose draft constitution of June 1990 turned its Serbian popula-tion (12 percent of the total population) into a minority, whereas formerly it had been recognized as a constituent nation within the Socialist Repub-lic of Croatia. When Slovenian leaders openly declared their intention to seek independence, Milošević expressed a fierce commitment to keeping Yugoslavia together.

At the same time, Croatia experienced its own nationalist revival, elect-ing Franjo Tuđman as its first president in the postcommunist era. The rule of his Croatian Democratic Union (HDZ) was marked by the use of traditional national symbols, which caused alarm among Serbs. Some of these emblems had last appeared in public during World War Two, when the Independent State of Croatia had initiated a racist program in which Serbs, Jews, Roma, and Croatian communists had been rounded up in concentration camps and killed. In the parts of Croatia where Serbs were the majority in late 1980s, there was thus an understandable fear that 1941 was about to be repeated. Militias started to form, assisted by Belgrade, which distributed arms among them. Out of this militancy emerged the new Serbian Democratic Party (SDS), established in Knin in 1990. For these Serbs, their only protectors were Milošević, Serbia, and the remain-ing supranational institution, the JNA.

With the assistance of the JNA and Milošević, the SDS succeeded in declaring, within Croatia, an independent Republic of Serb Krajina (called simply "Krajina").[9] In a referendum held on May 19, 1991, 93.2 percent of Croatian voters rejected the option of their republic remaining part of federal Yugoslavia, but kept open the possibility of some form of loose confederation. Within Krajina itself, 99 percent voted for Krajina's unification with Serbia, and for the Yugoslav state to subsist.[10] As pressure on Croatia increased, and sporadic violence began to break out, both the Croatian and Slovene parliaments declared that, henceforward, no federal regulations were valid in the territories under their control, unless they were also endorsed by their respective parliaments. This inevitably led to Serbian and JNA accusations of secession. As has been observed, this justified "all the forcible methods they applied in the following months as attempts to preserve the integrity and territorial sovereignty of the Socialist Federal Republic of Yugoslavia."[11] While the U.S. Secretary of State warned Croatia and Slovenia that the United States would not support their aspirations for independence, the Croatian and Slovenian representatives blamed Milošević and the JNA for the mounting violence and the disintegration of Yugoslavia. In the event, they achieved the autonomy to which they aspired, something recognized in January 1992 by the international community.

Elsewhere, the first multiparty elections were held in Bosnia-Herzegovina in November 1990. Out of these emerged a ruling tripartite coalition comprising representatives from the Muslim-dominated Democratic Action (SDA), with Alija Izetbegović as its president, the Croat HDZ (Croatian Democratic Union), and the Serb SDS. From the very start, the SDS obstructed the work of the new republic and, on January 9, 1992, announced the creation of a separate Serb Republic. It accordingly refused to participate in the referendum held at the end of February, which overwhelmingly supported the proposition that Bosnia-Herzegovina should be recognized as a sovereign and independent country, comprising Muslims, Serbs, and Croats. The response of the SDS, supported by the JNA, was the erection of barricades in Sarajevo and a brutish civil war.

THE WARS

The war that broke out in Slovenia in 1991 lasted for only a few days. Twenty thousand JNA troops were stationed on Slovene territory, but only small numbers were actively deployed. The historian Ivo Goldstein states,

the Slovenian territorials were easily able to resist the small and unmotivated JNA land forces, which mostly consisted of non-Serbs and surrendered in large numbers. . . . It seems that the JNA leaders were in a quandary and the army was not fully engaged in the Slovenian war episode. Several weeks later the Slovenian authorities and the JNA agreed that the latter should withdraw from Slovenia within three months. This was the end of Yugoslavia as it had existed for forty-six years.[12]

A woman digs through a garbage can in central Sarajevo in 1994 as a dog noses around the hallway. Despite
many goods making it into the city with a ceasefire,
few Sarajevans had enough money to afford the goods
they saw in the shop windows. Courtesy of AP Photo/
Rikard Larma.

As suggested, the significance of this short-lived conflict was huge. By
capitulating to Slovene independence, the JNA ensured that the ensuing
conflict, fought in Croatia (1991–95), lost its Yugoslav character and became a Serb-Croat conflict.

Between July and August 1991, Serbian militias in Croatia brought an
ever-expanding area under their control, in what Silber and Little have
characterized as "undeclared war."[13] In the words of another commentator, "Croatian villagers fled before the Serbian militias, while the Croatian
National Guard attempted to maintain some shred of order, scurrying
around the front-lines in commandeered grocery vans and adapted tourist buses."[14]

By October 1991, the town of Vukovar, whose prewar population had been around 50,000, was reduced to rubble, while JNA-backed Serbian militias kept Osijek (population 200,000, including 30,000 Serbs) under siege. Dubrovnik (population 60,000, including less than 6,000 Serbs) and several other towns were subjected to aerial bombardment. Air strikes were also carried out against the presidential palace in the capital of Zagreb.[15]

During seven months of intense fighting, between 6,000 and 10,000 people were killed in Croatia.[16] The total material damage was estimated at 18.7 billion U.S. dollars. Left homeless were 400,000 people, and one-third of the republic was occupied by hostile forces. Gross industrial production declined by 28.5 percent in 1991 alone, and was to drop another 14.6 percent in the course of 1992. Inflation, which had reached 123 percent in 1991, climbed to 665.5 percent the following year. Tourism, central to the Croatian economy, had crashed by 80.7 percent in 1991. To compound matters, the neighboring conflict in Bosnia-Herzegovina led to an influx of thousands of refugees. By summer 1994, there were more than 600,000 refugees in Croatia, mainly in Zagreb.[17] Although the war in Croatia ended in August 1995, when Krajina was retaken, this was at the cost of turning thousands of Serbs into refugees.

As the fighting in Croatia continued into late 1991, Bosnia's Serbs and, to a lesser extent, Croatian communities in Bosnia, mobilized in readiness for conflict. Serb leaders declared their intention to remain within the Yugoslav Federation or seek independence of Bosnia. Serb "autonomous areas" were set aside, and a plebiscite was held in these districts to demonstrate popular opposition to any secession from Yugoslavia. Tensions further mounted in early January 1992, when the JNA began transferring Bosnian Serb troops from Croatia into Bosnia.

So it was that the war in Bosnia-Herzegovina erupted, just when hopes were rising that matters elsewhere were under control. As has been observed, "When the European Community (EC) recognized both Slovenian and Croatian independence in January 1992, largely as a gambit to end the war in Croatia, it worked. Within two months, however, war had engulfed neighboring Bosnia."[18] The EC recognized Bosnia-Herzegovina as an independent state two months later, on April 6, 1992, two days after a general mobilization was ordered, one month after the first barricades were erected in the streets of Sarajevo, and one day after Serb paramilitary forces besieged Sarajevo's police academy and the JNA seized its airport. The first shots were fired, on April 5, at citizens participating in a peace rally outside the assembly, and two women were killed.

An earlier UN Security Council arms embargo against the whole of Yugoslavia (September 1991), designed to take the sting out of the conflicts, only served to consolidate Serb military superiority, as the JNA was already much better equipped and supplied than its opponents. For some historians, the UN thus assisted the process of ethnic cleansing, leaving many communities defenseless.[19]

Over the next three and a half years, Bosnian government forces were at war with radical Bosnian Serbs, actively supported by Serbia, who were fighting to expel non-Serbs from what was later declared an independent Serb republic (*Republika srpska*), with intentions to join Serbia proper.[20] For a short period, government troops were also at war with Bosnian Croats, actively supported by Croatia, who in July 1992 proclaimed their own autonomous territory, "Herzeg-Bosna."[21]

By December 1995, when the Dayton Agreements ended the war in Bosnia-Herzegovina, the total number of Bosnian citizens killed and missing 1991–95 was 97,207, out of whom 40.82 percent were civilians. Of the total number of killed and missing, 65.88 percent were Bosniaks (Muslim citizens of Bosnia).[22] More then 200,000 people were wounded, including 50,000 children.[23] It has been additionally calculated that infectious diseases spread extensively, and that infant mortality doubled. The estimated value of the country's assets destroyed was put anywhere between 15 billion and 20 billion U.S. dollars. Industrial production was reduced to between 5 and 10 percent of prewar levels, and up to 80 percent of agricultural equipment was wrecked. Between 2 million and 4 million land mines had been laid, making large portions of productive farm and forest areas unusable. At the end of the war, unemployment reached 90 percent, and per capita Gross Domestic Product (GDP) dropped nearly three-quarters, to 500 U.S. dollars in 1995.[24]

Violence had done much therefore to spread economic disintegration and poverty, and had given rise to new sources of conflict: the forced migrations of people and ethnic cleansing.[25] In the attempts to consolidate territorial control and political ascendancy, Bosnian Serbs, Croats, and even Muslims (nowadays officially called Bosniaks) violently displaced and killed members of rival ethnic groups. Victims of ethnic cleansing further included so-called Yugoslavs and Others, as they were registered in the Yugoslav census. They were attacked either by the regular military, or, more frequently, by paramilitaries and other irregular forces. In all cases, "this assault on civilian populations was both an aim and an instrument of war."[26] Amid this violence, the assault on Srebrenica stands as one of the most atrocious events. Almost 7,000 Bosniak (Muslim) men were slaughtered in the week in which the town was taken by Serb forces.[27] Cousens and Cater observe that "beyond the obvious responsibility borne by Serb authorities for this bloodletting, many others have been accused of contributory culpability: the commander of local Bosnian forces who never arrived to help defend the town, the UN authorities who never managed to order close air support when it was desperately needed, and the U.S. authorities who are alleged to have known in advance but done nothing to prevent the assault on the town."[28] Notably, Srebrenica was one of the six UN-protected safe areas in wartime Bosnia.[29]

The post-Yugoslav conflicts caused the most extensive population displacement Europe has witnessed since World War Two. At their close in

1995, it has been calculated that out of some 4 million refugees, anywhere between 500,000 and 600,000 were residing in different European countries, mainly Germany, Switzerland, and Sweden. The rest were "internal refugees." More than 2 million stayed in Bosnia-Herzegovina, some 700,000 in Croatia, and a similar figure congregated in Serbia and Montenegro.[30] Inevitably such upheavals forced people to adapt and overhaul their everyday life. It was a wholly discomforting experience.[31] Our concern, however, is with those who stayed behind, and who were entrapped by the fighting.

THE MYTH OF ETHNIC CONFLICT

In his study *Yugoslavia's Bloody Collapse*, the journalist Christopher Bennett claimed that intense media coverage of the post-Yugoslav wars had done little to promote an understanding of the conflicts. This lack of comprehension not only stemmed from the complexity of the situation and the competing claims of the belligerents, but also from "a deliberate campaign to confuse the issue by Western commentators and statesmen" who sought "above all, to justify the policy of inaction."[32]

Bennett himself has done much to disentangle the nature of the post-Yugoslav wars, in particular by dismissing the notion that the conflicts were a peculiarly Balkan phenomenon:

The wars fought in the Balkans in past centuries were not fought between south Slavs, but between and against the multinational empires of the Habsburgs and the Ottomans. . . . Far from being perennial enemies, Serbs from Serbia and Croats from Croatia were, until very recently, essentially strangers. Moreover, Serbs who lived within the Habsburg Empire had more in common with their Croat neighbors than they did with Serbs from Serbia, and Serbs, Croats and Muslim Slavs from Bosnia-Hercegovina had far more in common with each other than they did with either Serbs from Serbia or Croats from Croatia. . . . Given the separate traditions and identities of the various Yugoslav peoples, south Slav union was bound to be a difficult process, but there was no inherent animosity between Serbs, Croats and Slovenes damning the Kingdom bearing their name from its inception. The hatred . . . is, in fact, a very recent phenomenon and reflects the failure of south Slavs to develop a durable formula for national coexistence in the course of the twentieth century. It is hatred bred of fear which is rooted not in history, but in contemporary interpretations of the past and can be dated to the 1980s and the media offensive which accompanied Slobodan Milošević's rise to power in Serbia.[33]

In his book *The Myth of Ethnic War: Serbia and Croatia in the 1990s*, Gagnon makes a similar point and shows in great detail that the violence of the wars was part of a strategy used by conservative elites in Serbia and Croatia, "not in order to mobilize people, but rather as a way to *demobilize* those who were pushing for changes in the structures of economic and political power that would negatively affect the values and interests of those elites."[34] He continues:

The wars and violence seen in the 1990s were thus not an expression of grassroots sentiment in the sites of conflict. They were also far from being the democratic expression of the political and cultural preferences of the wider population. Rather, the violence was imposed on plural communities from outside those communities by political and military forces from Serbia and Croatia as part of a broader strategy of demobilization.[35]

Gagnon does not argue that ethnicity is meaningless, that history is irrelevant, or that Yugoslavia was a multiethnic paradise. Rather he argues against seeing ethnicity in and of itself as the cause of violence. Ethnic identification is social fact, but its meanings are contextual, never homogenous and never fixed. Importantly, Gagnon highlights the instrumental function of *violence as the cause of ethnic homogenization,* and ethnic homogenization as a tool in the hands of the elites as they try to create a political space that they can control.[36]

Indeed, other researchers engaged in the ethnographic studies of the post-Yugoslav wars have also dismissed notions that the fighting ensued primarily because of ethnic hatreds. They have shown that politicians and army leaders certainly attempted to exploit ethnic tensions, through the media and propaganda, yet there was frequently a shared understanding on the part of civilians that they were largely powerless to change the course of events.[37] Scholars have also pointed to the *experience of violence* as a basis for hatred. Yet, civilians did not necessarily equate all politicians as war criminals and did not necessarily perceive members of another ethnic group as the enemy: they did not necessarily hate them. Torsten Kolind's ethnographic study of a postwar situation in a Bosnian town where the Croats had victimized their Bosniak neighbors shows that on their return Bosniaks avoided the discourse of ethnic blame and hatred.[38] There are accounts of how, in appalling circumstances, people nonetheless worked together: stories of how a war prisoner's life was saved by an acquaintance wearing the enemy's uniform, of how an old Serb woman in Sarajevo was helped by a Bosniak man, of how people shivering in the shelters disregarded ethnicity in favor of shared experience. Within a project entitled "Positive Stories," the Research and Documentation Center in Sarajevo has collected numerous testimonies about Bosnian citizens of different ethnicities who helped each other during the war, thus expressing human courage and civilian solidarity.[39] Such stories confirm Gagnon's claim—confirmed by war ethnographers—that violence was a means of destroying social relations of people who previously in peacetime had no reason to think of belonging to a certain ethnic group.[40]

As a personal memoir, the author recalls watching live television coverage of NATO's bombing of Serbia in March 1999—a supposedly humanitarian measure aimed at protecting Kosovo Albanians—while sitting in a tiny hotel room in the centre of the Zagreb. It was one of two rooms that served as a living room and kitchen, and was used by a family of Croatian refugees from Vukovar who had lived there since November 1991. Their hometown, on the Croatian-Serbian border, had been wholly destroyed by the JNA and Serbian paramilitaries, who had also murdered wounded soldiers and civilians in the local hospital, dumping their bodies in mass graves. As civilians from Vukovar, the family had been victimized solely on the basis of their ethnicity, yet no remarks of ethnic hatred comments were uttered that afternoon. There was no cheering at the bombing of the Serbs, and no sense that Serbia was finally getting what it deserved. On the contrary, the atmosphere was permeated with awful memories and fear. These people knew that war was terrible, and they knew that the post-Yugoslav wars were not over. Everyone in the room was pale, reflective, and quiet. "Poor people," someone said in a quiet voice.

PLACE-BOUND EXPERIENCES

In both political discourse and in the media, the post-Yugoslav wars have been predominantly viewed through the prism of ethnicity. Several scholarly works have also adopted such an approach.[41] In an "introduction to the theories and cases of violent conflicts," one American professor of international studies devotes considerable attention "to the exclusivist character of ethnicity" as "a powerful mobilizing symbol."[42] Ethnicity may well be an important motivation for people caught up in violent conflicts. However, it can also interfere with an understanding of how war was experienced.[43] In the cases of Croatia and Bosnia-Herzegovina, several anthropologists have shown how ethnicity evolves in different contexts, as well as the situations in which ethnicity becomes irrelevant.[44]

An important insight into the effects of military violence has been achieved through ethnographic fieldwork; this has focused on the *places* in which civilian lives are organized. Violence intensifies the relationship between people and places, and also creates a strong identification with the place. This has little to do with primordial and constructivist concepts of ethnic and national belonging. It concerns a different level of identification; one that is situated in *a physical place* and *depends on experience.* This explains why memories of war—of bomb shelters, food shortages, poor hygiene, and of the awful choices posed by war—are usually communicated in relation to place, and in relation to what people did.[45]

The tendency to situate one's own identity in spatial terms is significantly intensified as a result of people's lived encounters of the violence of war. People become aware of the importance of their physical position within, and physical dependency on, the surrounding landscape and urban structure. The nonmediated experiences of place thus come to the fore.[46] Admittedly, when people are shot at because of their ethnic origins, it goes without saying that people become more conscious of their ethnicity. Yet, ethnicity might also cease to matter when the shared experience of violence (or of any catastrophe) forms the basis of a feeling of belonging to a place. It is especially striking that, among the three major ethnic groups in Sarajevo, there emerged a "fourth nation," comprising civilians who valued the multiethnic life in Bosnia, and who identified themselves as *Sarajevans*. They were not prepared to allow ethnic animosity to take over their personal social relations.[47]

The aim here is thus not to (re)construct the suffering of *ethnic groups*, but to reach beyond the issue of ethnicity by offering a necessarily partial, but nonetheless authentic narrative of the experiences of civilians struggling to continue their everyday life in the midst of violence, focusing in particular on the civilians in Croatia and Bosnia-Herzegovina.

LETTERS FROM ZAGREB

An image of everyday conditions in the midst of the war in Croatia may be gleaned by quoting the titles and subtitles from a single newspaper page (*Nedjeljni Vjesnik* of October 6, 1991, page 4): "Wild attacks on Karlovac"; "The bus-station hit, as well as the general store and the marketplace, the parks ploughed up"; "The villages by the river Kupa plundered and burnt-down"; "Not a single building intact in Duga Resa"; "Repair in between the alarms. In the last 24 hours two air strikes on the transmission tower"; "Alarm in children's hospital: No panics, says the 9-year old Srećko, we are used to going down there."

Newspapers, however, can only tell part of the story. More useful are interviews and letters, though these were initially hard to obtain.[48] Some half a year after the fiercest fighting in Croatia had stopped, it was barely possible to interview Zagreb inhabitants about their personal experiences. People were embarrassed to talk about the humiliation of life in the bomb shelters, of ducking sniper fire when traveling on the trams. They would express considerable anxiety for loved ones called up to fight, and considerable empathy for peoples of Vukovar, Osijek, Dubrovnik, and other towns under siege. But their own war experiences were "not worth mentioning" in comparison. Nonetheless the following letters, written by people from Zagreb, offer direct, diary-like insights into the key elements of their wartime experiences. It is an *ethnographic chronicle* of the war, a kaleidoscopic image made out of little bits of personal experiences and observations intertwined with fear and hope.

The first account is that of a 36-year-old woman, and vividly relays the ever-present danger of war that interrupted day-to-day life:

I will probably write this letter in sequels, in the intervals between the air-raid alarms. Today we were fleeing to the shelter three times already. I am cooking lunch now, watching TV and, while expecting another alarm, I'll try to describe the last few days. . . . Since Tuesday I am at home with A. (the schools are closed).

In the hall we keep things prepared for the shelter. We sleep in sweatsuits, so that we can leave the flat quickly. We eat earlier and visit the toilet as soon as we feel the need, so that we don't end up in the shelter hungry and with a full bladder. I cook in the morning, for who knows if I would have time for that later. All in all, our life got muddled, but we find comfort in the fact that we are still out of mortal danger. The two of us are very disciplined and go to the shelter every time, unlike N., who mostly stays in her flat. . . .

On Sunday (15 September) we experienced the first, still mild encounter with the war in Zagreb. . . . There was a decree on the blackout. Behind the closed blinds, with some weak light, you feel like tinned fish. Totally cut off from the outer world, you deal with the first symptoms of claustrophobia (how do the true claustrophobics feel?!), that are strengthened when, again, the planes fly through that darkness. After that—silence as in a grave, interrupted by harsh male voices: "Switch the light off!" Not pleasant in the least. The first stay in a darkened flat was upsetting me more than the stay in the shelter. In the shelter we somehow felt safe. However, in the following days the fear has been growing, of potential diversions, especially after the rumor about someone damaging the air pipes. . . . Different stories are spread, many hearsays and disinformation among them—fantastically efficient in the production of fear. That first night, after still no real war in Zagreb, I hardly slept. I spent it staring in the dark, fearing that I won't hear the air-raid alarms if I fall asleep. . . .

The next day I went to work, but, of course, never got there. The street was blocked. . . . I decided to go to M.'s and call the office from her place. I didn't want anyone to think that I was afraid. . . . But, half way to her, I saw small groups of people running and hiding in the entrances, someone was shouting that they should keep off the street. Together with some man I stopped—another man, living on the ground level, invited us to his flat. I made coffee for everyone there; we waited for it to calm down, i.e., for the Army [JNA, stationed in the town center; M.P.F.] to surrender. . . . Realizing that I am not going to work that day (no one was answering the phone anyway; they were warned earlier to leave the premises), I went home. . . . After lunch, I had a walk with N. . . . It was dreary . . . no people whatsoever, just a loving couple on the bench. A sunny late summer afternoon— idyllic, but too calm and thus ominous, frightening. . . . While we were returning home—another air-raid alarm. . . . The neighbors tell me that the phones will be connected tomorrow or the day after. At least something nice. The night—again in the dark apartment, but this time I am almost relaxed; I sleep.

Tuesday 17 September . . . At home we do everything we think is needed before a new air-raid alarm. I wash my hair (something I otherwise never do in the evening), but I am drying it in the shelter, since the alarm went off again at 23'30. We are shaken by a strong detonation before that. The machine-guns' yelping from afar doesn't bother us much any more. In the shelter we make beds (wire-beds, on two levels, so that three people can sleep one above the other), we lie down, listen to what is said on TV. With the horrendous comprehension that Šibenik and Varaždin are under attack, that Osijek, and especially Vukovar, are bleeding and burning, that our guys are attacked on Sljeme [the hill next to Zagreb; M.P.F.], that they [JNA; M.P.F.] shoot from the barracks [within Zagreb; M.P.F.] vindictively, not choosing their target, I am trying to relax in order to keep strength and stay collected, since I am afraid that the real horror is only to start here. I even fall asleep for a short while. The end of the alarm is heard two hours later, around half past one in the night. We return to the flat pattering in total darkness—oh God, we never saw so many stars above Zagreb.

(September 20, 1991)

The next extract is that from a 31-year-old woman, which relays the exhaustion experienced by civilians as a result of the war:

So, after the first horrendous experiences one gets used to the alarms, one can differentiate between dangerous shots and those less dangerous or very dangerous. Everyone is searching for a brighter side of life, and comfort in the fact that the Jews went to theaters, that people traveled. . . . We can travel, however, only in a north-west direction. . . . In a long-term perspective, we are the winners, but how many lives must be offered to the "altar of the homeland," how many more burnt down churches, villages . . . and what to say about Vukovar, Osijek, Vinkovci, Šibenik . . . in comparison to them, this in Zagreb was just a military game . . . 20, 30 days in the cellars. Where are the limits of human endurance?

Listening to the horrendous stories, my first war experience was trifling; yet, the war caught me unprepared; I suddenly realized that there is no more "they are not going to attack Zagreb" . . . It happened in a tram, on the corner of Z. And S. streets. A policeman is stopping the tram and shouting: "All out, in the shelter, lie down, sniper on the roof," then sirens, shelters. . . . Fear, uncertainty, helplessness, rage and obstinacy are all mixed . . .

(October 4, 1991)

Life for children was described by a 54-year-old woman:

In fact, this abnormal situation has its positive aspects. It drew people closer, so that now for the first time I really know who is living in the house. Everyone is caring for everyone else and if someone doesn't show up in the shelter, the search starts.

It is the same at school. I have five children in the class, from the regions enmeshed in war. They are in a very difficult situation. They came without anything. The other children provided them with all the books and all the supplies. It is incredible how from being little egoists they turned mature and capable of dealing with such actions.

That, perhaps, is the greatest value in this evil, which, I hope, we may keep also after this war is over. It is like that in the entire homeland. People are helping in all possible ways, they organize the collecting of help, the hosting of refugees. . . . That is something that is filling one with admiration; it is hard to believe that they can organize in such a short time. The caps are knitted, socks, gloves for the fighters. The cakes are baked and sent to the fronts, so that almost everyone is involved in this war, in their own way. . . .

We all hope this will end soon, and then we will have a lot to do in rebuilding what they have destroyed. Here people don't feel pain any more, but a great obstinacy. I think that obstinacy will help us all to go through these difficulties.

(October 11, 1991)

Christmas proved especially trying, as the following account of a 35-year-old man testifies:

The war in Zagreb is felt through the minor shortages, as for example yesterday. I went to buy the Christmas tree yesterday, but there weren't any left. The children that came with their parents were crying bitterly, and the parents were walking around in disbelief, hoping to find at least a branch. When a truck loaded with Christmas trees finally arrived, there were a hundred people around it at once. Not asking for the price, they bought everything that was in the truck. I gave up on the buying, so D. [his 3-year-old daughter; M.P.F.] and I decorated the tree of life instead.

(December 25, 1991)

As in the previous quote, a normality of sorts resumed as the following correspondent, a 34-year-old woman describes:

After a very, very long time, I am finally able to write a few lines again. Although I fear that the true end of this horror is still far away, we gradually got used to this insecure living, and I—at least at the moment—got rid of that forceful cramp which made every word on the paper look like a final shaping of all anxieties into a final sentence, a reality to stay. I could talk about everything, but I couldn't write. We are beginning to live a little again—this Sunday we went sledging with the friends, and the children were enjoying it again. It is that tiny difference which turns survival into life, which I became aware of only now.

(January 30, 1992)

THE BOSNIAN WAR FROM WITHIN

In addition to firsthand accounts such as those cited, civilian life under wartime can also be gleaned from documentary films. In one such film made by Erik Gandini in 1994, there is a scene showing young people skiing on a small slope in a neighborhood in the hilly town of Sarajevo in 1994, during one of the many soon-to-be-broken cease-fires negotiated with the Bosnian Serbs who had the town under siege.[49] The youngsters shout, laugh, and show off their skiing competence, enjoying their physical activities after having been cooped up for weeks, months, indeed, years. Venturing outside was always dangerous, and was only undertaken in order to obtain food and water. For the most part, people remained in their homes, or found themselves hiding in accidental places so as to avoid sniper fire. In so doing, civilians became experts in local geography.

The Gandini film is one of the rare live documents "from within," showing four friends in their early twenties who try to live their lives in a town under siege, while witnessing the many ways by which people were being killed, including "psychological death," as one of them calls it, that is, the killing of hope. It is a film about the retention of dignity. This is witnessed in the setting out of porcelain dishes on a white tablecloth in order to eat canned fish bought at an inflated price on the black market; in the snatched leisure moments when the youngsters perform in a rock band;

and in the walks home after curfew. By "staying normal," a dignity was upheld. In this way, the film records how the friends reflect on their hopes and dreams both before and after the war, the maintenance of personal hygiene, though this was especially difficult, and the celebration of New Year's Eve. In short, the film records how civilians endeavored to live, as well as how they struggled to survive.

Another document—an in-depth description and analysis of life in Sarajevo under siege, one that lasted for three and a half years—is provided by the anthropologist Ivana Maček in her study entitled *War Within: Everyday Life in Sarajevo under Siege.*[50] An eyewitness to events, she caught many of the paradoxes of civilian life in wartime: the peculiar tension that existed between destruction and creativity. Offering an account of individual experiences of war, something neglected by most other commentators, she discusses the norms of behavior, and the perceptions of reality, that were continuously defined and redefined as people tackled the shortages created by the fighting: of life in apartments without running water, heating, and electricity; of surviving on meager and basic foodstuffs; and of communicating without phones, trams, and buses. Whereas in peacetime civilians take a normal existence for granted, when under fire they become especially aware of the relativity, frailty, and artificial constructs of their environment. In so doing, Maček illustrated how, in the post-Yugoslav wars, civilians reevaluated their social bonds, their routines, the material value of things, and the very nature of familiar spaces.[51]

A further insight into daily life may be drawn from a graphic novel, *Safe Area Goražde: The War in Eastern Bosnia 1992–95*, published in 2000.[52] It is a comic book, with plenty of irony and sarcasm but little laughter, authored by Joe Sacco, an artist, reporter, and ethnographer, all in one. The insights offered in his book corroborate those offered by Gandini and Maček. In it, he depicts everyday experiences: the chopping of wood, the sharing of meager meals, children playing, and the empty school benches of pupils who had been killed. He also captures the staged events of the war: the photographer throwing candy at the children in order to get a good picture of the poverty in which people were living. Yet, for the most part, he captures the miseries and tensions of life under wartime: the massacre in Srebrenica; the feeble intervention of the UN; the efforts of civilians to assist one another, for instance the Serb rescuing his Bosniak neighbor from the paramilitaries; and the Sarajevans' contempt for the seemingly primitive refugees from eastern Bosnia. It is all there, in masterly drawings accompanied by authentic quotes from the people among whom Sacco was living when a resident in Goražde. And, in the middle of it all, an authentic story about the strong disappointment—in the context of dire needs and insecurity—of a girl for whom Sacco attempted to buy a pair of jeans. He managed to go as far as Sarajevo, but returned only with a copy, not the original Levi's 501s that she so much wanted.

THE PRESENCE OF DEATH

In peacetime, reality is marked by a daily timetable, the demands of a job and domestic routine. In war, it is defined by violence, unknown threats, and the possibility of an undignified and depersonalized death. Just as the death of a civilian in wartime cannot be interpreted as the product of personal guilt, so too survival cannot be viewed as a personal achievement. It is chance that decides on both, thus confirming the frailty of human existence and the impotence of civilians when under armed assault. Deep *humiliation* is implied in the passive position of civilians exposed to dangers that they cannot do anything about, except to try to hide from. In interviews conducted with survivors of the conflicts, a recurring theme was the embarrassment with which people recalled how they had evaded sniper fire and shrapnel and how they had avoided a death that had no reason, no meaning, and no dignity.

Death, however, became a normal aspect of everyday life in war. In Croatia, the names of people killed in armed attacks were communicated by the media in the summer of 1991; soon afterwards, television and radio reports took merely to recording the numbers killed. People had their own records of the killing. Children were especially aghast at what they saw: "My mum, brother and I saw a dead man with the upper part of the body missing. We were shocked."[53] Violent death, heroic death, death by chance, death with no meaning—the threat of dying was omnipresent and all too real. Wartime also blurred the differences between natural deaths and those as a result of the fighting. In one Vukovar shelter, the body of one old man could not be taken to the morgue because of the shelling and so remained close to where people were eating and children playing. Dying of old age in Vukovar in the autumn of 1991 was so unusual that the death of an old woman became a news item on the local radio program.[54]

As one of the two Sarajevo cemeteries was in the occupied territory, and the other became the front line, the citizens buried their dead in old cemeteries, around the mosques, in the parks, and even around some residential buildings. One cemetery established during the siege expanded into the auxiliary soccer field and other green areas around a soccer stadium. The funeral processions were often shelled, and the graves had to be dug at night in order to minimize the risk of getting shot from the surrounding hills. In 1995, from April to September, funerals and burials occurred only at night.[55]

STRIVING FOR NORMALITY

The strange experiences of wartime were partially overcome by attempts to retain a routine. On the one hand, people tried to keep up as many everyday customs as possible. On the other, they tried to make sense of a reality far too chaotic to be understood by their concept of normality situated in cultural contexts and norms of everyday life in peace. They thus had to negotiate the meaning of normal in the abnormal circumstances imposed by war. The following accounts, drawn from the author's ethnographic fieldwork carried out in Durovnik in April 1996, reveals this quest for normality:

We brought an old bed into the cellar. We also brought blankets and everything. . . . It remained there until recently [for five years; M.P.F.]. We had everything we needed—a house in six square meters! You ought to have a table to place all the important things—light, food, radio. . . . Some had petrol lamps, some had oil lamps, since we were out of petrol after a while. On the other hand, petrol was suffocating us—in regard to what the day was like. If the attacks were constant, everything was closed. . . . It remained totally closed for four days in October [1991, M.P.F.]— you couldn't breath. In such situations, you let the lamp burn only if necessary.

(a woman from Dubrovnik, interviewed in 1996)

The life in Aquarium? [Dubrovnik Aquarium, situated in one of the castles in the medieval town walls, served as one of the two biggest public shelters; M.P.F.] In the first days—the first ten or fifteen days—there were lots of people, we were five hundred, for sure. All those living close to the city walls, all, all that were close, but also from other parts of the Town [the old city is called "the Town" in Dubrovnik; M.P.F.], because Aquarium was the closest, the safest. . . . On the ground level, where the fish are kept, were the elderly, children and women. On the first floor, there were young people, fifteen to seventeen years old. It is interesting, in those three months—except for some virus that made people run to the toilet for one day—everyone was in good health, no one had a cold, no one asked for anything . . . they did not ask for any medicine. People were bringing in anything they could. From beach mattresses to real beds . . . Afterwards it became difficult to sleep in your trousers—so you would bring in the nightgowns, the blankets, you would bring in everything you needed to feel at home, since you were spending all that time in there. . . . There was a little kitchen there, something like a kitchen. However, we could boil some water there to make the tea for the kids. . . . The ones more courageous, went home. I went home to prepare some meal, then I would return.

(a woman from Dubrovnik, interviewed in 1996)

And everyone had a battery in the radio, and everyone would gather—when the news was on—so just one radio would be on at a time, so the batteries could be saved.

(a man from Dubrovnik, interviewed in 1996)

This continuation of minimal normality was crucial not only in attempting to deny or overcome the immediate circumstances of wartime, but also as a means of linking daily routines to the stability of life before the fighting, as these testimonies attest:

It was very funny when my daughter went to take a shower.—Where are you, N.?—I went to take a shower.—How on earth could you take a shower, we don't have but one pot, and it is for cooking, for washing the dishes and for cleaning the toilet!?—She would step in a plastic bucket and use a little cup . . . two liters of water at most . . . You can take a shower with one liter, too! Eventually we ended up with half a liter! And you still use it for the toilet afterwards; nothing is lost.— When the electricity was back, after a month, only then we realized how dirty we were. And you take a shower every morning. But the quality is sinking, it has to sink.

(a woman from Dubrovnik, interviewed in 1996)

Wherever the water cistern would come, they [the enemy soldiers on the hill above the city; M.P.F.] would start the shelling, so we were left without water. There were also big queues for water, it was really difficult for the people who had no . . . [no access to the rain-collecting wells; M.P.F.]. We had a little boat in the garden—we collected rain in it. It was Autumn, so there was rain. And it was warm. People were taking baths in the sea, even in November.

(a man from Dubrovnik, interviewed in 1996)

I exercised some kind of quiet resistance. I even did not go to fetch water for them [for the people staying in the block-house cellars that served as shelters; M.P.F.]; I did not want to. I thought—if I am thirsty, I'll go and drink at the well [many of the traditional rain collecting wells typical for the Mediterranean region are still used in Dubrovnik—for watering the gardens in peace; M.P.F.] but I refused to make reserves, to let something bother me.

(a man from Dubrovnik, interviewed in 1996)

We were saved by the sea, we were saved by the fish. People went fishing although they [the enemy soldiers on the hill above the city; M.P.F.] were shooting at them.

(a man from Dubrovnik, interviewed in 1996)

You cook two or three potatoes. When they [the enemy soldiers; M.P.F.] start to shoot, you turn it off and go to the cellar—the potatoes remain in warm water. When it is quiet again, you come back, peel the one onion you could buy—onions can last long—and when you mix it with one tuna fish from a can, you have a warm meal. You have eaten for that day. Imagine that you had only bread every day. I mean—*this* is a meal.

(a woman from Dubrovnik, interviewed in 1996)

Reflecting on these shortages, the "War Cookbook 1992/1993" from the *Sarajevo Survival Guide*[56]—a sarcastic imitation of a Michelin guide—speaks of resourcefulness, but more importantly, of dire hunger. Along with the recipes for garden snails that can be found in parks after the rain, for "Mayonnaise with No Eggs," "Bread-Crumbs Pate," and "Fir-Tree Juice," there is a recipe for "Cheese a la Olga Finci":

4 demitasses of milk powder (bought at the black market)
1 demitasse of oil (from humanitarian aid)
1 demitasse of water (boil it first!)

0.5 demitasse of vinegar, or one lemon
1 small spoon of garlic powder (present given by a good friend)
Mix it all with a plastic spoon which can be found in the USA lunch package. The mix will thicken immediately, just like a pudding. If you were lucky enough to grab a bunch of expensive parsley, cut it finely, pepper it, and add to the mix. All should be then taken to your balcony, where the temperature is -10C; you can as well leave it in the kitchen, where it is only -8C. It should get hard. Even if you had other ideas, this dish has to be served cold. Enjoy![57]

In a bitter effort to present humorously the reality of the unreal, or the normality of abnormal life during the years of siege, *Sarajevo Survival Guide* also quotes war prices: 200 DM (German marks) for 1.25 cubic yards of wood, and 50 DM more for home delivery; 170 DM for a bottle of whiskey; 120 DM for a couple of pounds of garlic; 40 DM for a quart of oil, or 2.2 pounds of beans, or a children's bicycle, or one lunch package; 10 DM for four batteries of 1.5 V, or for about a gallon of water.[58] At the same time, the salary of those who still worked was between 10 and 30 DM.[59]

MODES OF RESISTANCE

Through talking about air-raid alarms and shelters, about food, water, and hygiene, about neighbors, friends, and communities, about the importance of family ties and the care for children and elderly people, about obstinacy and courage, people also presented examples of how they modified their lives as a result of the sieges and shelling. They articulated an identity based primarily on strategies of survival, but they also demonstrated how everyday routines were an effective means of coping with wartime deprivation, fear, and anxiety.

In that connection, a modest, humble definition of *bravery* emerges from the narrative of people's lives in Dubrovnik, a very distant concept from that presented all too frequently by the heroes of war films. The bravery that people recognized and admired was the ability to retain as many peacetime routines as possible. The very act of going to work regularly, fetching drinking water for the people in the blockhouse shelter, washing the family's laundry at the beach, or repairing the neighbor's damaged roof were key in this respect, even though they were extremely dangerous patterns of behavior. There was always the possibility of being killed by a shell or sniper fire: the attackers holding the hill behind Dubrovnik were just under two miles away.

During the war, the regular evening walk on the main street was another brave action. It was not only a strategy of keeping routines going (people walked on the safer north side of Stradum, before being forced into side roads), it was also a way of obstinately maintaining an element of Mediterranean urban life and culture. It was a symbolic and practical move against victimization. By walking on the main street, the people of

Dubrovnik did not give in to the violence that had overtaken their town, as the following interviewee reveals:

My mother stayed in the Aquarium for a very long time, more than eight months, because she was very much afraid. Occasionally, she did come home in the morning, to prepare breakfast and lunch at the same time so she did not have to return. She never slept at home, but she would visit home for a couple of hours, depending on what kind of day it was, if it was quiet or not.

(a woman from Dubrovnik, interviewed in April, 1996)

Unlike the women mentioned above, and regardless of possible danger, many people decided to stay in their homes, not only during air raid or artillery attack alarms, but also during the actual attacks.[60] For some, the decision was based on a fatalism acquired through the fighting. For others, it was a minimal, very private, but conscious act of *resistance*. Some even felt safer in their homes than in the improvised shelters in the cellars. It was *the safety of normality* surrounding them, the familiarity of the place that could help them forget the danger. Refusing to sit in a public shelter was also a statement of resistance to a group identity imposed by the violence. Staying in one's own flat was very much a matter of keeping one's personal dignity—at least when circumstances permitted such a privilege. The Sarajevo journalist Ozren Kebo noted that when the calamity lasts as long as it did in Sarajevo under siege, insisting on dignity becomes obscene.[61]

Surviving the war thus went further than mere physical survival. For the maintenance of personal integrity, and for the perpetuation of a living community, it was imperative to uphold at least some traits of customary behavior, so as to escape from the unpredictability and pressures created by the war. It was a time and place for sleeping, eating, smoking, telling jokes, listening to music, playing cards, or reading to the children—acts that were carried out as though people's very lives were not under threat. It was the time for a young woman to take a walk on the main Dubrovnik street: hair washed, make-up on, all dressed in white.

In Sarajevo, in the partially destroyed Red Cross building in the "Sniper Alley," exhibitions by local artists were held once a week. In a shelled building where the chamber theater was situated, performances, presentations, and commemorations were held daily—occasionally even cocktail parties, where humanitarian aid was served. The daily newspaper *Oslobođenje* was published in a completely destroyed building—sometimes with a radically reduced edition due to the lack of paper.[62] *Sarajevo Survival Guide* summarized it as "cultural survival":

The besieged city defends itself by culture and thus survives. Groups and individuals create whatever they used to create before the siege. In impossible circumstances they produce films, write books, publish newspapers, produce radio programs, design postcards, stage exhibitions, performances, make blueprints for rebuilding the city, found new banks, organize fashion shows, shoot photographs, celebrate holidays, put on make up.[63]

OASES OF NORMALITY, IMITATIONS OF LIFE

Everyone is well-dressed, cafés are working, music. And everyone looks somehow normal, but it reality everyone is troubled by the same worries. . . . He goes to the town, sits down for a while in a café, with friends, makes himself look nice, but actually in their sub consciousness men think about their next trip to the front lines, what they would do, would they go outside of the town or will they be placed in the town, or would they be sent to a real battlefield, what will happen, for how long, will there be shooting again, what will happen at the negotiations, what will happen when the winter comes, what will happen at home, how to provide . . . who shall provide . . . Now, you're sitting in a café enjoying. There is music and everything is fine, beautiful, but when you come home you have to fetch water, you have to stand for hours, you have to drag those canisters. Two canisters on one shoulder, two on the other, two in the hands . . . you have to make a fire, sit by the candlelight at home. That is it, you know. But, like, we all make efforts to somehow look normal.[64]

Many people in Sarajevo presented their everyday life as an *imitation of life*. Although one of the people I interviewed in Dubrovnik also said that "you don't live like that *in life*," the everyday habits sustained by the people in that particular town may be interpreted as an attempt to strive for *oases of normality*, not imitations thereof. The difference lies in the dimensions of suffering that can be established in objective terms: the length of the siege, the availability of water and electricity, the relative lack of food and communication, the number of apartments blown up because of the ill-improvised gas pipes people were eager to install as it was getting colder, the number of people killed by mortar shells in marketplaces, the number of children killed by snipers. Time played a key part. Dubrovnik was under siege for three months, Sarajevo for more than three years. There is a difference in the weight people have lost; there is a difference in the overall consequences for people's health. In Dubrovnik water was collected from the nearby sea, whereas in Sarajevo people stood in queues lasting up to eight hours and became targets for snipers.

In Dubrovnik, it was possible to pick fruit in a Mediterranean backyard—"The fruit has saved us!" "Everything was bearing fruit so richly that autumn!" recalled contemporaries. In Sarajevo, as hunger took a grip of civilians, they discovered that wild grown plants could be eaten; nettles and dandelion found their way to the market. People planted seeds in window boxes on their balconies, around the houses, in the parks— seeds donated as humanitarian aid! Open Society Fund sent $2 million worth of pumpkin, carrot, tomato, lettuce, and corn seeds.[65] This kind of aid addressed people's needs but, at the same time, sent a clear message about the outer world accepting the *normality* of what the Sarajevans were enduring. As much as the seeds were well appreciated, they corroborated Sarajevans' belief that making Sarajevo into a symbol of terror suited the UN. As Ivana Maček explains, it silenced opinion in the West as it made identification with Sarajevans impossible. After two years of isolation, they were no longer dangerously like Westerners. The incomprehensible terror that informed their lives made them essentially different.[66] Killed in Sarajevo were 10,615 persons, out of whom 1,601 were children. More than 50,000 persons were wounded, a great number of whom remained invalids. The siege of the city lasted from May 2, 1992, to February 26, 1996, or 1,395 days, which is the longest siege in modern history.[67] Hence the sarcastic attitude of many Sarajevans towards the UNHCR (United Nations High Commissioner for Refugees) and UNPROFOR (United Nations Protection Forces) reflected in the *Sarajevo Survival Guide* published in 1993 and the Sarajevo *Survival Map* from 1996:[68]

UNHCR supplied the city with the numerous but not sufficient thermal foils for windows. On every window, from the outside, one can read their name: UNHCR—they are the owners of our lives.[69]

The role of the UNPROFOR was manifold. They served as hostages to the aggressor, they cleared the garbage, they rode in the trams as a protection against snipers, they gave out sweets, brought flour, destroyed the surface of Sarajevo streets with their tanks and transporters, representing the only city transportation throughout a long period, they repaired electrical transmission lines, they controlled the airport. . . . The most important form of protection of citizens was driving the transporters next to them shielding them from the sniper fire while they were crossing the Tito street. For a long time they were the most significant part of the city's commercial life because they were trading the goods available to them.[70]

The experiences of violent destruction of life-worlds acquired under siege were basically the same in both Sarajevo and Dubrovnik, as they were in numerous other towns, but the time span of the siege *does* make a difference. There *is* a limit to human endurance, if not to psychological stamina, and to physical staying power. Even more importantly, there is a danger of people forgetting their original, peacetime normality and succumbing to the normality of scarcity: the search for fresh vegetables while living under constant threat, being happy for receiving some seeds that can be planted on their balconies. Once again, people were struck by the changes in their environment. In the course of three years of armed destruction, isolation, and overall pauperization the surroundings changed markedly. *Sarajevo Survival Guide* suggests what gifts were appreciated most by people living under siege: a bottle of clean water, a candle, a bar of soap, shampoo, some garlic or an onion.[71] Markets, in peaceful times lively, with rich offerings, and abundant with color, became places where "one can see poverty at its worst. Merchandise from all the tables can fit into two nylon bags."[72] The nontransparent thermal foils imitating wired glass, and with UN-blue

UNHCR letters and symbols, made the apartments and town look even more like ruins, or construction workers' field barracks.[73] Sarajevan parks became places where citizens got their wood—it could be bought at markets, packed in bags. Even the park benches ended up in handmade stoves, as did innumerable books from home libraries.[74]

So, if the childish skiing on an innocently white slope in Sarajevo in 1994 was an *imitation of life*—an imitation of the normal skiing that those youngsters were used to in their past—the sledging in Zagreb in 1992 may be interpreted as an *oasis of normality.* In Zagreb, both parents and children knew there was no danger of sniper fire or bombing. The youngsters in Sarajevo could never be sure, not even on a day of a cease-fire.

In Dubrovnik, all the persons I interviewed stressed that they had freshly baked bread every morning during the siege in 1991–92:

The shelves were empty in our shop. The end has come. If that blockade has not been broken through, we would meet real hunger. Terrible hunger would have come. People were still sharing what they had, and we had bread—that is the most important. We went in the night. . . . We never lacked bread, and that was a very important thing.

"Honor to the bakers!" "All thanks to them!" These phrases repeatedly revealed an admiration for the people who had helped their fellow citizens keep a material link with their peacetime existence—a link that involved both the perpetuation of normality and a hope for a peaceful future. A loaf of bread placed on an improvised kitchen table in the shelter became an *oasis of normality.*

In Sarajevo, however, people could not buy bread regularly. It involved endless queues for foodstuffs that might have been sold out at the end of a lengthy wait. As one witness attests:

Many times it happened that we who worked there got a loaf of bread. And I felt simply embarrassed to go out with that bread when I knew that the ones standing on the other side of the entrance cannot get it. You know, bow your head, pass, go home. You feel terrible. It was really horrible to see these people who stood for hours in front of the bakery, in the worst cold, during the heaviest shelling, begging over the fence that someone give them bread. As if for the child, for the ill, I have nothing. . . . I shall pay you. . . . Terrible, really horrible.[75]

The bread produced in Sarajevo was insufficient, although the flour was provided by the UNHCR. The city bakery was continually shelled and often lacking energy supply and ingredients for baking. Only in 1994 could people buy subsidized bread in their local currency—the Bosnian coupon. The price of a loaf of bread was 60,000 coupons; an average Bosnian salary sufficed for a loaf a bread a day. One could, however, get 8.2 ounces per person only.[76]

The sentence "I'll go out to buy some bread" was loaded with meaning. Buying bread had to be negotiated on a daily basis, and always had an uncertain outcome. It might have evoked an image of peaceful normality, but in Sarajevo under siege it functioned only as an imitation.

STAYING BEHIND: HUMILIATION AND DIGNITY

The experiences presented in this chapter are held in the memory of the civilians who were exposed to the dangers of war and manifold deprivations, uncertainties, and fears. Their hardships, inner thoughts, and dilemmas never filled the daily reports on the wars in Croatia and Bosnia-Herzegovina in the 1990s. Given that they remained in their homes and did not become refugees, they were forgotten in the discourse of war articulated in the media. Yet this *forgotten majority*—people who stayed behind—struggled to retain their lives as best they could in spite of the violence around them.

Written by an ethnologist, and based on ethnographic research, the quotations, descriptions, and insights offered here do not attempt to give a complete or definite ethnographic insight into the experiences of everyday life in the post-Yugoslav wars 1991–95. However, they reveal the practical and narrative rootedness of identity in the spheres of everyday life in peacetime.

In wartime, routines are not recognized as suffocating—predictability and repetition are not perceived as boring. The everyday becomes a script, with a particular dramatic structure, which helps in the solving of problems when organizing day-to-day existence. At the same time, routines construct and confirm the individual and group identity in its prepolitical aspects, related to shared place-bound experiences.

Even when reduced to the very minimum, routine proved to be salutary for the psyche, inasmuch as it was structuring a certain order and at the same time evoking, imitating, or embodying peace. As in many other places enmeshed in war, it was comprehended as an area of human dignity, integrity, and authenticity.

The last word should be given to a man in his late fifties whom the author interviewed about his most important memories of war spent in his hometown. He mentioned that his sister's house was destroyed, so she became a refugee. He mentioned his plans for an early retirement and life in the countryside being crushed, since his grandfather's house in a nearby village was plundered and heavily damaged. He talked about how a wedding was organized overnight when his son was called up to the army, so that his recently pregnant girlfriend would not remain an unwed mother, but a widow, in case the son was killed. He recalled that he still feels pain in his back when remembering carrying containers with seawater uphill to his household. Yet, his worst, saddest, most difficult memory, he emphasized, was a scene he witnessed at one of the occasions when he was carrying one of these water containers. He saw an old man bearing a couple of eggs—a real treasure in a town under siege, as rare and as valuable as fresh vegetables—in a rubber net serving as a carrier bag. The man stumbled and dropped the eggs. The scene that followed poignantly reveals the kind of humiliation imposed on people not recognized as real victims of war, since they had the dubious privilege of staying behind, walking in their own streets: the old man was kneeling down on the pavement, trying to put some of the spilled eggs back in the broken shells.

NOTES

1. See Elizabeth M. Cousens and Charles K. Cater, *Toward Peace in Bosnia: Implementing the Dayton Accord* (Boulder, Colo., and London: Lynne Rienner Publishers, 2001), pp. 17–21.

2. See Stef Jansen, "The (Dis)comfort of Conformism: Post-war Nationalism and Coping with Powerlessness in Croatian Villages," in *Warfare and Society: Archaeological and Social Anthropological Perspectives*, ed. T. Otto, H. Thrane, and H. Vandkilde (Aarhus: Aarhus University Press, 2006).

3. See V. P. Gagnon, Jr., *The Myth of Ethnic War: Serbia and Croatia in the 1990s* (Ithaca, N.Y. and London: Cornell University Press, 2004), p. xvi.

4. See Gagnon, *The Myth of Ethnic War,* p. 32.

5. Gagnon, *The Myth of Ethnic War,* p. 32. This was also the motivation of an international team of researchers involved in the project *The Scholars' Initiative: Confronting the Yugoslav Controversies.* They defined the problem as follows: "Amid all the bitter debates about the Yugoslav conflicts, there has been one element of agreement by all sides, namely the pivotal role that history has played in shaping people's minds. Unfortunately, each national group employs a different array of facts, many of which are either distorted or blatantly untrue. The resulting, divergent recitations of history have divided nations by sowing mistrust, resentment and hatred between people who coexisted with one another for long periods of time. The deepest divide of all separates the great majority of ethnic Serbs (in both Serbia and *Republika Srpska*) from virtually all other national groups in Bosnia, Croatia, Kosovo, and Slovenia. In the hands of nationalist politicians, journalists, and academics, the tragic events of the 1990s have been misrepresented in ways that have intensified mutual recrimination, further widening the cultural gap between the Serbs and their neighbors." http://www.cla.purdue.edu/si/prospectus.pdf (accessed October 14, 2007).

6. "The Dissolution of Yugoslavia (1986–1991)," executive summary by Sabrina Ramet and Latinka Perović, of one of the projects encompassed by *The Scholars' Initiative: Confronting the Yugoslav Controversies,* available at http://www.cla.purdue.edu/si/Bullet[T2].pdf (accessed October 14, 2007).

7. "The Dissolution of Yugoslavia."

8. "The Dissolution of Yugoslavia." See also other results of international research project *The Scholars' Initiative,* at http://www.cla.purdue.edu/si/. The 10 other research themes are: "Kosovo Under Autonomy (1974–1990)"; "Independence and the Fate of Minorities (1991–92)"; "'Ethnic Cleansing' and War Crimes Committed (1991–95)"; "International Community and the FRY/Belligerents (1989–95)"; "The Safe Areas (1992–1995)"; "The War in Croatia (1991–1995)"; "Milošević's Kosovo: Rugova and the KLA (1990–99)"; "US/NATO intervention (1998–99)"; "The Hague Tribunal (ICTY)"; and "Living Together or Hating Each

Other?" *The Scholars' Initiative* attempted to bridge the gap that separates scholarly knowledge of the tragic events of the period 1986–2000 from the proprietary interpretations that nationalist politicians and media have impressed on mass culture. It also intended to narrow the cognitive gap between peoples by simultaneously validating evidence and discrediting unfounded, proprietary myths through a combination of sober scholarship and sustained interaction with media and public officials. The hope was that an international consortium of eminent scholars could furnish a common, and ostensibly legitimate, alternative account on which moderate opinion leaders can lean for support. The credibility of *The Scholars' Initiative* is based not only on the indisputable scientific credentials of its participants, but on the transparent impartiality of its methodology as it solicits and examines evidence presented by all sides, then jointly evaluates and (in)validates the documentary material through the application of universal scientific methodologies. http://www.cla.purdue.edu/si/prospectus.pdf (accessed October 14, 2007).

9. Cousens and Cater, *Toward Peace in Bosnia*, p. 19.

10. Ivo Goldstein, *Croatia: A History* (London: Hurst and Company, 1999), p. 222.

11. Goldstein, *Croatia: A History*, p. 226.

12. Goldstein, *Croatia: A History*, p. 227.

13. Laura Silber and Allan Little, *Yugoslavia: Death of a Nation* (New York: Penguin Books, 1997).

14. Sabrina Petra Ramet, *Balkan Babel: The Disintegration of Yugoslavia from the Death of Tito to the Fall of Milošević* (Boulder, Colo., and Oxford: Westview Press, 2002), p. 67.

15. Ramet, *Balkan Babel,* pp. 68–69.

16. The Croatian nongovernmental organization Documenta, led by Vesna Teršelić, intends to organize systematic documentation of the names of Croatian citizens killed and missing in the war 1991–95. According to Teršelić, the Croatian government quotes the figure of 12,000 killed and missing, but that figure does not encompass Croatian citizens of Serbian ethnic affiliation (VOANews.com, February 12, 2007). http://www.voanews.com/croatian/archive/2007–02/2007–02–12-voa9.cfm? (accessed October 20, 2007).

17. Ramet, *Balkan Babel,* p. 163.

18. Cousens and Cater, *Toward Peace in Bosnia,* p. 19.

19. Ethnographic research quoted in this chapter points to the perception from below, among the victimized civilians in Croatia and Bosnia-Herzegovina, that is in line with Christopher Bennett's observation that "having made it as difficult as possible for non-Serbs to organize effective resistance, the great powers refused to protect defenseless communities or even to acknowledge what was taking place in former Yugoslavia. And it is this indifference to the fate of the innocent victims of the conflict on the part of the UN Security Council, which has bordered on complicity in ethnic cleansing, that has brought shame on the great powers and brought the entire mediation process into disrepute"; Christopher Bennett, *Yugoslavia's Bloody Collapse: Causes, Course and Consequence* (New York: New York University Press, 1995), p. 238.

20. On May 19, 1992, the Yugoslav People's Army (JNA) was renamed the Army of Yugoslavia, and made a show of pulling out of Bosnia, but left behind some 50–80,000 troops of purportedly Bosnian Serb origin, together with their armory, to form the army of *Republika srpska*. This army was commanded by General Ratko Mladić, in 2008 still on the run from the indictment by the UN War

Crimes Tribunal in The Hague, which has charged him with the massacre of civilians in Srebrenica.

21. Cousens and Cater, *Towards Peace in Bosnia,* p. 19. Herceg-Bosna was proclaimed by the Croats in Western Herzegovina in July 1992, and was a quasi-state that aspired to eventual union with Croatia. It was created as an ad hoc defensive formation, but by the summer of 1993, its defensive character had been replaced by a more aggressive and expansionist stance towards central Bosnia. However, with the growing power of the governmental forces in central Bosnia, Herceg-Bosna came under a serious threat that was averted only by the intervention of units of the Croatian Army. Long after the Dayton Agreements and the formal annulment of its existence, Herceg-Bosna continued to license its own cars, bestow insignia on its own police force, and use the Croatian currency. It was officially abolished only in August 1996. The recovery by Croatia of control over its own Serb "Krajina" could not have been achieved without the cooperation of the Croatian Council of Defense (HVO) in Herceg-Bosna. That explains the support it got from the Tuđman government, which only formally assented to international agreements recognizing the integrity of Bosnia-Herzegovina in the later 1990s. See John A. Allcock, Marko Milivojević. and John J. Horton, eds., *Conflict in the Former Yugoslavia: An Encyclopedia* (Santa Barbara, Calif.: ABC-CLIO, 1998), pp. 113–114.

22. These and many other figures concerning "Human losses in Bosnia and Hercegovina 1991–95" are provided by the Research and Documentation Center in Sarajevo, at http://www.idc.org.ba/aboutus.html.

23. Cousens and Cater, *Toward Peace in Bosnia,* p. 25.

24. Cousens and Cater, *Toward Peace in Bosnia,* p. 25.

25. Carl-Ulrik Schierup, "Former Yugoslavia: Long Waves of International Migration," in *The Cambridge Survey of World Migration,* ed. Robin Cohen (Cambridge: Cambridge University Press, 1995), pp. 285–289, p. 288.

26. Cousens and Cater, *Toward Peace in Bosnia,* p. 59.

27. 6,951 Bosniaks (Muslims) were slaughtered in the week in which Srebrenica was taken by Serb forces, 95.26 percent of them men. Of the total number of killed and missing in Srebrenica, 75.13 percent were civilians. For these and other figures see Research and Documentation Center in Sarajevo, "Human losses in Bosnia and Hercegovina 1991–95," at http://www.idc.org.ba/aboutus.html.

28. Cousens and Cater, *Toward Peace in Bosnia,* p. 29.

29. See executive summary by Darko Gavrilović and Charles Ingrao, of "The Safe Areas (1992–1995)" (http://www.cla.purdue.edu/si/BulletT6.pdf), one of the projects encompassed by *The Scholars' Initiative.* "The UN created the Safe Areas to forestall ethnic cleansing and other human rights violations against the civilian populations of Bihać, Goražde, Sarajevo, Srebrenica, Tuzla and Žepa. This apprehension stemmed largely from the record of crimes committed by Croatian and Bosnian-Serb forces during 1991–1992. Whereas the international community was eager to 'do something' to protect civilians in the six besieged towns, France, Britain and the USA were primarily interested in *appearing* to 'do something' but were unwilling to incur the financial, military, and political sacrifices necessary to render the Safe Areas effective. Although non-permanent members of the UN Security Council such as Hungary, Pakistan, New Zealand and Venezuela sought 'protected zones' the UNSC's permanent members created a Safe Area system that lacked deterrence." See http://www.cla.purdue.edu/si/ExecutiveSummaryT6.pdf (accessed October 14, 2007).

30. Schierup, "Former Yugoslavia," p. 288.

31. See Julie Mertus, Jasmina Tesanovic, Habib Metikos, and Rada Boric, eds., *The Suitcase: Refugee Voices from Bosnia and Croatia* (Berkeley and Los Angeles: University of California Press, 1997) for a collection of personal narratives, letters, stories, and poems by such refugees.

32. Bennett, *Yugoslavia's Bloody Collapse,* p. 240.

33. Bennett, *Yugoslavia's Bloody Collapse,* p. 240.

34. Gagnon, *The Myth of Ethnic War,* p. xv.

35. Gagnon, *The Myth of Ethnic War,* p. xv.

36. Gagnon, *The Myth of Ethnic War,* p. 200.

37. See Ivana Maček, "Predicament of War: Sarajevo Experiences and Ethics of War," *Anthropology of Violence and Conflict,* ed. in Ingo W. Schröder and Bettina E. Schmidt (London and New York: Routledge, 2001).

38. See Torsten Kolind, "Post-war Identifications: Counterdiscursive Practices in a Bosnian Town" (PhD diss., Institute of Anthropology, Archaeology and Linguistics, The University of Aarhus, 2004). See also his "Non-ethnic Condemnation in Post-war Stolac," in *The Balkans in Focus: Cultural Boundaries in Europe,* ed. Sanimir Resic and Barbara Tömquist-Plewa (Lund: Nordic Academic Press, 2002).

39. See http://www.idc.org.ba/project/oralhistory_stories.htm.

40. Gagnon, *The Myth of Ethnic War,* p. 8. See too Ivana Maček, "War Within: Everyday Life in Sarajevo under Siege" (Uppsala: Acta Universitatis Upsaliensis, 2000), p. 23. This PhD dissertation defended at Uppsala University is forthcoming in a revised version under the title *Within the War: Life in Sarajevo under Siege* at University of Pennsylvania Press.

41. See Gagnon, *The Myth of Ethnic War,* pp. 195–200, for a critique of the dominant theoretical approaches that are used to explain conflicts described as "ethnic."

42. See Earl Conteh-Morgan, *Collective Political Violence: An Introduction to the Theories and Cases of Violent Conflicts* (New York and London: Routledge, 2004).

43. See Maja Povrzanović, "The Imposed and the Imagined as Encountered by Croatian War Ethnographers," *Current Anthropology* 41, no. 2 (2000): 151–62.

44. See Brian Bennett, ed., "Socio-cultural Analyses of the Political and Economic Democratization Processes in East/Central Europe," a special issue of *Collegium Antropologicum* 19, no. 1 (1995): 7–119; Kolind, "Post-war Identifications"; Stef Jansen, "Anti-nationalism: Post-Yugoslav Resistance and Narratives of Self and Society (PhD diss., University of Hull, 2000), published in Serbian as *Antinacionalizam: Etnografija otpora u Zagrebu i Beogradu* (Beograd: XX vek, 2005); Lada Čale Feldman, Ines Prica, and Reana Senjković, eds., *Fear, Death and Resistance. An Ethnography of War: Croatia 1991–1992* (Zagreb: Institute of Ethnology and Folklore Research, Matrix Croatica, X-Press, 1993); and Renata Jambrešić Kirin and Maja Povrzanović, eds., *War, Exile, Everyday Life: Cultural Perspectives* (Zagreb: Institute for Ethnology and Folklore Research, 1996). See too the documentary films of Tone Bringa: *We Are All Neighbors,* documentary film, directed by Debbie Christie, "Disappearing Worlds" series (Granada Television, 1993); and *Returning Home: Revival of a Bosnian Village,* documentary film, coauthored with Peter Loizios, (Saga Video, 2001). Both can be obtained from Film office (Susanne Hammacher) at the Royal Anthropological Institute in London, e-mail: film@therai.org.uk.

45. Maja Povrzanović Frykman, "Violence and the Re-discovery of Place," *Ethnologia Europaea* 32, no. 2 (2002): 69–88.

46. Edward S. Casey, *Getting Back into Place: Toward a Renewed Understanding of the Place-World* (Bloomington and Indianapolis: Indiana University Press, 1993), p. xiii.

47. Maček, "War Within," pp. 230–35.

48. Being affiliated to the Zagreb Institute of Ethnology and Folklore Research, I collected private letters written by people from Zagreb in late 1991, and over the next five years interviewed women and men of different ages and of different social backgrounds (mostly Croats, but also Serbs) not only from Dubrovnik and the Dubrovnik region, but also from Vukovar, Županja, Vinkovci surroundings, Osijek, Zadar, Šibenik, and Zagreb in the period from 1991 to 1996. Interviews/letters are anonymous and were not published in English. See Maja Povrzanović, "Identities in War. Embodiments of Violence and Places of Belonging," *Ethnologia Europaea* 27, no. 2 (1997): 153–62, and her article, "Children, War and Nation: Croatia 1991," *Childhood: A Global Journal of Child Research* 4, no. 1 (1997): 81–102.

49. Erik Gandini, *Raja Sarajevo/Sarajevogänget*, documentary film (Stockholm: Filmcentrum, 1994), available on VHS. See also Antonia D. Carnerud, *Dubrovnik, murar av vår förflutna*, documentary film (Stockholm: Filmcentrum, 1994), also available on DVD; and Keith Doubt, "Film and Video Resources for Understanding Events on Bosnia," in *Sociology after Bosnia and Kosovo: Recovering Justice* (Lanham, Md., Boulder, Colo., New York, and Oxford: Rowman and Littlefield, 1994), pp. 163–69.

50. Ivana Maček, "War Within."

51. For such ethnographic examples from Croatia in 1991–92, see Maja Povrzanović, "Culture and Fear: Everyday Life in Wartime," and Ines Prica, "Notes on Ordinary Life in War," both in Čale Feldman et al., *Fear, Death and Resistance;* Povrzanović, "Identities in War: Embodiments of Violence and Places of Belonging"; and Povrzanović Frykman, "Violence and the Re-discovery of Place."

52. Joe Sacco, *Safe Area Gorazde: The War in Eastern Bosnia 1992–95* (Seattle, Wash.: Fantagraphics Books, 2000).

53. Selections of Vukovar children's autobigraphical stories written in 1994 are translated into English in Ines Prica and Maja Povrzanović, "Narratives of Refugee Children as the Ethnography of Maturing," in *War, Exile, Everyday Life: Cultural Perspectives,* ed. Renata Kirin Jambrešić and Maja Povrzanović (Zagreb: Institute for Ethnology and Folklore Research, 1996), pp. 83–113.

54. See Alenka Mirković, *91,6 MHz—Glasom protiv topova* (Zagreb: Algoritam, 1997).

55. Suada Kapić, *Sarajevo Survival Map,* graphic design and illustration by Ozren Pavlović, text by Nihad Kreševljaković (Sarajevo: Fama International, 2006).

56. Maja Razović and Aleksandra Wagner, eds., *Sarajevo Survival Guide,* text by Miroslav Prstojević, photos by Željko Puljić (Sarajevo: Fama, 1993), for FAMA, distributed by Workman Publishing.

57. Razović and Wagner, *Sarajevo Survival Guide,* p. 22.

58. Razović and Wagner, *Sarajevo Survival Guide,* p. 45.

59. Razović and Wagner, *Sarajevo Survival Guide,* p. 68.

60. See Povrzanović Frykman, "Violence and the Re-discovery of Place."

61. Ozren Kebo, *Sarajevo—en bruksanvisning* (Stockholm: Bokförlaget DN, 1998).

62. See Razović and Wagner, *Sarajevo Survival Guide,* pp. 86–87.

63. Razović and Wagner, *Sarajevo Survival Guide,* p. 89.

64. Transcript of an interview quoted in Maček, "War Within," p. 90.

65. See Suada Kapić, *Sarajevo Survival Map.*

66. See Maček, "War Within," pp. 160–62.

67. See Suada Kapić, *Sarajevo Survival Map.*

68. Here a later edition of *Sarajevo Survival Map* is quoted, produced, and published by Fama International in 2006.

69. Razović and Wagner, *Sarajevo Survival Guide,* p. 17.

70. See Suada Kapić, *Sarajevo Survival Map.*

71. Razović and Wagner, *Sarajevo Survival Guide,* p. 39.

72. Razović and Wagner, *Sarajevo Survival Guide,* p. 40.

73. Maček, "War Within," p. 79.

74. See Suada Kapić, *Sarajevo Survival Map.*

75. Maček, "War Within," p. 90.

76. See Razović and Wagner, *Sarajevo Survival Guide,* p. 36.

Glossary

Attentisme. Literally, "waiting on events," a term used to describe the neutral position adopted by many French men and women following the defeat of their country in June 1940. Such a position avoided taking sides, as either a collaborationist or a resister. Some civilians who adopted an *attentiste* approach waited for their moment before joining the resistance. By 1942, and the occupation of all France, it was extremely difficult to maintain such neutrality.

Barbarossa. Code name given to the Nazi invasion of the Soviet Union, instigated on June 22, 1941, and which breached the nonaggression Nazi-Soviet Pact of August 1939. Hitler's invasion of the Soviet Union was intended to create *Lebensraum* or living space for the German peoples, and was expected to bring to a head war with Britain and the United States so as to confirm Nazi Germany as the leading global power.

Blitz. Name given to the German aerial assault on British cities in the period from August 1940 to May 1941. Such raids brought into relief the possibilities of strategic bombing, which affected civilian morale as much as they did damage to economic infrastructure.

Brest-Litovsk. Treaty of March 3, 1918, concluded between the Central Powers and Bolshevik Russia. Determined to honor his pledge to pull Russia out of World War One, which was viewed as "an imperialist struggle," and anxious to consolidate revolution at home, Lenin dispatched Trotsky to Brest—Litovsk, modern-day Brest on the Polish border, where he met German and Austrian delegates on December 3, 1917. Protracted negotiations ensued, but German military successes ensured that the Bolsheviks eventually had to agree to Germany's draconian terms, which involved a considerable loss of territory. The armistice of November 11, 1918, effectively nullified Brest-Litovsk.

Carlism. Reactionary political movement which, in the nineteenth century, was periodically engaged in dynastic struggles for the Spanish crown. In 1936 Carlists sided with the Nationalists in the Spanish Civil War.

Central Powers. Term given to the military alliance, initially comprising the German empire and Austria-Hungary, which confronted the Allies in World War One. Geographically located in the heart of Europe, hence the term *central,* Germany and Austro-Hungary were joined in October 1914 by the Ottoman empire, and Bulgaria a year later.

Četniks. Partisans, drawn largely from the army, who sought a restoration of the Yugoslav state under a Serbian monarchy. They also fought Tito's followers and were prepared to collude with the Nazis.

Cheka. All Russian Extraordinary Commission for Combating Counter Revolution and Sabotage. Founded immediately after the Bolshevik takeover, this was one of the many branches of the Russian secret police, and eventually became known as the KGB in 1954. It was responsible for prosecuting the Red Terror, running the gulags, and generally spreading fear among the civilian population.

Chemin des Dames. Site of the disastrous Nivelle offensive, launched on April 16, 1917, which led to heavy casualties, prompting mutinies in French units along the western front.

Cossacks. Peoples of southeastern Russia who, in the nineteenth century, increasingly saw themselves as a separate nation. Though some Cossacks fought with the Bolsheviks, the majority opposed the October Revolution and were vigorously persecuted by the Bolsheviks during the Civil War.

Dayton Agreements. Negotiated at Wright-Patterson Air Force Base in Dayton Ohio, these agreements brought an end to the war in Bosnia-Herzegovina. The agreements were officially signed in Paris on December 14, 1995.

Displaced Persons. European refugees at the end of World War Two who were cared for by the United Nations Relief and Rehabilitation Administration.

Duma. Russian parliament granted by Nicolas II after the 1905 Revolution. It possessed few powers and could be suspended by the tsar, as was the case in World War One.

Einsatzgruppen. Mobile killing units, formed largely out of the SS in 1938. They first saw action in the Polish campaign in 1939 and became notorious in 1941 when they followed the Wehrmacht into the Soviet Union with the task of eliminating all Jews, Communist Party officials, gypsies, and others. An integral part of the Final Solution, they were later deployed against Soviet resisters.

Exode. Literally *exodus,* was the term given to the floods of refugees from Luxemburg, Holland, Belgium, and France who fled the German advance in May and June 1940. It is estimated that between six and eight million civilians took to the roads. Though official plans had been put in place to cope with refugees, these arrangements were overtaken by the speed and scale of events.

Falange. Created in 1933 by José Antonio Primo de Rivera, the son of the dictator, this was an extreme right-wing political party whose ideology was close to fascism. The party was outlawed in March 1936 but was influential in the Civil War, despite the execution of Primo de Rivera, and it eventually merged with other Nationalist movements.

Franctireurkrieg. German term to describe the guerrilla war launched by irregular French forces in the Franco-Prussian War (1870–71), a method of fighting the Germans feared the French would use again in World War One.

Great Patriotic War. Russian term used to describe the war that the Soviet Union fought against Nazi Germany in the period 1941–45. Significantly the term is not extended to the war that the Allies were fighting with Hitler, nor the conflict that the USSR was fighting with Japan. The term was a deliberate propaganda device conjuring up memories of the Patriotic War of 1812 when the Russian peoples had resisted the invasion of Napoleon I's armies.

Guernica. Site of an appalling German bombing raid in the Spanish Civil War. In late afternoon on market day, April 26, 1937, the small market town of Guernica was bombarded for several hours by German bombers; civilians attempting to flee were mown down by surrounding Italian forces. The death toll is bitterly disputed but is now thought to number between 250 and 300 fatalities, though hundreds were injured. Later depicted in a famous painting by Picasso, Guernica came to symbolize civilian suffering under aerial bombardment.

Hague Conventions. Series of international agreements signed in 1899 and 1907 that attempted to deal with the methods of waging war, notably outlawing the use of particular weapons.

Kadets. Also known as the Constitutional Democratic Party, was founded at the time of the Russian Revolution of 1905 and sought progressive reform under a constitutional monarchy. After the 1917 February Revolution, the Kadets, previously the preeminent liberal party, found themselves on the right and were forced to disperse after the Bolshevik takeover.

Kinderlandesverschickung. German system of relief camps in the countryside that provided urban children with protection from air raids on their cities.

Kronstadt uprising. A protest in March 1921 on the part of Russian sailors at the Kronstadt naval base on the Gulf of Finland. Though they had initially supported both the February and October Revolutions, they were disenchanted with the restrictive political controls imposed by the Bolsheviks and the harsh living conditions of War Communism. The mutiny was brutally crushed by the Bolsheviks, signaling Lenin's unwillingness to tolerate dissent of any description.

Lend-Lease. Program of aid given by the United States to its allies in World War Two. Rather than providing credit and loans, as it had in World War One, the American preference was to supply material aid. The president himself had enormous powers in deciding and granting such assistance, which was eventually extended to 38 countries.

Maquis. Members of the French resistance who, from 1942–43 onwards, took refuge in the scrubland (the *maquis*) so as to avoid compulsory labor service in Germany. It is calculated that there were around 10,000 *maquisards* in the old occupied zone, and approximately 30,000 in the former nonoccupied zone. *Maquisards* lived off the land and depended on the support provided them by local communities. In 1944, the *maquis* engaged the Germans in a series of set battles, most famously at the Glières plateau in March 1944 where they were outgunned; however, they played a significant role at the Liberation, several enlisting in the French First Army, which fought in the battle for Germany.

Miliciens. Members of the paramilitary police force, the *Milice*, created by the Vichy government in 1943 to hunt for resisters, Jews, and deserters from the compulsory work service in Germany. Numbering around 30,000, and led by the collaborationist Joseph Darnand, the *miliciens* symbolized the extent to which Vichy had sacrificed itself to Nazi Germany.

Nationalists. Name given to the disparate supporters of General Franco in the Spanish Civil War.

Nazi-Soviet Pact. Infamous nonaggression treaty signed by Molotov and Ribbentrop by which both sides agreed to maintain neutrality should either country find itself at war. Secret articles permitted the Nazis and Soviets to pursue their territorial ambitions.

New Economic Policy. Was designed to replace the disastrous policies of War Communism that the Bolsheviks had introduced to fight the Civil War. Introduced in 1921, NEP permitted a mixed economy within the countryside and soon made good earlier agricultural losses. However, it agitated Stalin and hard-line Bolsheviks, who believed the system had given rise to a new middle class in the shape of the kulaks, better-off peasants. To reassert Bolshevik control, NEP was abandoned at the Fifteenth Party Congress in 1929, to be replaced by collectivization and state planning.

Nomenklatura. Refers to the official party and state positions in the USSR and the persons who occupied these appointments.

Provisional Government. Was created after the February Revolution, and thanks to the abdication of Tsar Nicholas II became the *de facto* government of Russia. Based in Petrograd, it suffered several challenges to its authority, notably from the Petrograd Soviet, and was overthrown by the Bolsheviks.

Race to the Sea. Took place in September-November 1914 when both sides on the western front attempted to outflank one another, the result being a series of trenches from the North Sea coastline to Switzerland.

Red Terror. Campaign launched by the Bolsheviks against their many enemies after the October Revolution. Though officially the Red Terror lasted but two months in September and October 1918, most historians agree that it lasted for the duration for the Civil War.

Reichstag. German parliament.

Romanovs. Ruling dynasty of imperial Russia overthrown by the revolutions of 1917.

Samizdat literature. Unofficial publications that appeared in the Soviet Union and its satellites, often deeply critical of communism.

Second International. European-wide organization of trade union and socialist parties, 1889–1916, which moved increasingly in a nonrevolutionary and social democratic direction, yet was still noted for its factionalism.

Socialist Revolutionaries. Russian political party, created in 1898, dedicated to the overthrow of tsardom and active in both the 1905 and February 1917 revolution, but outmaneuvered and eventually suppressed by the Bolsheviks.

Spanish Second Republic. Came into being in April 1931 with the fall of Alfonso XIII. Committed to a progressive constitution, the Republic was challenged by several traditional and reactionary forces, a struggle that culminated in the Spanish Civil War. The Republic struggled on until its final defeat by Franco in 1939.

Stasi. East German Secret Police.

Todt Organization. Was named after Fritz Todt, Hitler's chief architect, and before 1939 was charged with massive public works programs, notably the building of motorways. In the conflict itself, the OT was an integral part of the war economy, employing large numbers of foreign workers and POWs.

Union Sacrée. Literally *sacred union*, was a temporary burying of political and religious differences on the part of French politicians in August 1914 so that they could rally the nation behind the war effort.

Ustašas. Croat fascists who fought alongside German forces in World War Two and who initiated a campaign of genocide against Jews and Serbs. Their violence even shocked the Nazis.

Verdun. Site of one of the most murderous battles fought on the western front in World War One. In February 1916, German forces assaulted this small garrison town on the river Meuse. Though of little strategic value, Verdun was of tremendous symbolic importance, being the scene of repeated French resistance to German attackers in 1792, 1870, and 1914. The Germans thus knew the French would defend it to the last and, in Falkenhayn's words, hoped "to bleed France white," enabling Germany to win its war against the British and Russians. In the event, Verdun stood firm and came to symbolize French patriotism and resolve.

Vichy regime (1940–1944). Reactionary wartime government that presided over France after the defeat of June 1940. Following the Franco-German Armistice (June 25, 1940), France was divided into two principal zones, the largest of which was occupied by the Germans. Having quit Paris on June 10, the French government settled, on July 3, at the little spa town of Vichy, chosen because of ample accommodation.

Whites. Opponents of the Bolsheviks during the Russian Civil War. Drawn from disparate groups, and led by members of the former imperial army, the Whites often alienated popular support by their brutish treatment of civilians.

Bibliography

WORLD WAR ONE

There exists a gargantuan literature on World War One. Two excellent overviews are provided by David Stevenson, *1914–1918: The History of the First World War* (London: Penguin, 2005) and Hew Strachan, *The First World War: A New History* (London: Free Press, 2006). Other works well worth consulting include Ian Beckett, *The Great War 1914–1918* (London: Pearson, 2001), Marc Ferro, *The Great War, 1914–1918* (London: Routledge and Kegan Paul, 1973), Keith Robbins, *The First World War* (Oxford: Oxford University Press, 1984), François Cochet, *La Grande Guerre* (Paris: Nouveau monde édition, 2006), and Robin Prior and Trevor Wilson, *The First World War* (London: Cassell, 1999). For an introduction to the experience of civilians, see Roger Chickering and Stig Förster, eds., *Great War, Total War: Combat and Mobilisation on the Western Front, 1914–1918* (Cambridge: Cambridge University Press, 2000).

The Home Front

There is additionally an extensive literature exclusively on the home fronts. An introduction is to be found in John Horne, ed., *State, Society and Mobilization in Europe during the First World War* (Cambridge: Cambridge University Press, 1997), Frank P. Chambers, *The War Behind the War, 1914–18: A History of the Political and Civilian Fronts* (New York: Harcourt Brace, 1939), J. Williams, *The Other Battleground: The Home Fronts, Britain, France and Germany, 1914–1919* (Chicago: Henry Regnery, 1972), and John Horne, *Labour at War: France and Britain, 1914–1918* (Oxford: Oxford University Press, 1991). Specifically on France, see Jean-Jacques Becker, *The Great War and the French People* (Leamington Spa: Berg, 1986), Jean-Baptiste Duroselle, *La Grande Guerre des Français 1914–1918* (Paris: Perrin, 1994), Patrick Fridenson, ed., *The French Home Front, 1914–1918* (Oxford: Berg, 1992), and P. J. Flood, *France 1914–18: Public Opinion and the War Effort* (London: Macmillan, 1990). On Germany, an excellent starting point is Roger Chickering, *Imperial Germany and the Great War, 1914–1918* (Cambridge: Cambridge University Press, 1998), which may be complemented by Gerhard Feldman, *Army, Industry and Labor in Germany 1914–1918* (Princeton, N.J.: Princeton University Press, 1996), Jürgen Kocka, *Facing Total War: German Society, 1914–1918* (Leamington Spa: Berg, 1984) and Holger H. Werwig, *The First World War: Germany and Austria-Hungary, 1914–1918* (London: Arnold, 1997). On Britain, see Arthur Marwick, *The Deluge: British Society and the First World War* (London: Bodley Head, 1965), Jay Winter, *The Great War and the British People* (Cambridge, Mass.: Harvard University Press, 1986), John Bourne, *Britain and the Great War* (London: Hodder Arnold, 1989) and Geoffrey de Groot, *Blighty: British Society in the Great War* (London: Longman, 1996). On the response of the cities, where the effects of the conflict were quickly felt, see Jay Winter and Jean-Louis Robert, eds., *Capital Cities at War: London, Paris, Berlin, 1914–1919* (Cambridge: Cambridge University Press, 1997) and Pierre Darmon, *Vivre à Paris pendant la Grande Guerre* (Paris: Fayard, 2002). The funding of the war is considered in Hew Strachan, *Financing the First World War* (Oxford and New York: Oxford University Press, 2004).

Women's Roles

On gender, a good starting point is Susan Grayzel, *Women's Identities at War: Gender, Motherhood and Politics in Britain and France during the First World War* (Chapel Hill: University of North Carolina Press, 1999).

Presenting the War to the Home Front

On the ways in which the war was presented to the home fronts, see Harold Lasswell, *Propaganda Techniques in the World War* (London: Kegan Paul, 1927), James Squires, *British Propaganda at Home and the United States from 1914 to 1917* (Cambridge: Cambridge University Press, 1935), Eberhard Demm, "Propaganda and Caricature in the First World War," *Journal of Contemporary History*, 28 (1993): 163–192, and David Welch, *Germany, Propaganda and Total War, 1914–1918: The Sins of Omission* (London: Athlone, 2000).

Domestic Opposition

For domestic opposition to the war, see Martin Ceadel, *Pacifism in Britain, 1914–1945: the Defining of Faith* (Oxford: Clarendon Press, 1980), Cyril Pearce, *Comrades in Conscience: The Story of an English Community's Opposition to the Great War* (London: Francis Bourle, 2001), Peter Bock and Nigel Young, *Pacifism in the Twentieth Century* (Syracuse, N.Y. and New York: Syracuse University Press, 1999), and Charles Chatfield, *The American Peace Movement: Ideals and Activism* (New York: Twayne Publishers, 1992).

Devastation and Remembrance

The material devastation is brilliantly discussed in Hugh Clout, *After the Ruins: Restoring the Countryside of Northern France after the Great War* (Exeter: University of Exeter Press, 1996), while the issues of remembrance are treated in the many works by Jay Winter. See, in particular, his *Sites of Memory, Sites of Mourning: The*

Great War in European Cultural History (Cambridge: Cambridge University Press, 1995) and his *Remembering War: The Great War and Historical Memory in the Twentieth Century* (New Haven, Conn.: Yale University Press, 2006). Among older works, see Paul Fussell, *The Great War and Modern Memory* (London, Oxford, and New York: Oxford University Press, 1975) and George Mosse, *Fallen Soldiers: Reshaping the Memory of the World Wars* (Oxford: Oxford University Press, 1990) are well worth consulting.

General Reference

Among the many reference works on World War One, see Stéphane Audoin-Rouzeau and Jean-Jacques Becker, eds., *Encyclopédie de la Grande Guerre: 1914–1918. Histoire et culture* (Paris: Bayard, 2004); Spencer Tucker, *The European Powers in the First World War: An Encyclopedia* (New York and London: Garland, 1996); and Jay Winter, *The Experience of World War One* (Oxford: Grange Books, 1988).

THE RUSSIAN CIVIL WAR

The revolutionary events of 1917, the Russian Civil War, and the early years of Soviet consolidation remain matters for intense historiographical debate. Jonathan Smele has written an excellent bibliographical guide to this controversial and fascinating period. See: Jonathan D. Smele, *Russian Revolution and Civil War* (London: Continuum, 2003). It has some 2,000 entries in English, Russian, and French as well as other languages.

Events of 1917

The events of 1917 provide the immediate backdrop to the Russian Civil War. In February, the tsar abdicated and two organizations came to power: the Provisional Government and the Petrograd Soviet. Each represented different social and political groupings, a reflection of the deeply fractured nature of Russian society. The government embraced liberal and bourgeois aspirations, while the left-wing Soviet's membership was drawn from the city's urban proletariat, as well as soldiers and sailors. In many ways, the dynamics of a dual-power system presaged the divisions that marked the Civil War period. A good introduction to these matters is to be found in E. N. Burdzhalov, *Russia's Second Revolution: The February 1917 Uprising in Petrograd* (Bloomington: Indiana University Press, 1987). See, too, Orlando Figes and Boris Kolonitskii, *Interpreting the Russian Revolution: The Language and Symbols of 1917* (New Haven, Conn.: Yale University Press, 1999), an interesting analysis of the dynamics of social and political discourse in the revolution, which draws upon the vast range of written and visual propaganda printed in this period. Tsuyoshi Hasegawa, *The February Revolution: Petrograd 1917* (Seattle: University of Washington Press, 1981), provides a detailed, day-to-day assessment of February that may be complemented by George Katkov, *Russia 1917: The February Revolution* (London: Longmans, 1967).

The Bolsheviks

In October 1917, the Bolsheviks came to power. Historians sometimes view the Bolshevik takeover as a guarantee of civil war in Russia and some have argued that Lenin's party was deliberately set upon such a war. Certainly, by late November/early December 1917, an internecine conflict looked a certainty. The following texts, a fraction of a vast historiography, consider the reasons the Bolsheviks came to power, their policies, and who opposed and supported them, as well as providing an insight into the conditions in which the civil war was born: Abraham Ascher and Paul Stevenson, *The Mensheviks in the Russian Revolution* (London: Thames and Hudson, 1976); Daniel H. Kaiser, *The Workers' Revolution in Russia, 1917: The View from Below* (Cambridge: Cambridge University Press, 1987); Ronald Kowalski, *The Bolshevik Party in Conflict: The Left Communist Opposition of 1918* (London: Macmillan, 1991); David Mandel, *The Petrograd Workers and the Fall of the Old Regime: From the February Revolution to the July Days, 1917* (London: Macmillan, 1983); Evan Mawdsley, *The Russian Revolution and the Baltic Fleet: War and Politics, February 1917-April 1918* (London: Macmillan, 1978); Alexander Rabinowitch, *Prelude to Revolution: The Petrograd Bolsheviks and the July 1917 Uprising* (Bloomington: Indiana University Press, 1968); William G. Rosenberg, *Liberals in the Russian Revolution: The Constitutional Democratic Party, 1917–1921* (Princeton, N.J.: Princeton University Press, 1974); Adam B. Ulam, *The Bolsheviks* (Cambridge, Mass.: Harvard University Press, 1998); and Dmitrii A. Volkogonov, *Lenin: Life and Legacy* (London: Harper Collins, 1994).

Overviews and Documents

Historians have conventionally divided the Russian Civil War into its geographical and military fronts. Others have concentrated on the interventions of Britain, France, Czechoslovakia, and the United States. More recent historiography has focused on different aspects, such as the role of the Green movement, peasant reactions to the Civil War, and propaganda techniques. The following provide a good overview of these areas of historical debate: J.F.N. Bradley, *Civil War in Russia, 1917–1920* (London: Batsford, 1975); Geoff Swain, *The Origins of the Russian Civil War* (London: Longman, 1996); and Rex A. Wade, *The Bolshevik Revolution and the Russian Civil War* (Westport, Conn.: Greenwood, 2000), a good conspectus, which is accompanied by useful biographies of the major participants and some interesting documents. Other primary sources are located in: V. P. Butt, A. B. Murphy, N. A. Myshov, and Geoff Swain, eds., *The Russian Civil War: Documents from the Soviet Archives* (Basingstoke: Macmillan 1996), a selection of documents that emphasize the editors' belief that Bolshevik success was inevitable; Vladimir N. Brovkin, ed., *Dear Comrades: Menshevik Reports on the Bolshevik Revolution and the Civil War* (Stanford, Calif.: Stanford University Press, 1991); A. B. Murphy, ed., *The Russian Civil War: Primary Sources* (Basingstoke: Macmillan, 2000); and P. N. Wrangel, *The Memoirs of General Wrangel, The Last Commander-in-Chief of the Russian National Army* (New York: Duffield and Company, 1930), the autobiography of the White General who oversaw the final period of the White defeat.

Regional Aspects of the War

On the regional aspects of the war, see A. E. Adams, *The Bolsheviks in the Ukraine: the Second Campaign 1918–19* (London: Kennikat Press, 1973), which reminds us that a great deal of the Civil War was fought over Ukrainian territory, where political and national allegiances were changeable and difficult to manage for any group. The following also provide local perspectives: C. F. Smith, *Vladivostok under Red and White Rule: Revolution and Counterrevolution in the Russian Far East 1920–1922* (Seattle: University of Washington Press, 1975); N.G.O. Pereira, *White Siberia: The Politics of Civil War* (Montreal: McGill-Queens University Press, 1996); and Richard Sakwa, *Soviet Communists in Power: A Study of Moscow during the Civil War, 1918–21* (Basingstoke: Macmillan, 1988).

Allied Intervention

On the allied intervention, see J.F.N. Bradley, *Allied Intervention in Russia* (London: University Press of America, 1968), which looks at the British and French involvement; George A. Brinkley, *The Volunteer Army and Allied Intervention in South Russia, 1917–1921: A Study in the Politics and Diplomacy of the Russian Civil War* (DeKalb: University of Notre Dame Press, 1966); C. H. Ellis, *The British "Intervention" in Transcaspia, 1918–1919* (Berkeley: University of California Press, 1963); Peter Kenez, *Civil War in South Russia, 1919–1922: The Defeat of the Whites* (Berkeley: University of California Press, 1971), which tackles the beginning of the end of the Whites' campaign; and Jonathan D. Smele, *Civil War in Siberia: The Anti-Bolshevik Government of Admiral Kolchak 1918–1920* (Cambridge: Cambridge University Press, 1996), which considers the far eastern frontier in the Russian Civil War. On Kronstadt, see Paul Avrich, *Kronstadt 1921* (Princeton, N.J.: Princeton University Press, 1970).

Political Maneuverings behind the War

On the political maneuverings behind the war, see Vladimir N. Brovkin, *Behind the Front Lines of the Civil War: Political Parties and Social Movements in Russia, 1918–1922* (Princeton, N.J.: Princeton University Press, 1994); Andrea Graziosi, *The Great Soviet Peasant War: Bolsheviks and Peasants, 1917–1933* (Cambridge, Mass.: Harvard University Press, 1996); M. Malet, *Nestor Makhno and the Russian Civil War* (London: Macmillan, 1982), which considers anarchism in the Ukraine; and M. Palij, *The Anarchism of Nestor Makhno* (Seattle: University of Washington Press, 1976).

The actual campaigning is usefully discussed in Norman Davies, *White Eagle, Red Star: The Polish-Soviet War, 1919–1920* (London: Pimlico, 2003). This assesses an oft-forgotten part of military hostility in the immediate aftermath of the October Revolution. While the Bolsheviks encountered internal enemies of many colors, they also faced a protracted and bitter war against newly independent Poland. See too A. Denikin, *The White Army* (Cambridge: Ian Faulkner Publishing, 1992), an account by one of the principal protagonists of the White army.

Famine during the War

On the famine see Charles M. Edmonson, "The Politics of Hunger: The Soviet Response to Famine, 1921," *Soviet Studies* 29, no. 4 (Oct. 1977): 506–51, and Harold H. Fisher, *The Famine in Soviet Russia, 1919–1923: The Operations of the American Relief Administration* (New York: Macmillan, 1927), an account by a member of the ARA present in Russia during civil war and famine.

The Bolshevik Victory

For an understanding of the eventual victory of the Bolsheviks, see Peter Kenez, *The Birth of the Propaganda State: Soviet Methods of Mass Mobilization, 1917–1929* (Cambridge: Cambridge University Press, 1985) which examines how thousands of civilians were mobilized for the Red cause, and Joshua Sanborn, *Drafting the Russian Nation: Military Conscription, Total War and Mass Politics, 1905–1925* (DeKalb: Northern Illinois University Press, 2003), which looks at how compulsory conscription shaped the Russian army, in both Imperial and Bolshevik times.

THE SPANISH CIVIL WAR

The essential social and political background is well served in Gerald Brenan's classic account of long-term origins, *The Spanish Labyrinth* (Cambridge: Cambridge University Press, 1950), the work of Edward Malefakis, *Agrarian Reform and Peasant Revolution in Spain* (New Haven, Conn.: Yale University Press, 1970), and Paul Preston's *The Coming of the Spanish Civil War: Reform, Reaction and Revolution in the Second Republic*, 2nd ed. (London: Routledge, 1994). On the religious background, Frances Lannon's *Privilege, Persecution and Prophecy: The Catholic Church in Spain 1875–1975* (Oxford: Oxford University Press, 1987) is essential, while Mary Vincent's *Catholicism in the Second Spanish Republic: Religion and Politics in Salamanca 1930–36* (Oxford: Oxford University Press, 1996) explores the Church's identification with the political right into the first months of the war.

For the war years, in relation to the broad area of state, economy, and society in the Republican zone, Helen Graham's *The Spanish Republic at War, 1936–1939* (Cambridge: Cambridge University Press, 2002) is indispensable. Her introductory and suggestive *The Spanish Civil War: A Very Short Introduction* (Oxford: Oxford University Press, 2005) is also useful. There is much in this area in George Esenwein and Adrian Shubert's *Spain at War* (London: Longman, 1995), probably the most thorough overview, though Paul Preston's *A Concise History of the Spanish Civil War* (London: Fontana, 1996; reprint of *The Spanish Civil War* [New York: Grove Press, 1986]) is also highly engaging and authoritative.

Ideologies and the Cultural History of Spain

Several of the works already mentioned touch on the mentalities, culture, and ideologies of the war, but this area of the historiography is less developed than political questions. Several works relate to particular ideological strands. The best introduction to Spanish anarchism is Julián Casanova, *Anarchism, the Republic and Civil War in Spain, 1931–1939* (London: Routledge, 2004). Specifically for urban Barcelona, see Chris Ealham, *Policing the City: Class, Culture and Conflict in Barcelona, 1898–1937* (London: Routledge, 2005). Though it does not deal directly with the Civil War, Jerome Mintz, *The Anarchists of Casas Viejas* (Chicago: University of Chicago Press, 1982) reveals more of the reality of rural anarchism than many drier studies. On the Nationalist side, Martin Blinkhorn's *Carlism and Crisis 1931–1939* (Cambridge: Cambridge University Press, 1975) remains fundamental. Although largely a political and institutional study, Hilari Raguer's *Gunpowder and Incense: The Catholic Church and the Spanish Civil War* (London: Routledge, 2007 [Spanish original 2001]) presents the most recent research and views religion as a social phenomenon bound up with politics and ideology during the war.

More broadly, Michael Seidman's *Republic of Egos: A Social History of the Spanish Civil War* (Madison: University of Wisconsin Press, 2002), though it contains much information on daily life, is seriously marred by a highly reductive analytical framework. The recent volume edited by Chris Ealham and Michael Richards, *The Splintering of Spain: Cultural History and the Spanish Civil War, 1936–1939* (Cambridge: Cambridge University Press, 2005) sets out to explore particular aspects of daily life during the war. The chapters on the religious aspects of Republican violence in Andalucía (Mary Vincent), the exercise of Republican power in the city of Gijón (Pamela Radcliff), Carlist mobilization for the Nationalist rebellion in Navarra (Francisco Javier Caspístegui), and Holy Week processions in conquered Málaga, 1937–39 (Michael Richards) are particularly germane to the question of wartime mentalities. Another edited volume, Helen Graham and Jo Labanyi, eds., *Spanish Cultural Studies: The Struggle for Modernity* (Oxford: Oxford University Press, 1995) includes several chapters on particular areas of wartime culture. Sandie Holguín, *Creating Spaniards: Culture and National Identity in Republican Spain* (Madison: University of Wisconsin Press, 2002) includes one chapter on Republican cultural policy during the civil war. The posters of the war period, printed in large numbers in the Republican zone and giving insights into daily representations (many of them gendered), can be consulted widely online, and are also to be found in Jordi Carulla and Arnau Carulla, *La guerra civil en 2000 carteles: República, guerra civil, posguerra* (Barcelona: Postermil, 1997), 2 vols.

Eyewitness Accounts and Women's Experiences

Many of the published eyewitness accounts of the war are only available in Spanish, but Franz Borkenau's *The Spanish Cockpit* (London: Pluto, 1986 [originally 1937]) and Arturo Barea's *The Forging of a Rebel: The Clash* (London: Flamingo, 1984 [1946]) stand up well against the classic but problematic account by George Orwell, *Homage to Catalonia* (London: Penguin, 2003 [1938]). For the testimony of Spanish participants, see the brilliantly conceived *Blood of Spain: The Experience of Civil War 1936–1939,* by Ronald Fraser (Harmondsworth: Allen Lane, 1979).

There are a number of works in English devoted to the history of women and the war. Mary Nash's *Defying Male Civilization: Women in the Spanish Civil War* (Denver, Colo.: Arden Press, 1995) is essential, as is Martha Ackelsberg's *Free Women of Spain: Anarchism and the Struggle for the Emancipation of Women* (Bloomington: Indiana University Press, 1991). Shirley Mangini's *Memories of Resistance: Women's Voices from the Spanish Civil War* (New Haven, Conn.: Yale University Press, 1995) looks at gender-specific repression of the defeated.

The Violence of the Spanish Civil War

The benchmark work on Civil War violence (on both sides) is Santos Juliá et al., *Víctimas de la guerra civil* (Madrid: Temas de Hoy, 1999). The considerable further local and regional research carried out since the book's appearance has not substantially altered its conclusions. For the relationship of Francoist repression to culture, ideology, and economics, see Michael Richards, *A Time of Silence: Civil War and the Culture of Repression in Franco's Spain, 1936–45* (Cambridge: Cambridge University Press, 1998). For a detailed update summary of the historiography on Nationalist violence, see Michael Richards, "The Limits of Quantification: Francoist Repression and Historical Methodology,"in *¿Política de exterminio? El debate acerca de la ideología, estrategías e instrumentos de la represión*, ed. S. Gálvez, Dossier monográfico, *Hispania Nova: Revista de Historia Contemporánea* 7 (2007), http://hispanianova.rediris.es/7/ dossier/07d015.pdf, accessed May 27, 2008. For the essential relationship between Nationalist and Republican repression in a particular region, see Manuel Ortiz Heras, *Violencia política en la II República y el primer franquismo: Albacete, 1936–1950* (Madrid: Siglo Veintiuno, 1996). Most of the English-language historiography on the Republican terror is devoted to anticlerical violence (see, for example, the articles by Bruce Lincoln, Mary Vincent, and Julio de la Cueva, mentioned in the text).

WORLD WAR TWO

A good overview of World War Two is to be found in Peter Calvocoressi and Guy Wint, *Total War: Causes and Courses of the Second World War* (Harmondsworth: Allen Lane, 1972). Norman Davies, *Europe at War, 1939–1945: No Simple Victory* (London: Allen Lane, 2006) emphasizes the war in the east while Gerhard Weinberg, *A World at Arms: A Global History of World War* (Cambridge: Cambridge University Press, 1994) considers the military context. For a stimulating introduction to the many issues discussed within this essay, see Joanna Bourke's impressionistic *The Second World War: A People's History* (Oxford: Oxford University Press, 2001), R.A.C. Parker's solid *Struggle for Survival: The History of the Second World War* (Oxford: Oxford University Press, 1989), and the many essays in Roger Chickering, Stig Förster, and Bernd Greiner, eds., *A World at Total War: Global Conflict and the Politics of Destruction, 1937–1945* (Cambridge: Cambridge University Press, 2005). None of the aforementioned, however, place civilians to the fore in the manner of Robert Gildea, Olivier Wieviorka, and Anette Warring, *Surviving Hitler and Mussolini: Daily Life in Occupied Europe* (Oxford: Berg, 2006).

Civilian Displacement in Europe

On the displacement of the civilian populations, there is a special edition of *Contemporary European History* 16, no. 4 (2007), edited by Peter Gatrell. Older studies include Eugene M. Kulischer, *Europe on the Move: War and Population Changes, 1917–47* (New York: Columbia University Press, 1948), and G. Frumkin, *Population Changes in Europe since 1919* (London: George Allen and Unwin, 1951). For the experience of the *exode*, the most up-to-date and accessible account is Hannah Diamond, *Fleeing Hitler: France 1940* (Oxford: Oxford University Press, 2007). On the more general experience of refugees, see Tony Kushner and Katherine Knox, *Refugees in an Age of Genocide: Global, National and Local Perspectives during the Twentieth Century* (London: Cass, 1999), which may be supplemented by the collection of essays edited by Martin Conway and José Gotovitch, *Europe in Exile: European Exile Communities in Britain, 1940–45* (Oxford: Berghahn, 2001). Anne Applebaum, *Gulag: A History of the Soviet Camps* (London: Penguin, 2004) examines the fate of East Europeans while Ulrich Herbert, *Hitler's Foreign Workers: Enforced Foreign Labour in Germany under the Third Reich* (Cambridge: Cambridge University Press, 1997) discusses how Europeans were coerced into sustaining Hitler's war machine. It is difficult to know where to begin with the vast literature on the Holocaust, but a useful starting point, situating the fate of Jews in the broader framework of mass violence, is to be found in Omer Bartov, *Mirrors of Destruction: War, Genocide and Modern Identity* (Oxford: Oxford University Press, 2000).

Germany's Role

Hitler's plans for a Greater Germany are neatly summarized in Philip Bell, "Europe in the Second World War," in *Themes in Modern European History, 1890–1945,* ed. Paul Hayes (London: Routledge, 1992), pp. 249–73, and are developed more fully in Norman Rich, *Hitler's War Aims: The Establishment of the New Order* (New York: Norton, 1974), and Bernard Kroener, R.-D. Muller, and Hans Umbreit, eds., *Germany and the Second World War,* vol. 5 (Oxford: Oxford University Press, 2000). See, too, the relevant sections of Michael Burleigh, *The Third Reich: A New History* (London: Pan, 2000).

Civilians in Britain, France, Germany, and Other European Countries

There is a mass of literature on individual countries, which can only be hinted at here. On Britain, see Angus Calder, *The People's War: Britain 1939–1945* (London: Cape, 1969), Juliet Gardiner, *Wartime: Britain, 1939–1945* (London: Headline, 2004), Sonya Rose, *Which People's War? National Identity and Citizenship in Wartime Britain, 1939–1945* (Cambridge: Cambridge University Press, 2003), and Jose Harris, "Britain and the Home Front during the Second World War," in *The World War Two Reader,* ed. Gordon Martel (London: Routledge, 2004).

On France, Robert O. Paxton's *Vichy France: Old Guard and New Order, 1940–1944* (New York: Knopf, 1972) is a classic, but may be usefully supplemented by Robert Gildea, *Marianne in Chains: In Search of the German Occupation, 1940–45* (London: Macmillan, 2002), Julian Jackson, *The Dark Years: France 1940–1944* (Oxford: Oxford University Press, 2002), and Richard Vinen, *The Unfree French: Life Under the Occupation* (London: Penguin, 2006).

On other countries, see Mark Mazower, *Inside Hitler's Greece: The Experience of Occupation, 1941–44* (London and New Haven, Conn.: Yale University Press, 1993), Gerhard Hirschfeld, *Nazi Rule and Dutch Collaboration: The Netherlands under German Occupation, 1940–1945* (Oxford: Berg, 1988), Richard J. B. Bosworth, *Mussolini's Italy* (London: Allen Lane, 2006), and K. C. Berkhoff, *Harvest of Despair: Life and Death in Ukraine under Nazi Rule* (Cambridge, Mass: Harvard University Press, 2001). On the Polish experience, see Thomas Gross, *Polish Society under Germany Occupation* (Princeton, N.J.: Princeton University Press, 1979); Israel Gutman, *The Jews of Warsaw: Ghetto, Underground, Revolt* (Bloomington: Indiana University Press, 1982); Norman Davies, *Rising 44: The Battle for Warsaw* (London: Viking, 2004); Richard C. Lukas, *Forgotten Holocaust: The Jews under German Occupation, 1939–1944* (London: Hippocrene Books, 2001 ed.); and Józef Garlinski, *Poland in the Second World War* (London: Macmillan, 1985).

The German home front and war economy are treated in the multivolume collection edited by Bernard Kroemer and colleagues, cited above, and also in Martin Kitchen, *Nazi Germany at War* (London: Longman, 1995). A brilliant local perspective is provided in Jill Stephenson, *Hitler's Home Front: Wurttemburg under Nazi Rule* (London: Hambledon Continuum, 2006). The wider picture is found in Richard Overy's *Why the Allies Won,* 2nd ed. (London: Pimlico, 2006) and his

The Dictators: Hitler's Germany and Stalin's Russia (London: Allen Lane, 2004). On the USSR, useful starting points include John Barber and Mark Harrison, *The Soviet Home Front: A Social and Economic History of the USSR in World War II* (London: Longman, 1991) and S. J. Linz, *The Impact of World War II on the Soviet Union* (Totowata, N.J.: Rowman and Allanheld, 1985). For a broader comparison of economies at war, see Mark Harrison, ed., *The Economics of World War Two: Six Great Powers in International Comparison* (Cambridge: Cambridge University Press, 1998); and Alan Milward, *War, Economy and Society, 1939–1945* (Berkeley: University of California Press, 1977). Corelli Barnett, *The Audit of War: The Illusion and Reality of Britain as a Great Nation* (London: Macmillan, 1986) advances a provocative hypothesis that has never been entirely challenged.

Women's Roles

On the frontline experience of civilians, especially those subjected to bombing, see the many publications listed in the endnotes. On questions of gender, starting points include K. Anderson, *Wartime Women: Sex Roles, Family Relations and the Status of Women during World War II* (Westport, Conn.: Greenwood, 1981); and M. R. Higonnet, Jane Jenson, Sonya Michel, and M. C. Weitz, eds., *Behind the Lines: Gender and the Two World Wars* (New Haven, Conn. and London: Yale University Press, 1987). Penny Summerfield, *Women Workers in the Second World War: Production and Patriarchy* (London: Croom Helm, 1984) considers the UK front while Jill Stephenson, *Women in Nazi Germany* (London: Longman, 2001) questions many long-standing assumptions.

Collaboration and Resistance

The issues of collaboration and resistance may be approached through Rab Bennett, *Under the Shadow of the Swastika: The Moral Dilemmas of Resistance and Collaboration in Hitler's Europe* (Basingstoke: Macmillan, 1999); Henri Michel, *Shadow War: Resistance in Europe* (London: Deutsch, 1972); and Werner Rings, *Life With the Enemy: Collaboration and Resistance in Hitler's Europe, 1939–1945* (London: Weidenfeld and Nicolson, 1982), though the last two mentioned are beginning to show signs of age. The self-deceiving world of collaboration may be usefully approached through biographies of the leading protagonists. See notably Martin Conway, *Collaboration in Belgium: Léon Degrelle and the Rexist Movement* (New Haven, Conn.: Yale University Press, 2005) and Hans Fredrik Dahl, *Quisling: A Study in Treachery* (Cambridge: Cambridge University Press, 1989). On partisans, Tony Judt presents a useful collection of essays in *Resistance and Revolution in Mediterranean Europe, 1939–1948* (London: Routledge, 1998) while those pieces edited by Stephen Hawes and Ralph White in *Resistance in Europe, 1939–1945* (Harmondsworth: Penguin, 1975) are still worth consulting. An outstanding study of underground protest in a single country is to be found in H. R. Kedward, *Resistance in Vichy France* (Oxford: Oxford University Press, 1978), a book whose innovative methodology could helpfully be applied to many other occupied countries.

Reference Works

Among reference works, I.C.B. Dear, ed., *The Oxford Companion to World War Two* (Oxford: Oxford University Press, 2001) provides a mass of information and useful analysis. See too John Campbell, ed., *The Experience of World War II* (London: Grange Books, 1989). Extensive primary documentation is to be found in the on-line collection *Conditions and Politics in Occupied Western Europe, 1940–1945* (London: Thomson, 2006).

THE COLD WAR

Those interested in the New Military History can approach the subject through John Keegan, *The Face of Battle: A Study of Agincourt, Waterloo and the Somme* (London: Cape, 1976), which is an outstanding exemplar of the genre. Potential future military developments are covered in Bruce D. Berkowitz, *The New Face of War: How War will be Fought in the 21ˢᵗ Century* (New York: Free Press, 2003).

There are numerous primary sources relating to the Cold War, mainly of an official kind, in Gale Stokes, ed., *From Stalinism to Pluralism: A Documentary History of Eastern Europe since 1945* (New York: Oxford University Press, 1991). All aspects of the Cold War are put into their spatial context in John Swift, *The Palgrave Concise Historical Atlas of the Cold War* (London: Palgrave MacMillan, 2003), which has maps plus useful supporting text; and Richard Crampton and Ben Crampton, *Atlas of Eastern Europe in the Twentieth Century* (London: Routledge, 1996). An outstanding conspectus of events since 1945 is provided by Tony Judt, *Postwar: A History of Europe since 1945* (London, William Heinemann, 2005). Eastern Europe is covered in Richard Crampton, *Eastern Europe in the Twentieth Century and After* (London: Routledge, 1997) and Geoff Swain and Nigel Swain, *Eastern Europe since 1945* (Basingstoke: Palgrave MacMillan, 2003).

The Origins of the Cold War

Approaches to the Cold War are well covered in Odd Arne Westad, ed., *Reviewing the Cold War: Approaches, Interpretations, Theory* (London: Frank Cass, 2000). The conflicts's origins are discussed in Herbert Feis, *From Trust to Terror: The Onset of the Cold War, 1945–1950* (London, Anthony Blond, 1970); Melvyn P. Leffler and David S. Painter, eds., *The Origins of the Cold War: An International History* (London: Routledge, 1994); and Martin McCauley, *The Origins of the Cold War, 1941–1949*, 2ⁿᵈ ed. (London: Longman, 1995). Thomas Andrew Bailey, *America Faces Russia: Russian-American Relations from Early Times to our Day* (New York: Oxford University Press, 1950) places responsibility on the Soviet Union, an account challenged by William Appleman Williams, *The Tragedy of American Diplomacy* (Cleveland, Ohio and New York: World Publishing Co., 1959). The development of the debate on the origins and course of the Cold War can be traced in the many excellent writings of John Lewis Gaddis. See especially his *The United States and the Origins of the Cold War, 1941–1947* (New York: Columbia University Press, 1972); *We Now Know: Rethinking Cold War History* (New York: Oxford University Press, 1997); and *The Cold War* (London: Allen Lane, 2005).

The Superpowers and Manifestations of the Cold War

Relations between the United States and the Soviet Union are covered in Peter G. Boyle, *American-Soviet Relations from the Russian Revolution to the Fall of Communism* (London: Routledge, 1993). Relations within the Eastern Bloc are dealt with in Gerard Holden, *The Warsaw Pact: Soviet Security and Bloc Politics* (Oxford: Basil Blackwell, 1989). The nuclear arms race is discussed in John Newhouse, *The Nuclear Age: From Hiroshima to Star Wars* (London: Michael Joseph, 1989); while the spread of arms is dealt with by Frederic S. Pearson, *The Global Spread of Arms: The Political Economy of International Security* (Boulder, Colo.: Westview Press, 1994). On spying, see James Adams, *The New Spies: Exploring the Frontiers of Espionage* (London: Hutchinson, 1994); Stephen E. Ambrose and Oleg Gordievsky, *KGB: The Inside Story of its Foreign Operations from Lenin to Gorbachev* (London: Hodder and Stoughton, 1990); Gerald W. Hopple and Bruce. W. Watson, eds., *The Military Intelligence Community* (Boulder, Colo.: Westview Press, 1986). Events in 1956 and 1968 when military force was used to suppress dissent are treated in Miklós Molnár, *Budapest 1956: A History of the Hungarian Revolution* (London: George Allen and Unwin, 1971); and Jiri Valentina, *Soviet Intervention in Czechoslovakia, 1968: Anatomy of a Decision* (Baltimore, Md.: John Hopkins University Press, 1979).

Culture Wars

On the "culture wars" and the use of "soft power" see Frances Stonor Saunders, *Who Paid the Piper? The CIA and the Cultural Cold War* (London: Granta, 1998); her *The Cultural Cold War: The CIA and the World of Letters* (New York: The Free Press, 2000); and David Caute, *The Dancer Defects: The Struggle for Cultural Supremacy during the Cold War* (Oxford: Oxford University Press, 2003). Ron Robin, *The Making of the Cold War Enemy: Culture and Politics in the Military-Industrial Complex* (Princeton, N.J.: Princeton University Press, 2003) shows their significance for the conflicts in Korea and Vietnam.

Freedoms and Repressions

The literature on the Red Scare in America is vast, but useful are David Caute, *The Anti-Communist Purge under Truman and Eisenhower* (New York: Simon and Shuster, 1998) and D. K. Johnson, *The Lavender Scare: The Cold War Persecution of Gays and Lesbians in the Federal Government* (Chicago: University of Chicago Press, 2004).

Notions of civil society and of Central Europe are dealt with in Timothy Garton Ash, *The Uses of Adversity: Essays on the Fate of Central Europe* (New York: Vintage, 1990). The ideas of two leading dissidents are available in English: György Konrád, *Antipolitics: An Essay* (London: Quartet, 1984) and Václav Havel, *The Power of the Powerless* (London: Unwin Hyman, 1985). On the latter, see Michael Simmons, *The Reluctant President: A Political Life of Václav Havel* (London: Methuen, 1991).

Proxy Conflicts

Studies on the proxy conflicts include Bevin Alexander, *Korea: The Lost War* (London: Pan, 1987); Callum MacDonald, *Korea: The War before Vietnam* (Basingstoke: MacMillan, 1986); Noel Barber, *The War of the Running Dogs: How Malaya Defeated the Communist Guerrillas, 1948–1960* (London: Collins, 1971); Ahron Bregman, *Israel's Wars, 1947–1993* (London: Routledge, 2000); Joseph J. Collins, *The Soviet Invasion of Afghanistan: A Study in the Use of Force in Soviet Foreign Policy* (Lexington, Mass.: Lexington Books, 1986); Michael Griffin, *Reaping the Whirlwind: The Taliban*

Movement in Afghanistan (London: Pluto Press, 2001); Arthur Gavshon, *Crisis in Africa: Battleground of East and West* (Boulder, Colo.: Westview Press, 1984); Michael Gonzalez, *Nicaragua: What Went Wrong?* (London: Bookmarks, 1985). The literature on Vietnam is vast. Good starting points are Gabriel Kolko, *Anatomy of a War: Vietnam, the United States and the Modern Historical Perspective* (New York: The New Press, 1994); Gary R. Hess, *Vietnam and the United States* (Boston: Twayne Publishers, 1990); Michael Maclear, *Vietnam: The Ten Thousand Day War* (London: Thames Mandarin, 1989); Robert D. Schulzinger, *A Time for War: The United States and Vietnam, 1941–1975* (Oxford: Oxford University Press, 1997). Spencer C. Tucker, ed., *Encyclopedia of the Vietnam War: A Political, Social and Military History,* 3 vols. (Oxford: ABC-Clio, 1998) is a mine of information and includes documents. The air campaign is discussed in Mark Clodfelter, *The Limits of Air Power: The American Bombing of North Vietnam* (New York: Free Press, 1989). The two incidents when the Cold War almost became "hot" are discussed in Walter Phillips Davison, *The Berlin Blockade* (Princeton, N.J.: Princeton University Press, 1958); Avi Shlaim, *The US and the Berlin Blockade, 1948–1949: A Study in Crisis Decision Making* (Berkeley: University of California Press, 1983); and Mark White, *The Cuban Missile Crisis* (Basingstoke: MacMillan, 1996).

THE POST-YUGOSLAV WARS

The number of titles devoted to the historical, political, and sociological analyses of Yugoslavia, and especially to the wars of the 1990s, is overwhelming. An overview may be gleaned through the critical literature reviews authored by scholars who themselves have written important books in the field. See, for example, "Anti-bibliography: Reviewing the Reviews," in Sabrina P. Ramet, *Balkan Babel: The Disintegration of Yugoslavia from the Death of Tito to the Fall of Milošević* (Boulder, Colo., and Oxford: Westview Press, 2002), pp. 391–403; the bibliographical note in Christopher Bennett, *Yugoslavia's Bloody Collapse: Causes, Course and Consequences* (New York: New York University Press, 1995), pp. 252–255; and the bibliographical summary in V. P. Gagnon, Jr., *The Myth of Ethnic War: Serbia and Croatia in the 1990s* (Ithaca, N.Y. and London: Cornell University Press, 2004), pp. 195–200.

The Legitimacy of the State of Yugoslavia

Any effort towards an understanding of why and how Yugoslavia disintegrated must bear in mind the fact that the survival of a state is dependent upon whether its citizens recognize its legitimacy. Sabrina P. Ramet, in her book *Balkan Babel: The Disintegration of Yugoslavia from the Death of Tito to the Fall of Milošević* (Boulder, Colo., and Oxford: Westview Press, 2002), offers numerous examples of post-1918 challenges to the legitimacy of Yugoslavia. The copious statistical evidence presented in the volume shows in detail how economic decline after Tito's death led, in the 1980s, to a persistent questioning of the system's legitimacy. Chapters on the media, rock music, gender relations, and the status and influence of religious institutions up to 1991 enable the reader to contextualize the post-Yugoslav wars and assess their wider impact.

Another book by Sabrina P. Ramet, *Nationalism and Federalism in Yugoslavia 1962–1991* (Bloomington: Indiana University Press, 1992), a reissue of a work first published in 1984, offers an analysis of how the Yugoslav republics and autonomous

provinces interacted, and shows how the 1974 constitution initiated decentraliza-
tion. On a similar theme, see Sabrina P. Ramet and Lj. S. Adamovich, eds., *Beyond
Yugoslavia: Politics, Economics, and Culture in a Shattered Community* (Boulder, Colo.,
San Francisco, and Oxford: Westview, 1995).

For the wider background, see the many things by John B. Allcock, notably his
Explaining Yugoslavia (London: Hurst, 2000), an historical sociological study that
brings together politics, economics, demography, culture, and lifestyles. He also
coedited, with Marko Milivojević and John J. Horton, *Conflict in the Former Yugoslavia: An Encyclopedia* (Santa Barbara, Calif.: ABC-CLIO, 1998), a reader-friendly
collection of cross-referenced short articles that makes the complexity of post-
Yugoslav wars understandable for the wider audience.

Origins

Other books on the origins of the 1990s wars include Branka Magaš's *The Destruction of Yugoslavia: Tracking the Break-up 1980–92* (London: Verso, 2002). See, too,
Branka Magaš and Ivo Žanić, eds., *The War in Croatia and Bosnia-Herzegovina, 1991–
1995* (London: Frank Cass, 2001), with contributions from politicians and military
personnel who had a role in events. Laura Silber and Allan Little, *Yugoslavia: Death
of a Nation* (New York: Penguin Books, 1997) is a well-known study that accompanied a television documentary. The authors interviewed many of the politicians
who played crucial roles in the political and military developments of the 1990s.

The renowned study by Ivo Banac, *The National Question in Yugoslavia* (Ithaca,
N.Y.: Cornell University Press, 1984) remains the standard source on the formation
of Yugoslav state in 1918. For a fine introduction to the history of particular countries and provinces, see Noel Malcolm, *Bosnia: A Short History* (New York: New York
University Press, 1994), and Noel Malcolm, *Kosovo: A Short History* (London: Paper-
mac, 1998); Ivo Goldstein, *Croatia: A History* (London: Hurst, 1999); and Leslie Ben-
son, *Yugoslavia: A Concise History* (Basingstoke: Palgrave, 2001). See also John R.
Lampe, *Yugoslavia as History: Twice There was a Country* (Cambridge: Cambridge
University Press, 2000); S. K. Pavlowitch, *The Improbable Survivor: Yugoslavia and Its
Problems* (Cleveland: Ohio State University Press, 1998); Carl-Ulrik Schierup, ed.,
*Scramble for the Balkans: Nationalism, Globalism and the Political Economy of Recon-
struction* (Basingstoke: MacMillan, 1999); Marcus Tanner, *Croatia: A Nation Forged
in War* (New Haven, Conn.: Yale University Press, 1997); and Mark Thompson,
A Paper House: The Ending of Yugoslavia (New York: Pantheon, 1998).

Balkan and European Contexts

For books situating the wars of the 1990s into a broader Balkan and European
context, see Bennett, *Yugoslavia's Bloody Collapse*; Lenard J. Cohen, *Broken Bonds:
Yugoslavia's Disintegration and Balkan Politics in Transition* (Boulder, Colo., San Francisco, and Oxford: Westview Press, 1995); and Misha Glenny, *The Fall of Yugoslavia*
(London: Penguin Books, 1996).

The Postwar Era

For a starting point on the postwar era, see Elizabeth M. Cousens and Charles K.
Cater, *Toward Peace in Bosnia: Implementing the Dayton Accords* (Boulder, Colo., and

London: Lynne Rienner Publishers, 2001); Keith Doubt, *Sociology after Bosnia and Kosovo: Recovering Justice* (Lanham, Md., Boulder, Colo., New York, and Oxford: Rowman and Littlefield, 2000); Stef Jansen, "Troubled Locations: Return, the Life Course, and Transformations of 'Home' in Bosnia-Herzegovina," *Focaal* 49 (2007): 15–30, and the extensive bibliography on refugees accompanying that article.

Ethnic Questions in the Post-Yugoslav Wars

An outstanding challenge to the widespread notions of linkage between ethnicity and violence is offered by V. P. Gagnon, Jr., in his *The Myth of Ethnic War* For its detailed analysis of the intersection between politics and society, this book won the Best Book Award in European Politics and Society, given by the American Political Science Association. Gagnon's book shows why it is wrong to suppose that ethnicity itself is the main cause of war. A similar approach has been taken up by the anthropologist Stef Jansen, in his PhD Dissertation (at University of Hull), "Anti-nationalism: Post-Yugoslav Resistance and Narratives of Self and Society," based on field research among the *Zamir* (Pro-peace) network activists in Zagreb and Belgrade, men and women who were actively resisting nationalism in their respective surroundings in the 1990s. This study remains unavailable in English but has been published in Serbian: *Antinacionalizam: Etnografija otpora u Zagrebu i Beogradu* (Beograd: XX Vek, 2005).

Index

About the Editor and Contributors

EDITOR

Nicholas Atkin is professor of Modern European History at the University of Reading, United Kingdom. His publications include *Church and Schools in Vichy France, 1940–1944* (New York: Garland, 1991); *Pétain* (London: Longman, 1997); *The French at War, 1934–1944* (London: Longman, 2001); *The Forgotten French: Exiles in the British Exiles, 1940–1944* (Manchester: Manchester University Press, 2003); and the *Fifth French Republic* (Basingstoke: Palgrave, 2005). With Frank Tallett, he authored *Priests, Prelates and People: European Catholicism since 1750* (New York: Oxford University Press, 2003), and together they have edited *Religion, Society and Politics in France since 1789* (London: Hambledon, 1991); *Catholicism in Britain and France since 1750* (London: Hambledon, 1996); and *The Right in France from the Revolution to Le Pen*, 2nd ed. (London: Tauris, 2003). He is currently writing a study on British tourism to France since the 1850s.

CONTRIBUTORS

François Cochet is professor of Contemporary History at the University Paul Verlaine-Metz in France. He is a specialist on the face of battle and the experiences of prisoners of war. His books include *L'héroïsation au quotidien: Rémois en guerre 1914–1918* (Nancy: Presses Universitaires de Nancy, 1993); *Soldats sans armes, la captivité de guerre, une approche culturelle* (Bruxelles: Bruylant, 1998); *Les soldats de la Drôle de Guerre* (Paris: Hachette, 2004);

and *Survivre au front (1914–1918), les soldats entre contrainte et consentement* (Saint-Cloud: SOTECA/14–18 Editions, diffusion Belin, 2005).

Maja Povrzanović Frykman is associate professor of International Migration and Ethnic Relations (IMER), Malmö University, and external associate of the Institute of Ethnology and Folklore Research in Zagreb. Since the war started in Croatia in 1991, her main topics have included identities in war, violence, and place, and narratives on exile experiences. Her research among the labor- and refugee-migrants from Croatia and Bosnia-Herzegovina in Sweden addresses the relations between ethnicity, place, and community through the concepts and practices within the semantic domains of diaspora and transnationalism. She is the author of *Forgotten Majority: Civilians Remembering the War in Croatia 1991–92* (in Croatian) (Zagreb: Institute of Ethnology and Folklore Research, forthcoming). She is the coeditor of *War, Exile, Everyday life: Cultural Perspectives* (Zagreb: Institute of Ethnology and Folklore Research, 1996), and editor of *Beyond Integration: Challenges of Belonging in Diaspora and Exile* (Lund: Nordic Academic Press, 2001), and *Transnational Spaces: Disciplinary Perspectives* (Malmö: Malmö University, 2004).

Sam Johnson is senior lecturer in Modern European History at Manchester Metropolitan University, and a research fellow in the Department of Hebrew and Jewish Studies at University College, London. Her research is mainly focused on Jewish-Gentile relations in Europe in the late nineteenth and early twentieth centuries. She is currently completing a monograph on British responses to Eastern Europe's Jewish question, 1880–1925. She is involved in a second project, based at UCL, which deals with contemporary xenophobia and anti-Semitism in Central and Eastern Europe. Since 2006, she has been managing editor of the scholarly journal *East European Jewish Affairs.*

Michael Richards is reader in Spanish History at the University of the West of England, and author of *A Time of Silence: Civil War and the Culture of Repression in Franco's Spain, 1936–1945* (Cambridge: Cambridge University Press, 1998), and coeditor of *The Splintering of Spain: Cultural History and the Spanish Civil War, 1936–1939* (Cambridge: Cambridge University Press, 2005). He has published many articles on the cultural and social history of twentieth-century Spain and is currently completing a book on postwar social memory.

Frank Tallett is senior lecturer in History at the University of Reading, United Kingdom. Alongside the many things he has edited with Nicholas Atkin, he is the author of *War and Society in Early Modern Europe, 1485–1715* (London: Routledge, 1997). He has additionally written several articles on military and religious history. With David Trim, he has recently edited *European Warfare, 1350–1750* (Cambridge: Cambridge University Press, forthcoming).

Recent Titles in the
Greenwood Press "Daily Lives of Civilians during Wartime" Series

Daily Lives of Civilians in Wartime Africa: From Slavery Days to the Rwandan Genocide
John Laband, editor

Daily Lives of Civilians in Wartime Early America: From the Colonial Era to the Civil War
David S. Heidler and Jeanne T. Heidler, editors

Daily Lives of Civilians in Wartime Modern America: From the Indian Wars to the Vietnam War
David S. Heidler and Jeanne T. Heidler, editors

Daily Lives of Civilians in Wartime Asia: From the Taiping Rebellion to the Vietnam War
Stewart Lone, editor

Daily Lives of Civilians in Wartime Europe, 1618–1900
Linda S. Frey and Marsha L. Frey, editors